D1738410

POLITICAL PARTIES IN
THE SOUTHERN
STATES

POLITICAL PARTIES IN THE SOUTHERN STATES

Party Activists in Partisan Coalitions

EDITED BY

Tod A. Baker
Charles D. Hadley
Robert P. Steed
Laurence W. Moreland

PRAEGER

New York
Westport, Connecticut
London

Library of Congress Cataloging-in-Publication Data

Political parties in the Southern states : party activists in partisan
    coalitions / edited by Tod A. Baker . . . [et al.].
        p.   cm.
    Includes bibliographical references.
    ISBN 0–275–93027–0 (alk. paper)
    1. Political parties—Southern States.   I. Baker, Tod A.
JK2295.A133P65   1990
324.275—dc20   89–26557

Library of Congress Catalog Card Number: 89–26557
ISBN: 0–275–93027–0

First published in 1990

Praeger Publishers, One Madison Avenue, New York, NY 10010
An imprint of Greenwood Publishing Group, Inc.

Printed in the United States of America

∞

The paper used in this book complies with the
Permanent Paper Standard issued by the National
Information Standards Organization (Z39.48–1984).

10   9   8   7   6   5   4   3   2   1

Contents

Tables and Figure

TABLES

FIGURE

Preface: The Comparative State Party Activist Survey

The Comparative State Party Activist Survey (CSPA Survey), directed by Robert P. Steed, Laurence W. Moreland, and Tod A. Baker, was a survey of delegates attending state political party conventions in twelve states during the spring and summer of 1984. The twelve states were Maine, Connecticut, Indiana, North Dakota, Utah, Oklahoma, Texas, Louisiana, Arkansas, Mississippi, South Carolina, and North Carolina. This project was an outgrowth of a similar study of state convention delegates in 1980 (for a description of the 1980 survey, together with a series of studies resulting from the project, see Ronald B. Rapoport, Alan I. Abramowitz, and John McGlennon, editors, *The Life of the Parties: Activists in Presidential Politics* [Lexington, Ky.: University Press of Kentucky, 1986]). The present volume utilizes the data on the six southern states included in the CSPA Survey to explore some fundamental aspects of the changing southern party system.

In each state surveyed, a researcher or a research team administered the questionnaires produced by the CSPA Survey directors, coded the data, and sent the data to the survey directors for integration into a full dataset. The response rates and the researchers for each state are as follows:

Arkansas: Republicans: 51% (n = 262); Democrats: 60% (n = 356). Researcher: Arthur English, University of Arkansas at Little Rock.

Louisiana: Democrats: 45% (n = 336). Researcher: Charles D. Hadley, University of New Orleans.

Mississippi: Republicans: 35% (n = 206); Democrats: 35% (n = 514). Researcher: Stephen D. Shaffer, Mississippi State University.

North Carolina: Republicans: 44% (n = 327); Democrats: 62% (n = 954). Researchers: Charles Prysby and Lee Bernick, University of North Carolina at Greensboro.

| South Carolina: | Republicans: 75% (n = 743); Democrats: 51% (n = 526). Researchers: Laurence W. Moreland, Robert P. Steed, and Tod A. Baker, The Citadel. |
| Texas: | Republicans: 39% (n = 430); Democrats: 35% (n = 380). Researcher: John R. Todd, University of North Texas. |

These reported response rates are approximate inasmuch as the party organizations did not have precise figures on the number of delegates in attendance at the conventions. The number of respondents for the research reported in this volume is 5,034, and the average response rate is 48 percent.

In each state except Texas, questionnaires were administered to all delegates at their respective state conventions, and the response rate thus reflects the percentage of returns from the entire population. In Texas, because access to the conventions was not possible, the questionnaire was administered by mail to a random sample of delegates, and the response rate reflects the return rate of the sample. In Louisiana, there was no Republican state convention in 1984.

All the following chapters, with the exceptions of Chapter 1 and Chapter 11, rely on analyses of these CSPA Survey data for the southern states. In each case, unless otherwise noted, all tables are derived from those data, and no source notes are included. The questionnaire, with marginals, is included in the Appendix.

We are indebted to a number of people whose assistance at various stages of this project was instrumental to its ultimate completion. First, we gratefully acknowledge the help of our colleagues who were involved in collecting the data at the state conventions. The cooperation and assistance of party officials in each state was also critical for the completion of these surveys. Essential financial support was generously provided by The Citadel Development Foundation and University of New Orleans College of Liberal Arts research grants. We also are appreciative of the early editorial assistance provided by Colin S. Cavel while a graduate student at the University of New Orleans. Two long-time students of the American party system, William Crotty and Lewis Bowman, gave welcome encouragement and graciously agreed to involve themselves in the development of the manuscript by writing introductory and concluding chapters. Finally, we are grateful to our editors at Praeger for their patience and encouragement throughout the project and for their efforts to smooth the publication process.

POLITICAL PARTIES IN
THE SOUTHERN
STATES

Introduction: The Study of Southern Party Elites

William Crotty

The studies in this volume examine a number of issues and draw from a number of approaches basic to understanding political developments in the United States. The concerns addressed include the role and value of elite studies in identifying and interpreting trends to be found in broader mass politics; the increasing institutionalization of U.S. politics, in particular, the contribution to this occurrence made by the changes in the presidential nomination system and, more specifically, the initial reforms introduced into the process in the early 1970s, reforms whose ramifications are continuing to be felt (Darcy et al.; Shaffer; Steed, "Party Reform . . . "). Also addressed is the status of the much-discussed, much-debated realignment of southern politics, its present condition and continuing consequences for the representation of policy concerns, and the definition of policy positions and clientele group support within the political parties and within the region. Closely identified with this are the future consequences of the changes for the nation and the South, the most studied, distinctive, and, for generations, unyielding of political systems.[1] Each to some degree is addressed in the research that follows.

OVERVIEWING TRENDS IN SOUTHERN POLITICS

In forming a counterpoint to developments in the rest of the United States, a politics of privilege, racial, and, to an extent, economic and political repression has characterized the South. The roots of its politics are found in a history socially and economically distinct from the rest of the nation. The hallmarks of southern regionalism were first and foremost the "peculiar institution" of slavery that has left its imprint on all phases of southern development up to the present day. Writing in the immediate post–World War II years, V. O. Key, Jr., made the point:

Southern sectionalism and the special character of southern political institutions have to be attributed in the main to the Negro. The one-party system suffrage restrictions departing from democratic norms, low levels of voting and of political interest, and all the consequences of these political arrangements and practices must be traced ultimately to this one factor. All of which amounts to saying that the predominant consideration in the architecture of southern political institutions has been to assure locally a subordination of the Negro population and, externally, to block threatened interferences from the outside with these local arrangements.[2]

The South continues to contend with its racial legacy. Much has changed (as the chapters in this book make very clear) and much remains to be done. Race relations and the political consequences that still derive from these relations are in the process of a fundamental redefinition. The authors of a more recent work on the manifestations of southern political change, Earl Black and Merle Black, write:

Only in the early 1960s did southern blacks, victimized and handicapped by two centuries of slavery and another century of legal segregation, succeed in shaking the foundations of white racism. Race relations in the contemporary south reflect neither strict segregation nor thorough integration; rather, they embody a complex blend of old and new practices, old and new attitudes. Our analysis has shown remarkable areas of progress as well as a lengthy agenda of still controversial and unresolved interracial differences concerning the intermediate color line.[3]

Race and the present accommodation to a new social order still influence southern politics with enormous implications for politics in both the region and nation. If, in addition to race, one adds an agrarian plantation economy over which a civil war was fought to resolve issues of constitutional uncertainty, economic dominance, and individual worth, one begins to get a rough idea of how much the region developed outside the main currents of American history.

Southern regionalism with its correspondingly destructive politics evolved within a broader political system committed to ideals of openness, democratic representation, equality, and fairness—guarantees the southern one-party system worked effectively to repress. One consequence was a curiosity that invited the attention of the nation and the investigations of some of the principal scholars in the discipline.[4] The problems encountered in terms of representative capacities are fundamental to understanding the adaption of a democratic system within a hostile cultural framework: the domination of a political system by a self-selected and racially dominant elite; and the consequences of related political factors such as low participation in elections, an issue-less politics, and a generalized apathy for the mass of the electorate. In a comparative view, one not adequately developed, such investigations as those in this volume could well have continuing consequences for understanding the evolution of traditional, noncompetitive, and unrepresentative party systems worldwide, the dominant forms of party representation in Latin America, Africa, and Asia and their movement toward more democratic political expression. The relative scarcity of competitive democratic systems, whether two-party or multiparty, lends particular significance to a one-party system in transition toward a more open and competitive system consistent with national norms and practices. Regional party change, then, has a broader extranational relevance, although an open question at this point. The extent to which the South, in responding to industrialization, urbanization, migration (Moreland, "Immigration . . . "; Baker, "Urbanization . . . "; Steed, "Party Reform . . . "), the legal and social changes in race relations (Hadley and Stanley), homogenization of cultural values, and major political views through a ubiquitous media, can serve as an example for systems operating outside a broader concentration of national societal forces is unclear. These are questions to be explored. At present, it is enough—and a needed first step—to trace the changes taking place in the South in an effort to identify their broader consequences. The authors in this volume set this as their principal task.

The transformations in progress within the region are remarkable. The authors in this book make this point very clear. In the context of what often seems to be the glacial manifestation of broad social change, the South has undergone—and continues to undergo—a broad political revolution. Although the region, even more than others, might well be uncomfortable with such a characterization, the ramifications of what is occurring are far-reaching enough to justify being called revolutionary. To compare the South today to where it was a short generation or so ago is not only to identify massive change and a political restructuring of enormous consequence, it also enables one to look at a politics of excitement and transformation rare for a discipline such as political science. It is unusual that change can be so profound, so geographically bounded, so identifiable, and so politically consequential as that which has taken place over the last four decades in the South. As a consequence, these developments are receiving renewed attention in the writings and research of a newer generation of scholars.[5]

Within this context is the emerging role of blacks in regional and national politics. African-Americans, again within a generation, emerged from the shadows of discrimination and political impotency in the South to form a highly visible and powerful voting bloc that has formulated one of the clearest political agendas in the country.[6] The consequences of a core liberal constituency with clearly articulated policy goals and the electoral muscle to follow through on its objectives makes for a politics of issue and ideology rare on a mass level for this country. As the studies in this volume develop, the changes are profound, perhaps even going beyond what most had expected (Moreland, "Ideological Bases . . . "; Baker, "Religious Right . . . "; Prysby; Steed, "Civil Rights . . . "; Hadley and Stanley; Steed, "Party Reform . . . "). Blacks constitute the largest single core constituency in the South and one of the main building blocks, along with similarly inclined liberal white southerners, of the region's new Democratic politics. It is a politics at 180–degree variance from the "good old boy" white dominance of the 1876–1964 period and, using a different set of criteria, the

Republican party politics of the contemporary period. If the South's biracial Democratic coalition is significantly liberal, and the studies in this volume repeatedly demonstrate that it is (Steed, "Party Reform . . . "; Hadley and Stanley; Steed, "Civil Rights . . . "; Moreland, "Ideological Bases . . . "; Prysby), the South's Republicans are boisterously and self-consciously conservative. The result is a politics polarized along a broad policy spectrum of economic concerns, social welfare policies, and military and foreign policy approaches. The competing policy attachments are clear (Moreland, "Ideological Bases . . . "; Prysby; Steed, "Party Reform . . . ") and result in what has to be the most distinct choices among cohesive and competitive political agendas for southern electorates. From generations of being saddled with an issue-less politics of racial and economic privilege, the South is now being exposed to one of the most issue-oriented sets of party coalitions and electoral policy alternatives in the nation.

The role of the emergent forces of a black liberation in shaping this politics is suggested by the analyses found in this volume (Hadley and Stanley; Steed, "Civil Rights Activist . . . "; Steed, "Party Reform . . . "; Moreland, "Ideological Base . . . "). It is worth reemphasizing that a newly found black articulateness in policy matters combined with the mobilization of the black electorate and its representation of these concerns within the higher reaches of the Democratic party (the Republican party holds little attraction for blacks) could be the source for a significant national movement within presidential politics. The mobilization of these forces during the 1980s, particularly the support given Jesse Jackson in his two presidential runs, lends emphasis to such a proposition. The coalition base in the South may well push the national parties toward increasingly polarized liberal-conservative positions. The process could result in a further ideological clarification of the national parties, a trend reinforced by what is occurring in the South.

Such a development would constitute something of a reversal of roles for the southern and national parties, with the pressure for change toward more coherent policy positions being responsive in significant part to the demands of a new southern electorate, one with clear needs and priorities and one becoming increasingly assertive in its demands. Such a situation applies to both the Democratic and Republican parties. It constitutes, as several authors in this book have labeled it, the "southernization" of national politics (Moreland, "Ideological Bases . . . "; Steed, "Party Reform . . . "). If one choses to look for some ironies and role reversals, again over a very short period, this clearly ranks among the more unusual.

Finally, in this context and in direct relation to the studies in this book, there is the question of party decline. The argument over party decline has generated considerable heat: Have the parties really declined? Who is responsible? What are the consequences? Could it be that the political parties, rather than declining, are really stronger than at any point in their modern history?

There are advocates for each position and data to be marshaled in support of alternative contentions.[7] The problem is that the concept of party decline is a muddled one employing a number of often conflicting indicators subject to differing interpretations. The conceptualization and data patterns are stronger in the subareas addressed (party affiliations, the reform financing of campaigns, and the restructuring of presidential selection as examples) and in identifying the consequences of these changes than they are in dealing with the broader notion of party strength and its relevance in contemporary society. When the variety of indicators are drawn together and each is given separate weight by individual analysts, the results, as well as the debate, can become confusing.

At this point, it may be enough to say that the role of the parties within the political system is changing and that the changes have potentially enormous, but unclear, consequences for political representation in the United States. The rate of change and its direction are contested. Virtually all would agree that the process of remodeling the relationship of parties to their environment—from immediate responses to candidate strategies or short-run election outcomes, to more fundamental developments in campaign finance, to crises that arise in national politics (Vietnam, Watergate, Iran-Contragate) and the reformating of nomination decision-making—is, in effect, a second-stage reaction to fundamental changes in the society. These include areas such as technology and mass communications as well as in population patterns, demographic developments and politically relevant attitudes.[8] In short, what is taking place could be considered the normal transition of a party system during the postwar period to a national culture undergoing redefinition. The end result should be political parties more suited to the demands of a twenty-first century political system. This perspective has not been the dominant one. The parties' response to all of this and the significance of the changes are debated both in empirical terms and, where the heat radiates from, a normative context as to what a party should or should not be and what strengthens or weakens its social role.[9]

The empirical studies needed to flesh out the changing developments and their consequences are of value and this is where the present research makes a particular contribution. Certainly the South, more so than the nation at large, has witnessed the impact of the social and technological forces (Moreland, "Immigration . . . ''; Baker, "Urbanization . . . ''; Steed, "Party Reform . . . ''). The South's exposure and subsequent readjustment was concentrated in a much briefer time span. Its end result may well be that a more issue-based, competitive, and polarized party politics is being brought into sharper relief.

All of this took place within a few decades. The process in the nation is taking significantly longer and the end product may not be a party politics consistent with contemporary southern developments. This is yet to be decided. To complicate matters further, it may be that southern politics and parties are developing quicker institutionally and organizationally than parties in other regions. This appears to represent a reasonable conclusion from the Cotter, Gibson, Bibby, and Huckshorn study of state party developments over time.[10] To take the matter one step further: The evidence is at best fragmentary and isolated—confined essentially to selected cities—but it does not appear that the state-level party developments identified by Cotter and his associates have yet penetrated the local level.[11] The result leaves southern parties less structured at this level than those in the non-South (weak as their base structures may be), nonsouthern parties that have had generations of experience in serving local electorates and in nursing their own organizational needs. Such a conclusion is best stated as a research proposition rather than a fact. If true, however, it may indicate a continuingly weak organization base for southern parties statewide, a base hidden in part by the emerging Republican vote in presidential elections and by the clear changes in demographic characteristics and loyalty patterns of the Democratic vote.[12]

The picture emerging may be that of a fragmented party structure, one stronger at the state level, a forceful advocate for its objectives in national party circles and a factor of consequence in presidential elections. But below the state level, the Republican party may be relatively unstructured and no better organized now than it has been in the past. This would leave something of a void organizationally in the party at the county and local levels. It represents a problem area and there are at present no clear indications as to how it would be addressed.

This is speculative. The extensive data needed to develop the exact dimensions of state-level party organizational development and responsibilities is only now being collected (Bowman and associates, forthcoming), but it does suggest keeping an open mind as to the extent, relevance, and change within the southern parties at all levels.

It would be unwarranted to assume that the revolution in southern party politics uniformly has affected each level of party structure. What has to be identified is where and in what manner the change has taken place and where little or no change is apparent. Being overly optimistic in assuming the spread and impact of what has occurred serves no good scientific purpose.

Another peculiarity emerges. The parties that developed within the South may be closer in issue positions and concerns to national parties than are those of the other regions. The possibility is more apparent for the Republican than the Democratic party. The studies in this volume indicate an issue position/candidate appeal at the *presidential* level for motivating party service, particularly for inducing switchers to abandon their party of acculturation for a new political identification. The authors of the following studies also find that the shift reflects a convergence of ideological views. The party defectors are politically comfortable within their new parties—more so than they were in their old parties—and relatively indistinguishable from those whom they have joined. The major differences evident are with the party loyalists they left (Prysby; Moreland, "Ideological Bases . . . '').

The argument could be made that the realignment of southern politics, while responsive to forces within the region's electorate and directly related to its economic development, is essentially a top-down phenomenon.[13] This is particularly true, and more worrisome, for the Republicans. The party's activists are attracted by national party stands, especially evident in situations of clear political choices in presidential elections. The party must build on a weak to nonexistent organizational base at the local level (Prysby). It may be, again from suggestive evidence, that the Republican party with its strong national orientation and issue commitment has little interest in and little to offer voters in state legislature, local and even most congressional and statewide races. If so, this is a curious phenomenon of a truncated politics with a clearly unfinished political agenda, one, despite optimistic predictions, more than likely to take generations to mold into any type of harmonious, politically relevant organism of consequence to localized electorates.

The Democratic party's structure and appeal are less tenuous below the state level. However inadequate, it has some sense of organization and political affiliation to build upon. It is significantly less dependent on party switchers and regional in-migrants for its activist support (Prysby; Moreland, "Immigration . . . ''). Its issue base (as for example in black representation and civil rights) is generic to the traditional concerns of the region (Hadley and Stanley; Steed, "Civil Rights . . . ''). The Democratic party may fare poorly in presidential elections, as it has done in the past, but it remains relatively strong in congressional and state elections. In fact, the farther one penetrates downward in the electoral calendar, the more dominant the Democratic party is.

The transformation of the region's politics then is incomplete. What has occurred is profound. The impact has been enormous, but the final direction, consequence, and time frame for what remains of the transformation has yet to be assessed. The process is underway. The early results are impressive. Yet much remains to be done.

ACTIVISTS IN THE SOUTH

The research in this book proceeds from a common analytic base and a complementary set of assumptions. The commitment was made to analyze the political views and personal attributes of delegates to the national nominating convention in the 1984 presidential election year. Six states were chosen as representative of the South and at the same time providing a range of analytic opportunities sufficient to identify the principal dimensions underlying the change in the politics of the region. The states were Arkansas, Louisiana, Mississippi, North Carolina, South Carolina, and Texas.

Currently, there may be more reliable studies available of mass electorates, their views, and the dynamics affecting their change than there are of elite groups.[14] The reason for this is difficult to explain. Why few to no base lines exist for comparing elite party transformations from the early 1960s to the present is equally hard to explain. In part, the answer may lie in a more recent awareness of the broader impact of the presidential nominating reforms, mentioned earlier, in fueling change. Research studies probing the relevance of national convention delegate views and characteristics for broader audiences boast a long and honorable lineage. Herbert McClosky's early study of national convention delegates was used to set the issue-center of the two parties and relationship of elite views to the parties' base.[15] This particular line of inquiry was not exploited extensively until the post-reform era. Then a series of studies followed in succession attempting to establish the impact of the reforms in recentering the parties.[16] They employed extensive, in-depth analyses of national convention delegates to graph changes in elite party composition and representation at its most critical level—the selection of a presidential candidate and the creation of a national policy agenda.[17] John S. Jackson III and his associates took this approach and expanded it by comparing representative party officials (state and county chairs) with national convention delegates in terms of their policy commitments and political profiles.[18] Different cadres of officials often took contrasting directions in the intensity of their ideological/pragmatic commitments and the nature of issue stands. National convention delegates tend to be more ideological than other cadremen. They exhibit more clearly defined policy positions, a point to remember when attempting to place the studies that follow in context.

In another approach, Ronald B. Rapoport, Alan I. Abramowitz, John McGlennon, and L. Sandy Maisel, as well as a number of the authors represented by studies in this volume, pushed the boundaries farther. In the process they placed the nominating system and the representational value of studying national convention delegates in a broader context, by examining the representativeness of state convention delegates in presidential selection and by identifying the broader pool from which the national level representatives are chosen and its defining qualities.[19]

Each of these studies and approaches has relevance for placing the present analyses in context. Such factors as religion, race, sex, age, ideology, residence and immigration patterns, coalition formation and representativeness, and elite change set the dimensions of greatest relevance in tracing the outlines of a realigning politics and setting it within a broader activist-based literature. The hope would be that, contrary to previous experiences, the present studies could be continued at intervals of successive (or in alternative) election cycles to provide a mapping of the attitudinal and, in a more restricted degree, institutional changes taking place within southern politics. If so, with these studies as a base point, the questions raised by the authors in the individual chapters as to extent and permanence of the changes identified and their consequences could be clearly tracked. Their relevance for a broader mass base politics could be further developed. Such would constitute a worthy candidate for overtime analysis.

AREAS OF SUBSTANTIVE FOCUS

The following briefly addresses questions raised by each of the different foci that conceptually provide the thematic development for the book. Three stand out: elite studies; the nationalization of U.S. politics with particular reference to presidential nominations; and regional political realignment in the context of the South's political distinctiveness. The aspect of the problems addressed also can be used to comment on the party decline/reinvigoration controversy. Questions are raised in each of the areas that provide a common set of themes for the studies in this book and several alternative directions for development are sketched.

Elite Studies of Political Activists

Elite research itself raises a number of analytic questions that serve as the basis for political research and as an aid to the understanding of the dynamics of political change.[20] Elite research focuses on the influentials within the party system, their political attitudes, candidate support patterns, recruitment avenues, demographic characteristics, socialization patterns, degree of professionalism, policy commitments, ideological zeal, motivational explanations for initial and continued political involvement, group ties, career aspirations in politics and their political and community representativeness. The list is long but the presumption is that a reasonable exploration of the key areas that identify activists helps define the institution, its internal change and the continuity in progress, its vitality and responsiveness, and its relevance for the broader political environment. To the extent subgroup characteristics can be isolated, the assumption is that they will explain changes in the policy commitments and group support patterns of the party. It can be argued that a political party, like any institution, has its own distinctive life cycle, overtime pattern of stimulus, response, and stability in direct response to its environment. Since the party is a product of its immediate social environment and political culture, any identified changes in the response pattern assist in evaluating the adequacy and relevance of the party's fulfillment of its societal functions.

A key to such research is the activists chosen to carry the burden of the investigation and the characteristics focused on in the analysis. In the studies in this volume, the focus is on national convention delegates literature, a fruitful point of departure for research into changes in the political system. The characteristics analyzed, from age, sex, and race to issue positions and liberalism/conservatism, represent the standard indicators used to define the activists' attitudinal world.

If elite studies such as this are reasonably correct in their assumptions as to relevance, it is important to ask such questions as: What basic differences exist between the two political parties on a state level and in the regional parties? Are there sharp group and policy factions within one or both parties? If so, what ramifications does this have for future party development? For party representativeness? How has the national Republican party built its activist base? Are there significant numbers of defectors from one or both of the political parties? If so, who defects and why and in which direction do most defectors go? Do defectors increase intraparty or interparty polarization? (Depending on the answer to these questions, the South may have a politics of fragmented parties, not greatly institutionalized beyond the traditional one-partyism of the region or, alternatively, a polarized system of relatively cohesive parties with competing agendas, the presumed objective of most two-party politics.) What is the role of specific subgroups of national interest such as African-Americans and women in the region's politics? And, perhaps most basic of all, how has the region's politics changed and to what extent are its parties representative of the changes taking place in the broader society? Elite studies such as these, more specifically the chapters in this book, should begin answering such questions. The argument here is that they do, as indicated by the various threads and findings brought together in the final chapter of Lewis Bowman.

The Nomination Process and the Nationalization of U.S. Politics

The reforms that took place within the presidential nomination process in the wake of the 1968 election, the forces and events pushing for reform and, more debated, the consequences of the reforms, have been presented in detail in other places and are covered by Steed, Darcy et al., Shaffer, and Hadley and Stanley in their pieces in this volume. The nominating reforms were in response to broad social changes taking place in American society during the 1960s, social changes that laid the basis for new forms of campaign technology, political funding, and media use and emphasis. The end result was a transformed political environment that brought permanent change to party operations and the party system.

All of this and their consequences are developed elsewhere.[21] The nominating reforms gave impetus to the movements that affected the most vital of party activities, the selection of a presidential nominee. The reforms have had nationwide impact. As the studies in this book make clear, their consequences were profound within the southern parties. It is well to remember that the reform movement essentially began in the South with the demands of the Mississippi Freedom Democratic Party and its allies, a group of black and white civil rights activists, for representation in the 1964 Democratic National Convention. The immediate result was the division of Mississippi's convention seats between the insurgent group and the traditional white racist party that had represented the state since Reconstruction. It was a tacit admission of the validity of the insurgent group's call for representation and an indication that the days of racial discrimination within the party would end.[22]

The controversy over accreditation was referred to an obscure party committee for resolution before the next national convention. With the quiet backing of the power centers within the Democratic party, by 1968 all state parties (in reality, these provisions applied only to the southern parties, one reason they received such broad support) were required to open their doors to members of all races and to be able to *prove* their unprejudiced behavior. The penalty was the threat of not being permitted to participate in the quadrennial deliberations of the national convention.

The imposition of such standards and the use of national sanctions to implement them were unprecedented in party politics. While little noticed at this time—

specifically, the procedures of enforcement and their assumptions were not of concern to the media, the public or even, on a broad basis, party officials—these developments laid the basis for the changes that followed. The problem arose with the much more widespread and intense threat to party legitimacy that was mobilized through Eugene McCarthy's and Robert Kennedy's anti-Vietnam challenge to incumbent Lyndon Johnson in 1968, one focused on the question of political accountability and the openness and responsiveness of party procedures.[23] For better or worse, the results since then have transformed representation within the presidential selection process.[24]

In the studies that follow, of particular interest is the role of blacks in reshaping party priorities in the South and in influencing the sharp divergence on policy matters between the parties. These tendencies are charted in several of the chapters (Hadley and Stanley; Moreland, "Ideological Bases . . . "; Prysby) and may result in the clearest exposition of the issue-relevant, programmatic parties thought to be desirable by many political scientists.[25] The South of even recent memory hardly began to meet such standards. V. O. Key, Jr., wrote:

The South, unlike most of the rest of the democratic world, really has no political parties . . . the South must depend for political leadership, not on political parties, but on lone-wolf operations, on fortuitous groupings of individuals usually of a transient nature, on spectacular demagogues odd enough to command the attention of considerable numbers of voters, on men who have become persons of political consequence in their own little bailiwicks, and on other types of leaders whose methods to attract electoral attention serve as substitutes for [the] leadership of a party or organization.
. . . Technically the description of the politics of the South amounts to the problem of analyzing the political struggle under a system of nonpartisan elections, i.e., a system in which no party nominations are made and no party designation appears on the ballot.[26]

Within a generation, the South will have jumped from the chaotic one-partyism (or no-partyism) described by V. O. Key, Jr., to something approaching the coherent groups of the like-minded policy advocates many have advocated.

An extension of the manner in which presidential activists in each of the states represent the mass electorate, the degree to which their views reflect those of party activists at other levels (state legislators, county and local public officials, county chairs and local party workers) and the strength and nature of the ties between activists in the nominating process and the traditional centers of party operations would reveal whether the cadremen studied accurately reflect the views of the party—especially the Democratic party—more broadly cast. The bet is that they do not. If correct, then the question becomes whether presidential activists in southern states are an isolated phenomenon whose energies and views were channeled into the areas most open and least threatening to the state party and its leaders or if the views of activists developed in this book represent the vanguard of the grass-roots transformation, eventually to affect all levels of southern politics. More broadly one might ask if the immediate future will see an americanization of southern politics (that is, political parties divided along the economic class lines prevalent in the North) or a southernization of national politics. The latter would be typified by the clear group issue-based and pro-grammatic (and even ideological) contrasts found in the cohesive activist groups studied in the chapters that follow. An alternative, of course, would be some accommodation between the models. It is curious to be talking of such alternatives within the context of a study of southern party elites. Such a thing would have been unthinkable a few short decades ago.

Realignment, the South and a Traditional One-Party System

Much has been written on realignment, especially on realignment within the South.[27] The topic receives repeated attention in the chapters that follow (Steed, "Party Reform . . . "; Prysby; Moreland, "Ideological Bases . . . "). Clearly, and unlike other areas of U.S. politics, a realignment is underway in the region and its early political ramifications have been noteworthy. The research in this book makes this abundantly clear.

Two issues might warrant additional attention. First is to tease out the relevance of the findings for the party decline/party revitalization controversy. Second is to develop a depiction of the nature of the regional party system—with particular emphasis on the in-state parties—to emerge from the transformations.

The research included here would appear to support a position of party re-vitalization. Perhaps that is the only reasonable direction the tribal and person-alistic politics of the region could have taken. The changes documented or implied (for lack of adequate comparative data) are nonetheless impressive. Possibly, however, a broader set of questions should be asked. Political parties, as Walter Dean Burnham has argued, are the most effective societal vehicle ever created to "generate countervailing collective power on behalf of the many individually powerless against the relatively few who are . . . powerful."[28] This point is par-ticularly relevant in the South with its history of discrimination, status politics, economic exploitation, minimal public sector policy allocations, and closed po-litical systems. Political parties perform functions of electoral mobilization, re-cruitment, and aggregation critical to democratic representation and equitable resource allocation. How well do the new parties of the South perform these functions? Can a Republican party tied to a national party's ideological leanings provide the incentives to activists and relevance for larger publics to succeed at the state and local levels? Are the Democrats fast becoming a minority party in the region's presidential politics? If so, why? Does this trend portend the party's future at successively lower levels? If anything, the resistance to change at the lower levels—in this case, conversion to the opposition party—seems to be more formidable than might have been thought. Why? The resilience of a party system is impressive, although not well understood. The compromises resulting from such accommodations and the representational structures eventually emerging provide a point of departure for speculation and future analysis that moves well beyond the parameters of the decline/revitalization exchange. The initial reaction might be that the political parties in the South are becoming a more vital part of and influence on political decisionmaking and therefore a stronger contribution to democratic representation. The differential development of the two parties within the region in those regards could well merit exploration.

At one time, it was enough to hope that the South might evolve from its peculiarly personalistic system into the pluralistic approach shared by most of the rest of the United States. The changes in the South, however, came rapidly and occurred at a time when political parties throughout the nation were in a period of transition. While not as profound as that being experienced in the South, the national changes are quite significant nonetheless.

A reading of the studies in this volume—and questioning the extent to which the activists examined represent the broader party evolution—suggests the emergence of a system modeled along the lines of the programmatic parties. The personalistic and clientelistic parties of the prealignment era seem to have been dropped precipitously by both Democrats, for whom it had more historical relevance, and by the increasingly competitive Republicans. For reasons that are unclear, the New Deal party model based on a pluralistic conception of interest group bargaining that dominated U.S. politics during most of the twentieth century appears to hold little attraction. Is the New Deal model less relevant for a more homogeneous (even if changing) southern culture? Did the New Deal model represent the party response to a specific historical era and set of economic conditions, now changing? Is the interest-group pluralism model not a natural stepping-stone between the anarchist and unrepresentative clientelistic style and the seemingly more advanced and demanding programmatic model? Or should we look for the answers elsewhere, more in the politics of the region: Are the activists in presidential-level politics too ideological and too policy-sensitive to be broadly representative of the range of social forces in the culture? Are they too cohesive to permit of the give-and-take, coalition-building, and compromising necessary to build a long-term party base? Or are the characteristics identified and dynamics implied indicative only of short-term forces? Are they products of a transitional period and/or a reaction to the choices and alternatives possible within the immediate political environment? Could they be primarily reactions to recent elections and the current electoral cycle? The answer to these and other questions will have to await future developments and further research. It is enough at this point for the studies that follow to outline the major issues to be explored and to identify the characteristics and broader political ramification of those who participate in the presidential selection process.

CONCLUSION

Political change is one of the most exciting and difficult aspects of U.S. politics to study. The research studies in this volume explore change within the context of regional politics and the issues raised for a party system undergoing transition. Within this context, the results may well go beyond expectations.

The political parties in the South moved rapidly over the last several decades to meet the demands of a social order in flux. The chapters that follow make clear how profound this change was. An examination of delegates from South Carolina and Virginia in the 1988 presidential election year indicates that the process, with all its imponderables and aberrations, continues (Steed and McGlennon). The effort of the South to assert itself as a regional power of consequence within the Democratic party through the device of the Super Tuesday primaries served to reemphasize the debilitating cleavages within the party as symbolized by the candidacies and support patterns of the principal contenders, Albert Gore (traditional white and "Old South"), Michael Dukakis (moderate white and more liberal) and Jesse Jackson (black). Not surprisingly, the fundamental political divisions associated with race, gender, income and education, residency, religious fundamentalism and ideology remain. The sample is limited but its results would probably be little different for the other states in the region.

How confusing the cross-alignments are at present can be suggested by visualizing a cross-tabulation of "New South" with "Old South" values and voting patterns and then superimposing on this race. In 1988, blacks who supported Jackson were closer to more traditional white southern Democrats who favored Gore on moral and social values but in line with Dukakis's "New South" Democratic delegates in favoring liberal economic priorities. The Gore and Dukakis delegates, predominantly white, then divided on both economic issues and social positions.

The Republicans in turn, and clearly with less serious political consequences, divided principally in relation to issues of religious fundamentalism and public morality (school prayer, a literal interpretation of the Bible, abortion) between delegates supporting George Bush and those favoring Pat Robertson. The Robertson delegates were also more economically conservative than Bush's, less politically experienced and loyal to the Republican party and more committed to the fortunes of an individual candidate. Whatever their differences, the recent history of the South indicates that at the presidential level, Republicans are more able to smooth over their divisions and, in the indicator of greatest political weight, win the state-level presidential elections. Such a formula continues to elude the Democrats.

The broader questions that remain to be answered relate to what the research in this book portends for the future. These will be left for other observers of southern politics to address. One factor predictably will remain constant: the South, as always, will continue to provide one of the most intriguing areas for the exploration of the most fundamental of political questions available in U.S. politics.

NOTES

1. V. O. Key, Jr., *Southern Politics in State and Nation* (New York: Alfred A. Knopf/Vintage Books, 1949); Avery Leiserson, ed., *The American South in the 1960's*

(New York: Praeger, 1964); Donald R. Matthews and James W. Prothro, *Negroes and the New Southern Politics* (New York: Harcourt, Brace and World, 1966); Allan P. Sindler, ed., *Change in the Contemporary South* (Durham: Duke University Press, 1963); William C. Havard, ed., *The Changing Politics of the South* (Baton Rouge: Louisiana State University Press, 1972); and Numan V. Bartley and Hugh D. Graham, *Southern Politics and the Second Reconstruction* (Baltimore: Johns Hopkins University Press, 1975).

2. Key, *Southern Politics*, 665.

3. Earl Black and Merle Black, *Politics and Society in the South* (Cambridge, MA: Harvard University Press, 1987), 168–170.

4. Key, *Southern Politics*; Leiserson, ed., *The American South*; Sindler, ed., *Change in the Contemporary South*; Donald S. Strong, *Urban Republicanism in the South* (University, Ala.: University of Alabama Bureau of Public Administration, 1960); Matthews and Prothro, *Negroes and the New-Southern Politics*; Alexander P. Lamis, *The Two-Party South* (New York: Oxford University Press, 1984); Harold W. Stanley, *Voter Mobilization and the Politics of Race* (New York: Praeger, 1987); and Black and Black, *Politics and Society in the South*.

5. Black and Black, *Politics and Society in the South*; Lamis, *The Two-Party South*; Stanley, *Voter Mobilization and the Politics of Race*; Robert P. Steed, Laurence W. Moreland, and Tod A. Baker, eds., *Party Politics in the New South* (New York: Praeger, 1980); Moreland, Baker, and Steed, eds., *Contemporary Southern Political Attitudes and Behavior: Studies and Essays* (New York: Praeger, 1982); and Baker, Steed, and Moreland, eds., *Religion and Politics in the South: Mass and Elite Perspectives* (New York: Praeger, 1984).

6. Lawrence J. Hanks, *The Struggle for Black Empowerment in Three Georgia Counties* (Knoxville: University of Tennessee Press, 1987); Robert J. Norrell, *Reaping the Whirlwind: The Civil Rights Movement in Tuskegee* (New York: Alfred A. Knopf, 1985); Hanes Walton, Jr., *Invisible Politics: Black Political Behavior* (Albany: State University of New York Press, 1985); Michael B. Preston, Lenneal J. Henderson, Jr., and Paul Puryear, eds., *The New Black Politics: The Search for Political Power* (New York: Longman, 1982); Rod Bush, ed., *The New Black Vote: Politics and Power in Four American Cities* (San Francisco: Synthesis Publications, 1984); Paul Kleppner, *Chicago Divided: The Making of a Black Mayor* (DeKalb: Northern Illinois University Press, 1985); Lucius J. Barker, *Our Time Has Come: A Delegate's Diary of Jesse Jackson's 1984 Presidential Campaign* (Urbana: University of Illinois Press, 1988); Melvin G. Holli and Paul M. Green, *The Making of the Mayor: Chicago 1983* (William B. Eerdmans, 1984); and Bob Faw and Nancy Skelton, *Thunder in America: The Improbable Presidential Campaign of Jesse Jackson in 1984* (Toronto: Paperjacks, 1988).

7. William Crotty, *American Politics in Decline*, 2nd ed. (Boston: Little, Brown, 1984); Martin P. Wattenberg, *The Decline of American Political Parties: 1952–1984* (Cambridge, MA: Harvard University Press, 1986); David E. Price, *Bringing Back the Parties* (Washington, D.C.: Congressional Quarterly Press, 1984); Larry J. Sabato, *The Party's Just Begun: Shaping Political Parties for America's Future* (Glenview, IL: Scott, Foresman/Little, Brown, 1988); and Xandra Kayden and Eddie Make, Jr., *The Party Goes On* (New York: Basic Books, 1986).

8. See, for example, Everett Carll Ladd, Jr., *American Political Parties* (New York: W. W. Norton, 1970); Everett Carll Ladd, Jr., and Charles D. Hadley, *Transformation of the American Party System* (New York: W. W. Norton, 1975).

9. Jeane Kirkpatrick, *Dismantling the Parties: Reflections on Party Reform and Party Decomposition* (Washington, D.C.: American Enterprise Institute, 1978); and Nelson W. Polsby, *Consequences of Party Reform* (Oxford: Oxford University Press, 1983).

10. Cornelius P. Cotter, James L. Gibson, John F. Bibby, and Robert J. Huckshorn, *Party Organizations in American Politics* (New York: Praeger, 1984).

11. Anne H. Hopkins, "Campaign Activities and Local Party Organization in Nashville," 65–88, and Richard W. Murray and Kent L. Tedin, "The Emergence of Two-Party Competition in the Sunbelt: The Case of Houston," 39–63, in William Crotty, ed., *Political Parties in Local Areas* (Knoxville: University of Tennessee Press, 1986).

12. See, for example, Harold W. Stanley, "Southern Partisan Changes: Dealignment, Realignment or Both?" *Journal of Politics* 50 (February 1988): 64–88.

13. Stanley, "Southern Partisan Changes."

14. See Black and Black, *Politics and Society in the South*; and, for an earlier era, Matthews and Prothro, *Negroes and the New Southern Politics*.

15. Herbert McClosky, Paul J. Hoffman, and Rosemary O'Hara, "Issue Conflict and Consensus among Party Leaders and Followers," *American Political Science Review* 56 (1960): 406–429.

16. Kirkpatrick, *Dismantling the Parties*; Price, *Bringing Back the Parties*; Polsby, *Consequences of Party Reform*; and William Crotty, *Decision for the Democrats* (Baltimore: Johns Hopkins Press, 1978).

17. Warren E. Miller and M. Kent Jennings, *Parties in Transition: A Longitudinal Study of Party Elites and Party Supporters* (New York: Russell Sage Foundation, 1986); and Miller, *Without Consent: Mass-Elite Linkages in Presidential Politics* (Lexington, Ky: The University Press of Kentucky, 1988).

18. John S. Jackson III, Barbara L. Brown, and David Bositis, "Herbert McClosky and Friends Revisited," *American Politics Quarterly* 10 (1982): 158–180; and Jackson, Jesse C. Brown, and Barbara L. Brown, "Recruitment, Representation, and Political Values," *American Politics Quarterly* 6 (1978): 187–212. See also Robert S. Moatjoy, William R. Shaffer, and Ronald E. Weber, "Policy Preferences of Party Elites and Masses: Conflict or Consensus," *American Politics Quarterly* 8 (1980): 319–344.

19. Ronald B. Rapoport, Alan I. Abramowitz, and John McGlennon, eds., *The Life of the Parties: Activists in Presidential Politics* (Lexington, Ky.: University Press of Kentucky, 1986).

20. For a related discussion focusing on local political parties, see William Crotty, "The Comparative Study of Local Parties: An Agenda for Research," In Crotty, ed., *Political Parties in Local Areas*, 1–38.

21. William Crotty and John S. Jackson III, *Presidential Primaries and Nominations* (Washington, DC: Congressional Quarterly Press, 1985); Polsby, *Consequences of Party Reform*; James W. Ceaser, *Reforming the Reforms: A Critical Analysis of the Presidential Selection Process* (Cambridge, Mass.: Ballinger, 1982); William Crotty, *Party Reform* (New York: Longman, 1983); Larry J. Sabato, *PAC Power* (New York: W. W. Norton, 1985); Sabato, *The Rise of Political Consultants: New Ways of Winning Elections* (New York: Basic Books, 1982); R. Kenneth Godwin, *One Billion Dollars of Influence: The Direct Marketing of Politics* (Chatham, NJ: Chatham House, 1988); Frank J. Sorauf, *Money in American Elections* (Glenview, IL: Scott Foresman/Little, Brown, 1988); and John Chubb and Paul Peterson, eds., *The New Direction in American Politics* (Washington, D.C.: Brookings Institution, 1986).

22. Crotty, *Decision for the Democrats*.

23. Crotty, *Decision for the Democrats*; Byron E. Shafer, *Quiet Revolution: The Struggle for the Democratic Party and the Shaping of Post-Reform Politics* (New York: Russell Sage Foundation, 1983); and Price, *Bringing Back the Parties*.

24. Crotty and Jackson, *Presidential Primaries and Nominations*; and Byron E. Shafer, *Bifurcated Politics: Evolution and Reform in the National Party Convention* (New York: Russell Sage Foundation, 1988).

25. American Political Science Association, *Toward a More Responsible Two-Party System* (New York: Rinehart, 1950); and E. E. Schattschneider, *Party Government* (New York: Rinehart, 1942).

26. Key, *Southern Politics*, 16.

27. Philip E. Converse, "On the Possibility of Major Political Realignment in the South," in Angus Campbell, Philip E. Converse, Warren E. Miller, and Donald E. Stokes, *Elections and the Political Order* (New York: John Wiley and Sons, 1966), 212–242; Bruce A. Campbell and Richard J. Trilling, eds., *Realignment in American Politics: Toward a Theory* (Austin: University of Texas Press, 1980); James Sundquist, *Dynamics of the Party System: Alignment and Realignment of Political Parties in the United States* (Washington, DC: Brookings Institution, 1973); Jack Bass and Walter DeVries, *The Transformation of Southern Politics: Social Change and Political Consequence since 1945* (New York: Basic Books, 1976); Lamis, *The Two-Party South*; Black and Black, *Politics and Society in the South*; and Havard, ed., *The Changing Politics of the South*.

28. Walter Dean Burnham, *Critical Elections and the Mainsprings of American Politics* (New York: W. W. Norton, 1970), p. 133.

Part I
Party Reform and Party Systems

Party Reform, the Nationalization of American Politics, and Party Change in the South

Robert P. Steed

Writing in the late 1940s, V. O. Key, Jr., identified four major interrelated points of southern political distinctiveness: (1) the one-party system; (2) the Jim Crow system of social, economic, and political segregation; (3) malapportionment; and (4) low voter participation related to disenfranchisement and the one-party system. At the very foundation of this system was the overriding concern of most white southerners with maintaining the pattern of white supremacy established in the 1890s and carefully nourished over the first half of the twentieth century.[1] In Key's view, if and when the South experienced significant change in these elements, the region would be well on its way toward losing its special characteristics and becoming more integrated into national political patterns and practices.

The changes, fueled by the experiences of World War II[2] and the developments of the immediate postwar world, began even as Key wrote. Southern Democratic solidarity began to crack with the 1948 Dixiecratic movement, which was generated by southern white dissatisfaction with what seemed an unreasonably liberal national Democratic party stance on civil rights.[3] It continued to waver less intensely into the 1950s as the Republican party began to make some modest inroads into metropolitan areas in presidential elections.[4] At the same time, and closely related to these rudimentary changes in party politics, the fabric of southern life began to change in other ways. The region became more urbanized and industrialized. Its economy, spurred by this "bulldozer revolution,"[5] was accompanied by rising education and income levels. The composition of the population changed as well. Blacks, seeking better jobs and less discrimination, continued the out-migration begun during the war; nonsoutherners, moreover, moved into Dixie at increased rates. Most significantly, the region's system of racial segregation came under attack and began to crumble in spite of stubborn resistance, especially in the Deep South. Pressure from increasingly militant and persistent civil rights groups, together with a series of actions by the national government (e.g., the Supreme Court's decision in *Brown* v. *Board of Education* and Congress's passage of civil rights legislation in 1957, 1960, and 1964), began to restructure the South's racial policies. Blacks slowly gained more access to the ballot as various Jim Crow barriers were attacked and removed. The crowning blow in this struggle was the passage of the 1965 Voting Rights Act.[6]

These changes fired the modifications in the party system by altering the structure of political competition and redefining the political agenda, especially in regard to racial issues.[7] The Democratic party's national and state electoral coalitions changed. It attracted the vast majority of newly enfranchised black voters, who tended to associate their political interests with the party that nationally had championed their cause most vigorously (particularly since 1964). At the same time, and at least partly in response to the party's new racial composition, some who had traditionally affiliated themselves with the Democratic party bolted that party in favor of independent status or Republican affiliation. The Republican party benefited not only from dissatisfaction within the Democratic party but also from other changes underway. In-migration of Republicans from other regions was especially important in states such as Florida, Virginia, and Texas. Increased educational and economic levels, coupled with a lessening importance attached to the racial issue, helped to overcome the historical animosity toward the GOP. There were renewed efforts to build viable Republican state party organizations in the region, efforts enhanced by the party's newfound respectability and its heightened attractiveness for strong candidates and organizational leaders. In short, dramatic changes in the South were reflected in the greater ability of the parties to define and structure political conflict in the region.[8]

The elements identified by Key as defining southern political distinctiveness have, therefore, changed, and, as he predicted, this has been accompanied by the region's becoming more fully integrated into national politics. While the importance of the agents and processes of change outlined above is reasonably well documented, it is arguable that these explanations generally have overlooked the national convention delegate selection reforms begun by the Democratic party in the late 1960s and early 1970s as an agent of southern political transformation. This is surprising insofar as research on party delegate selection and presidential nomination reforms has excited political parties scholars not only because of their effects on the parties themselves but because they have had a number of broader, and often unintended, consequences for other elements of the political system.

The immediate impact of the early reforms was evident in the composition, orientations, and actions of the delegates to the 1972 Democratic convention,[9] but the long-term impact ranged far beyond that specific event. It affected such diverse matters as the rising influence of the electronic media, the increasing importance of interest groups (especially political action committees), candidate nomination strategies, and, at least in the view of some observers, the declining influence of party organizations in nominations, elections, and governmental organizational activities. James W. Ceaser summarized the impact of these reforms:

American politics has just passed through an extraordinary era of reform, the consequences of which have been as profound as those of the reform period that accompanied the Progressive Movement earlier in this century. No major national institution, with the possible exception of the Supreme Court, has escaped the influence of the recent reforms, and their effects are certain to continue—and perhaps to increase—throughout this decade, even as the impetus for reform begins to diminish.[10]

In light of the widespread impact of these reforms on the national party system, it seems reasonable to expect they had an impact on changes in the southern party system as well. This chapter pursues this line of inquiry by identifying and examining possible contact points between party reform and southern political change. Since the changing South provides the context for the examination of reform consequences for regional political patterns, attention will be directed primarily toward the critical reforms of the 1968–1972 period. Although the entire reform process is of interest, this period is especially relevant because it witnessed the operation of the McGovern-Fraser Commission, arguably the most significant of all the reform efforts, and it coincided with a critical juncture in southern political development: the Voting Rights Act of 1965, which brought about changes in the southern Democratic electoral coalition, the turmoil of the civil rights struggle, the strong 1968 southern showing made by George Wallace's American Independent Party, and the Republican party's increased southern electoral effort and subsequent support. A brief summary of recent party reform will provide the foundation for identifying and discussing possible connections between these reforms and southern political change.

THE NATURE AND CONSEQUENCES OF PARTY REFORM

Over the past two decades the major political parties in the United States undertook a series of actions designed to alter the delegate selection process for their national nominating conventions.[11] The reform effort touched both the Republican and Democratic parties, but in terms of drama, longevity, interest, attention, conflict, and impact, it clearly was most pronounced in the latter.[12]

For the Democrats, the recent national convention delegate selection reform movement can be traced to 1964 when the Special Equal Rights Committee was established to examine problems relating to minority (black) representation among state delegations. This committee's work was important primarily because it set some vital precedents for its successors and began an attack on a persistent representational problem that would continue to be addressed in a variety of ways by later reform commissions.

Since that time, the Democrats have had roughly a dozen reform commissions.[13] By most accounts, the keystone to the reform enterprise was the Commission on Party Reform and Delegate Selection, popularly known as the McGovern-Fraser Commission. Established during the final throes of the tumultuous 1968 Democratic Convention in Chicago, it was a major effort to democratize the delegate selection process by opening it to greater participation by the party's rank-and-file. It increased the opportunities for convention participation by groups—specifically blacks, women, and young people—that had heretofore been numerically underrepresented. Concomitantly, the reforms recommended and ultimately enforced upon the state parties were designed to reduce the influence of party regulars or professionals in the national nominating process.

Through skillful use of the media and an aggressive approach to its work, the McGovern-Fraser Commission moved boldly to adopt a set of guidelines to achieve its underlying goals for the selection of future national convention delegates.[14] These guidelines addressed a variety of concerns and called, among other things, for the adoption of easily available written rules regarding the selection of national convention delegates. They recommended affirmative action to represent blacks, women, and young people (under age 30) in proportion to their percentages in a state's population as well as the timely selection of delegates in the year of the national convention. Seventy-five percent of all delegates were to be selected at the congressional district level or lower, and no more than 10 percent of all delegates could be selected through state committees. The unit rule by which a state's delegation would cast its entire vote in accordance with the wishes of a majority was banned, and adequate public notice of all meetings involving delegate selection was required.

Upon the development of these rules, the commission proceeded to engage in strong enforcement rhetoric designed to bring state parties into compliance by the 1972 presidential nominating process. While its authority to demand compliance was, as William Crotty maintains, "somewhat illusionary" and certainly unprecedented in the annals of modern party history,[15] the McGovern-Fraser Commission emitted an aura of authority that led to virtually complete success. Against a long-accepted tradition of allowing state parties almost complete autonomy in the selection of their national convention delegates, the commission's ability to enforce its regulations on the state parties with the backing of the federal courts represented a new departure in U.S. party politics.[16] The magnitude of the accomplishment can be easily indicated. In 1970, when the push for compliance began in earnest, no state met all of the fifteen basic standards set forth by the commission, and states were out of line on average with two out of three of the specified guidelines. By 1972, 40 of the states (plus the District of Columbia and the territories) were in full compliance while the remaining ten were in substantial compliance. State parties met 99 percent of the guidelines overall, and over 98 percent of the delegates to the 1972 convention were selected by procedures prescribed by the commission (primaries and open caucuses or conventions). The percentages of blacks and women among state delegations approximately tripled compared with 1968 (from 13 percent to 42 percent for women and from 6 percent to 16 percent for blacks) and the percentage of young delegates increased over fivefold (from 4 percent to 22 percent). Moreover, all state parties adopted new written rules consistent with the principles advocated by the commission.[17]

The McGovern-Fraser Commission's sweeping reforms and unprecedented success set the context for all the succeeding commissions that have addressed the questions raised by the events surrounding the 1968 Democratic convention. As summarized by Crotty:

The period following the introduction of McGovern-Fraser and the election of 1972 was one of consolidation and reconsideration. The emphasis of reform during this phase was on reassessing, and constantly modifying, the reform guidelines. This was particularly true in presidential selection; each election begat a new "reform" committee which in turn begat a new set of rules for the succeeding election.[18]

The central thrust of the post–1972 reform effort has been to modify the changes made by McGovern-Fraser. While some changes were accomplished, the basic reforms of the 1969–72 period endured.

Critical in this retention of the spirit of the new rules was the work of the Mikulski Commission. Established by the Democratic regulars mainly to rid the party of the McGovern-Fraser Commission guidelines, this commission essentially endorsed the reforms and held the line by recommending modest adjustments designed to make the new rules more palatable to the critics. Along with a number of procedural changes (e.g., a relaxation of provisions relating to proxy voting and quorum requirements), the major changes enacted by the Mikulski Commission involved the adoption of less stringent affirmative action programs, a requirement that all national convention votes being contested in a primary or a caucus be allocated proportionately among all contenders receiving at least 10 percent (later amended to 15 percent) of the vote cast, and a requirement that participation in party convention affairs (primaries and caucuses) be limited to Democrats. It also recommended a rule that all contenders approve delegates running in their behalf and a modification of the selection process to allow state committees to choose up to 25 percent of the states' national convention delegations.[19]

Having thus survived a strong challenge, the fundamental reforms continued in the face of additional efforts to alter them. Subsequent commissions have tinkered with various of the McGovern-Fraser rules, but the system has not returned in either form or spirit to 1968. Party organizational regulars recaptured some of their influence in the presidential nominating process through the establishment of noncontested slots for specified party and elected officials among state delegations to the national convention ("super delegates"), a practice begun by the Hunt Commission in 1984 and expanded by the Fairness Commission in

1988. However, the board dimensions of reform persist: more heterogeneous group representation, greater opportunities for rank-and-file participation, closer ties or commitments between contenders and delegates, and the necessity of state party adherence to national party rules on delegate selection supported by such court decisions as *Cousins* v. *Wigoda* (1975) and *Democratic Party of the United States of America* v. *LaFollette* (1981). In setting rules for the 1984 Democratic national convention the Hunt Commission made some headway in modifying earlier reforms (particularly those that had weakened the party), but even there the commission's staff director concluded that "The [Hunt] commission's most conspicuous party-strengthening moves—enhancing the role of party leaders and elected officials and (partially) unbinding the national convention—represent rather modest changes. . . . "[20] Similarly, in considering rules for the 1988 national convention the Fairness Commission did little to reverse the reform impetus beyond increasingly slightly the number of superdelegates.

Students of party reform identified a variety of consequences for the parties and for the political system. The precise details change a bit with time as the party rules continue to be altered, but the broad outlines of reform impact have been constant. For example, since 1968 rank-and-file participation in delegate selection processes clearly increased, primaries proliferated, and the overall selection process was compressed into a relatively short three-month period. A wider range of groups (especially those targeted by affirmative action programs) became more involved in the nominating process. Delegates continued to be divided among various contenders in conjunction with requirements relating to proportional representation or at least "fair reflection" of candidate strength, and preconvention ties between delegates and contenders were solidified.

These developments, in turn, had some obvious effects on the nature of presidential nomination campaigns. They increased the number of people seeking the presidential nomination, lengthened the overall selection process, and made it more costly in terms of time, money, and energy. The reformed selection process led to more opportunities for an increasingly important role for the media, particularly in the early states, and the media, in turn, exaggerated the influence of the early primary and caucus states far beyond their normal proportionate significance in the national political arena. Strategically, contenders for the nomination found they must place added emphasis on entering a number of early states contests. Candidates must attract sufficient monetary contributions to remain competitive, and they must be able to make effective use of the media to establish their desired image and to attract the widespread grassroots support necessary for success.

The national convention itself also changed under these reforms. Delegates' flexibility was reduced tremendously, if not lost altogether, because of their required commitment to specific candidates. This led recent conventions to become virtual rubber stamps for the primary/caucus battles that preceded them. Negotiation and compromise on a host of matters before the convention were made more difficult, thus undermining whatever deliberative quality it once had.

Additionally, the national convention delegates elected under the new rules have been consistently more ideological and programmatically polarized than the parties' respective electorates (with the Democrats becoming more liberal and the Republicans becoming more conservative).[21] This, in turn, raises some serious questions about the degree to which the national conventions and their nominees can be considered representative of the party rank and file. Paradoxically, the democratization effort seems to have produced greater representation of selected groups (as the reformers hoped) while not diminishing the socioeconomic and ideological representatives of the delegates in the aggregate.

Beyond their impact on the presidential nominating process, the reforms critically affected the political parties themselves, a point that should not be surprising given the close connection between parties and the nominating function. In broad terms, it may be argued that the reforms weakened the parties. For one thing, they reduced the role of party officials in the nominating process in favor of candidate-centered organizations and rank-and-file participation (although this has been modified slightly in recent years with rules increasing the number of party leaders and elected officials in a state's delegation). Related to this, the reformed procedures facilitated the capture of the process by participants in low turnout contests, thus giving them disproportionate influence on party affairs. Additionally, the new reforms tended to elevate the media to a place of greater prominence in the quest for delegate support at the expense of state and local party organizations. Collectively, these changes constricted the party's incentive structure for workers and hindered its efforts to utilize delegate appointments as inducements for party support. Similarly, the continued reduction of the convention's deliberative component, begun with the emergence of television coverage in the 1950s, cut deeply into the party officials' traditional role in mediating among diverse groups in the party coalition in the interest of holding the party together for a strong general election campaign.

Perhaps Jeane Kirkpatrick's charge that "the most important sources of party decomposition are the *decisions* taken by persons attempting to reform the parties . . . "[22] is a bit strong, but there can be little doubt that they have hurt the parties. David Price summarized the impact in these terms:

The adverse consequences for party organizations are unmistakable: reduced decision-making powers, reduced incentives for serious involvement, a reduced capacity to influence who attends the convention (and hence to discipline and reward party members), and a weakened position from which to deal with candidates and their organizations.[23]

As the reforms weakened the connection between the party and its nominee, they contributed to the difficulties facing the party in its attempt to organize the government. This is seen most clearly in the relationship between the president and Congress. One of the devices available to bridge the separation of powers in our system historically has been the party. But if there is little or no party tie on the part of the president, and if he won the nomination and then the office with little help from party leaders in Congress or out, there may be little common ground or mutual self interest available for the construction of such a bridge. As Richard Rose has written, "Insofar as a politician concentrates his attention upon the relatively contentless concerns of campaigning, distancing himself from any organization besides his own personal following, he loses a stable commitment of party loyalty to invoke against the sub-governments of Washington."[24]

Finally, some observers have commented on the consequences of reform for the operation of our democratic system. On the one hand, the new rules democratized the system by opening the nominating process to greater participation by the party-in-the-electorate. On the other hand, in weakening the role of the party and in increasing the roles of personal campaign organizations, the media, and political action committees, the reforms took something of an antidemocratic twist insofar as such changes have a negative impact on the public's ability to hold these elements of the system accountable.[25] Here, as with other elements of reform impact, the reforms rippled out into the larger political system with both intended and unintended consequences that extend far beyond the initial goals of the reformers.

PARTY REFORM AND CHANGING SOUTHERN POLITICS

While the rationale for party reform was not couched in terms of southern party change, the reforms were integrally connected to political change in the region. The most obvious connection was associated with the civil rights movement and related changes in the Democratic party in the South. Historically, the southern Democratic party was a white man's party devoted largely to the maintenance of the one-party system and white supremacy. While there certainly were exceptions, the fundamental question of race had been pretty much settled around the turn of the century and was little debated for the next 50 years. As long as race remained off the center of the national political stage, southern Democrats remained basically loyal to the national New Deal Democratic coalition in spite of its inclusion of groups—Catholics, southern and eastern European ethnics, organized labor—for whom most southerners had little affinity.

When the national party began to take a more progressive course on the race issue, southern Democrats found it increasingly difficult to remain loyal to the party. From 1948 to 1968, this unhappiness with the national party surfaced repeatedly in the form of third party movements (the Dixiecrats in 1948 and the American Independent Party in 1968) and unpledged elector movements. It also surfaced in periodic endorsements of candidates other than the national ticket by southern Democratic party leaders. Sometimes their displeasure even extended to endorsements of the Republican candidates as happened in some areas in the region in 1964. While some longtime Democrats such as Strom Thurmond and Albert Watson openly switched their permanent allegiance to the Republican party, the majority continued to try to work within the party. For the most part, these Democrats fought a rearguard action aimed at stemming the national party's liberal tide on the race issue. They stubbornly hung onto their traditional policy orientations through the 1950s and well into the 1960s in spite of eroding solidarity and resolve within their ranks.

By the mid–1960s the southern state parties and the region were under increased pressure from the national party and the national government to allow blacks to participate fully in the political system. After the passage of the 1964 Civil Rights Act and the 1965 Voting Rights Act, black voter registration and participation increased dramatically.[26] This electoral alteration, of course, was enough in itself to make state Democratic party leaders back away somewhat from the hard line racial stances that had been common.[27] However, there still was resistance within the party to bringing the newly enfranchised blacks into party operations. The growing acceptance of black participation in the party-in-the-electorate was not paralleled by acceptance of black participation in party organizational circles. This circumstance was reflected in the virtual exclusion of blacks from state conventions and from state delegations to national conventions before 1968. National party concern with this problem increased with such activities as the Mississippi Freedom Democratic Party's challenge to that state's regular—all white—Democratic delegation to the 1964 national convention. It helped prompt the national party to establish the Special Equal Rights Committee, the first step on the recent reform road.[28] The efforts of this committee, coupled with some key delegation challenges at the 1968 Democratic national convention, succeeded in cracking the racial barriers in the southern delegations. (See Table 1.1.)

The guidelines developed by the McGovern-Fraser Commission calling for affirmative action for blacks constituted a significant advance in the drive for fuller participation. By 1972 a noticeable change was evident in the racial composition of every southern delegation. As shown in Table 1.1, in extreme cases black representation jumped many times as compared with 1968, and in every state except Georgia the proportionate increase was at least double that of 1968. Even after subsequent reform commissions lessened the emphasis on affirmative action, black participation in southern state delegations persisted and spread downward into state level party activities. By the end of the decade, large-scale black participation became the accepted norm within most southern state and local Democratic parties as evidenced by surveys of state conventions and local party committees. For example, a 1980 survey of state conventions in three southern states (Virginia, South Carolina, and Texas) revealed that a large portion of the delegates participating in each state convention was black.[29] A white party spokesman at the 1984 Democratic state convention in South Carolina claimed that his state party was now the most fully integrated in the nation.[30] In short, the racial composition of the southern Democratic parties clearly changed over the 1970s. While it may have been inevitable given the other changes then underway in the region, it seems clear that the push by the party reforms provided further impetus.

Table 1.1
Percentage Black Southern Delegates by State, 1964–1972

State	1964	1968	1972
Alabama	0	4	27
Arkansas	0	1	18
Florida	0	6	14
Georgia	7	27	34
Louisiana	0	17	41
Mississippi	0	19	56
North Carolina	0	5	20
South Carolina	0	14	34
Tennessee	0	11	33
Virginia	0	9	29

Source: Democratic National Committee as reported in William Crotty,
    Party Reform, 124-127.

Reforms helped move southern Democratic parties to integrate their organizations and contributed in other ways to changing their traditional party image. For example, affirmative action requirements for women originally recommended by the McGovern-Fraser Commission became mandated at 50 percent for 1980 and beyond. This helped push the Democrats away from the region's traditionally nonsupportive posture regarding the participation of women in politics.[31] The sex quotas combined with affirmative action for blacks remade the image of the southern Democratic party in a mold quite far removed from its former image as the party most associated with the defense of fundamental southern political values. This, in turn, was reflected in the nature of political orientations within the two parties on a series of social and economic questions.[32] In very real terms, to the extent a party can now be identified as the repository of traditional southern values, it is the southern Republican state parties. Whether this would have happened anyway is a matter for speculation. However, there seems little doubt that the past two decades of party reform coincided closely with the internal changes within the southern party system.

A somewhat less obvious and testable possibility concerns the contribution of the reforms to the growing disaffection of native white southerners with the region's Democratic party. Since there is some evidence that this group has been unhappy with the liberality of the national party during the 1950s and 1960s, it would seem logical that the unhappiness would extend to the state and local parties when those parties fell victim to the same trends. For a time, southerners could maintain their Democratic affiliations at the state level while denouncing and abandoning the party at the national level.[33] However, the changing image and policy positions of the state parties make this increasingly difficult. The problem appears aggravated by the fact that the reforms worked to reduce the discretion of state parties in a number of critical matters. For example, delegate selection rules that limit the decision-making possibilities for individual delegates at the national conventions run counter to values (states' rights and strong individualism) that have long been important features of southern political culture.[34]

The Republican party, with its less sweeping interest in reform, avoided these types of infringements on the authority of state parties and individual delegates. This point may not cause much stir among the electorate as a whole, but, in all likelihood, it is not lost on party activists. Southern Democratic parties have lost adherents over the past two decades both within the electorate and among party leaders. While there is no sure way to ascertain the roots of this movement, there is indirect evidence that changing party image is part of the reason for switches in party allegiance among southern convention delegates and local precinct officials.[35]

The key impact of the party reforms undoubtedly is related to the declining role of race in southern politics and the altered nature of the Democratic party in the South. Another contact point between party reform and southern political change relates to the role of the reforms in the erosion of the traditional isolation of the southern political system from the national political system.[36] The declining sense of southernness, of course, has been related to a variety of factors, but at least one possible factor is the increased attention now given to southern states in the nomination process. As Kathy B. Smith and Craig Allen Smith have pointed out, election campaigns that include the South and that bring media attention to the region contribute to a closer integration of the area into national politics.[37]

Since the one-party South was normally written off by the Republican party, there was little attention paid to the region by either party's candidates in this century until the appearance of some halting two-party competition in the 1950s.[38] The proliferation of primaries after 1968, in part a response to the McGovern-Fraser Commission reforms, added a number of southern states to the list selecting their delegates in this fashion (see Table 1.2). In combination with other reforms (proportionately in particular), these primaries elevated the strategic importance of various of the states in the region. In the 1984 Democratic nomination struggle, for example, a number of the southern primaries were critical to the chances of Walter Mondale, John Glenn, Jesse Jackson, and Gary Hart in particular, all of whom gave serious attention to the southern states.[39] Similarly in 1980, the South Carolina Republican primary proved critical for John Connally, Howard Baker, and Ronald Reagan. The 1988 Super Tuesday primaries, preceded by the South Carolina Republican primary, continued this trend, especially since they became a crucial feature of the nomination struggle in both parties.[40] What one study concluded about the importance of presidential speeches in the region should

Table 1.2
Southern States Having Presidential Primaries, 1968–1988

1968	1972	1976	1980	1984	1988
Alabama	Alabama	Alabama	Alabama	Alabama	Alabama
Florida	Florida	Florida	Florida	Florida	Florida
	N.C.	N.C.	N.C.	N.C.	N.C.
	Tenn.	Tenn.	Tenn.	Tenn.	Tenn.
		Georgia	Georgia	Georgia	Georgia
		Texas	Texas*	Texas - R	Texas
		La.- D	La.	La.	La.
		Ark.	Ark. - D	Miss. - R	Ark.
			S.C. - R		S.C. - R
			Miss.- R		Virginia
					Miss.

D = Democratic primary only
R = Republican primary only
* = Democratic primary did not choose or allocate delegates

Source: 1968-1984 lists adapted from David Price, Bringing Back the
        Parties, 208-209; 1988 list from data compiled in
        Cultural Information Service, Following the 1988 Campaign
        (New York: CIStems, 1988).

apply as well to the increased primary attention and its impact on the nationalization of southern politics:

The increased sense of relationship between the South and the nation should continue to
transform the Southern political culture. Since a relational context for policy discussions
fosters a sense of Southern inclusion, national policy initiatives should prove less threatening than before.[41]

Finally, from a nationalization perspective, the reforms also served to push
the national party system toward the traditional southern party system in some
ways. They made parties less central in the nominating process, contributed to
the increased personalism of U.S. electoral politics, reduced the parties' linkage
capacity for different parts of the governmental system, and negatively affected
their ability to enforce accountability among public officials. Ironically, therefore, they moved national party politics more toward the traditional mold of the
southern party system, characterized as it was by a highly personalistic, fac-
tionalized, and discontinuous politics.[42] The nationalization impact, therefore,
tended to draw the national and southern state party systems together. In both
instances, the resulting convergence underscores the erosion of distinctiveness
in the southern party system.

CONCLUSION

The reforms undertaken mainly by the national Democratic party over the past
two decades clearly have had far-reaching consequences for the party and political

systems. While extensive attention has been directed at various impacts of reform, little attention has been given its possible consequences for regional political patterns and practices. Studies of southern party change have paid scant attention to the possibility that party reform was a factor contributing to an alteration of that region's party system. This chapter suggests that these reforms were intertwined with the recent changes in the southern party system. For students of southern politics, the identification of connections between party reform and the post–World War II partisan developments in the region adds another element in the continuing effort to put these changes in focus. It helps provide a context for considering the changing nature of contemporary party coalitions in the South.

These observations have some obvious limitations. For example, there has been no systematic effort to gather new data to specifically address certain aspects of this argument. Studies of party switching within the electorate and among party leaders, to take one case, were not structured to examine the relationship between the impact of reforms on the Democratic party's image and changes in party identification. Secondary analyses of existing data, therefore, do not really get to that point very directly. Current efforts to follow this line of investigation would be hampered seriously by the problems of recall data, especially for those who switched their party allegiance in the critical period of the early-to-mid–1970s. A similar problem relates to the scarcity of data on such matters as the symbolic inclusion of the South in national political affairs, especially as a direct result of the increased number of primaries in the region. While a case can be made that this has had the effect described above, additional attitudinal data would clarify the point.

Still, the limits of the discussion should not override the rather convincing evidence that the party reforms of the 1960s and 1970s interacted with a host of other factors to contribute significantly to southern political change. The overall pattern, more than any single part, points toward such a conclusion. Thus the already impressive list of reform consequences can be expanded to include reform connections with the nationalization of southern politics; and the study of southern politics and southern party development can expand its list of agents of change to include recent party reforms.

NOTES

1. V. O. Key, Jr., *Southern Politics in State and Nation* (New York: Alfred A. Knopf, 1949), 3–12. Additional materials may be found in C. Vann Woodward, *Origins of the New South* (Baton Rouge: Louisiana State University Press, 1951), esp. chap. 12; George B. Tindall, *The Emergence of the New South 1913–1945* (Baton Rouge: Louisiana State University Press, 1967); and Numan V. Bartley and Hugh D. Graham, *Southern Politics and the Second Reconstruction* (Baltimore: Johns Hopkins University Press, 1975), chap. 1.

2. Morton Sosna, "The GI's South and the North-South Dialogue during World War II" (paper presented at the Fourth Citadel Conference on the South, Charleston, South

Carolina, 11–13 April 1985); and Bartley and Graham, *Southern Politics and the Second Reconstruction*, 18.

3. On the events surrounding the southern revolt in 1948, see Alexander Heard, *A Two-Party South?* (Chapel Hill: University of North Carolina Press, 1952), chap. 2.

4. Alexander Lamis, *The Two-Party South* (New York: Oxford University Press, 1984), 20–24; Donald S. Strong, *Urban Republicanism in the South* (University, Ala.: University of Alabama Bureau of Public Administration, 1960); Donald S. Strong, *The 1952 Presidential Election in the South* (University, Ala.: University of Alabama Bureau of Public Administration, 1956); Jack Bass and Walter DeVries, *The Transformation of Southern Politics: Social Change and Political Consequence since 1945* (New York: Basic Books, 1976), chap. 2; and Bartley and Graham, *Southern Politics and the Second Reconstruction*, 81–92.

5. Bartley and Graham, *Southern Politics and the Second Reconstruction*, 19–20. Also, C. Vann Woodward, *The Burden of Southern History* (New York: Vintage Books, 1960), 6–7.

6. See Steven F. Lawson, *Black Ballots: Voting Rights in the South, 1944–1969* (New York: Columbia University Press, 1976); Pat Watters and Reese Cleghorn, *Climbing Jacob's Ladder, the Arrival of Negroes in Southern Politics* (New York: Harcourt, Brace and World, 1967); Frederick D. Wright, "The History of Black Political Participation to 1965," in *Blacks in Southern Politics*, ed. Laurence W. Moreland, Robert P. Steed, and Tod A. Baker (New York: Praeger, 1987), chap. 1; and Mark Stern, "The Democratic Presidency and Voting Rights in the Second Reconstruction," in *Blacks in Southern Politics*, ed. Moreland, Steed, and Baker, chap. 3.

7. For a good discussion of how political rhetoric changed during this period, see Earl Black, *Southern Governors and Civil Rights* (Cambridge, Mass.: Harvard University Press, 1976).

8. A large literature addresses the changes that have taken place in the southern political system over the past three and a half decades. Among the more useful materials are John C. McKinney and Edgar T. Thompson, eds., *The South in Continuity and Change* (Durham: Duke University Press, 1965); Avery Leiserson, ed., *The American South in the 1960's* (New York: Praeger, 1964); Lamis, *The Two Party South*; Samuel D. Cook, "Political Movements and Organizations," *Journal of Politics* 26 (February 1964): 130–153; Allan P. Sindler, ed., *Change in the Contemporary South* (Durham: Duke University Press, 1963); Bernard Cosman, *Five States for Goldwater* (University, Ala.: University of Alabama Press, 1966); Donald S. Strong, "Further Reflections on Southern Politics," *Journal of Politics* 33 (May 1971): 239–256; James L. Sundquist, *Dynamics of the Party System: Alignment and Realignment of Political Parties in the United States* (Washington, D.C.: Brookings Institution, 1973); Bartley and Graham, *Southern Politics and the Second Reconstruction*; William C. Havard, ed., *The Changing Politics of the South* (Baton Rouge: Louisiana State University Press, 1972); Bass and DeVries, *The Transformation of Southern Politics*; Black, *Southern Governors and Civil Rights*; Bruce A. Campbell, "Change in the Southern Electorate," *American Journal of Political Science* 21 (1977): 37–64; Bruce A. Campbell, "Patterns of Change in the Partisan Loyalties of Native Southerners, 1952–1972," *Journal of Politics* 39 (August 1977): 730–761; Paul Allen Beck, "Partisan Dealignment in the Postwar South," *American Political Science Review* 71 (June 1977): 477–496; Louis M. Seagull, *Southern Republicanism* (Cambridge, Mass.: Schenkman, 1975); Alan I. Abramowitz, "Ideological Realignment and the Nationalization of Southern Politics: A Study of Party Activists and

Candidates in a Southern State'' (paper delivered at the 1979 annual meeting of the Southern Political Science Association, Gatlinburg, Tennessee, 1–3 November 1979); Donald S. Strong, *Issue Voting and Party Realignment* (University, Ala.: University of Alabama Press, 1977); Tod A. Baker and Robert P. Steed, "Southern Political Elites and Social Change: An Exploratory Study," in *Politics '74: Trends in Southern Politics*, ed. Tinsley Yarbrough (Greenville, N.C.: East Carolina University Press, 1974); Douglas S. Gatlin, "Party Identification, Status, and Race in the South: 1952–1972," *Public Opinion Quarterly* 39 (Spring 1975): 39–51; Louis D. Rubin, Jr., ed., *The American South: Portrait of a Culture* (Baton Rouge: Louisiana State University Press, 1980); John Shelton Reed, *One South: An Ethnic Approach to Regional Culture* (Baton Rouge: Louisiana State University Press, 1982); Carol A. Cassel, "Change in Electoral Participation in the South," *Journal of Politics* 41 (August 1979): 907–917; Robert P. Steed, Laurence W. Moreland, and Tod A. Baker, eds., *Party Politics in the South* (New York: Praeger, 1980); Laurence W. Moreland, Tod A. Baker, and Robert P. Steed, eds., *Contemporary Southern Political Attitudes and Behavior* (New York: Praeger, 1982); Tod A. Baker, Robert P. Steed, and Laurence W. Moreland, eds., *Religion and Politics in the South* (New York: Praeger, 1983); David Castle and Harold W. Stanley, "Partisan Realignment in the South: Making Sense of Scholarly Dissonance" (paper delivered at the 1982 annual meeting of the Southern Political Science Association, Atlanta, Georgia, 28–30 October 1982); Robert P. Steed, Laurence W. Moreland, and Tod A. Baker, "The Civil Rights Movement and Southern State Party Elites" (paper delivered at the 1982 annual meeting of the Southern Political Science Association, Atlanta, Georgia, 28–30 October 1982); Robert P. Steed, Laurence W. Moreland, and Tod A. Baker, "In-Migration and Southern State Party Elites" (paper presented at the 1981 annual meeting of the Southern Political Science Association, Memphis, Tennessee, 5–7 November 1981); Ernest M. Lander, Jr. and Richard J. Calhoun, eds., *Two Decades of Change: The South since the Supreme Court Desegregation Decision* (Columbia: University of South Carolina Press, 1975); Alexander Lamis, "The Rise of the Two-Party South: Dynamics of Electoral Politics in the American South since the Early 1960s" (paper delivered at the 1984 annual meeting of the American Political Science Association); Corwin Smidt, "Changing Patterns of Partisan Affection in the South: 1972–1980" (paper presented at the 1984 Citadel Symposium on Southern Politics, Charleston, South Carolina, 29–31 March 1984); Charles Prysby, "The 1980 Election in the American South: Implications for the 1980s" (paper delivered at the 1982 Citadel Symposium on Southern Politics, Charleston, South Carolina, 25–27 March 1982); Walter A. Rosenbaum and Margaret Aiesi, "Realignment and the Diffusion of Partisan Competition in the Urban South: Two Case Studies" (paper delivered at the 1978 Citadel Symposium on Southern Politics, Charleston, South Carolina, 16–18 February 1978); Robert P. Steed, Laurence W. Moreland, and Tod A. Baker, eds., *The 1984 Presidential Election in the South: Patterns in Southern Party Politics* (New York: Praeger, 1985), esp. the introductory chapter ("Southern Politics: A Prelude to Presidential Politics in 1984") by William C. Havard and the concluding chapter ("The 1984 Presidential Election in the South: Race and Realignment") by Harold W. Stanley; and Earl Black and Merle Black, *Politics and Society in the South* (Cambridge, Mass.: Harvard University Press, 1987).

9. Material on the activists at the 1972 national convention includes Denis G. Sullivan, Jeffrey L. Pressman, Benjamin I. Page, and John J. Lyons, *The Politics of Representation: The Democratic Convention of 1972* (New York: St. Martin's Press, 1974); Jeane Kirkpatrick, *The New Presidential Elite* (New York: Russell Sage Foundation, 1976); James

W. Soule and Wilma E. McGrath, "A Comparative Study of Presidential Nomination Conventions: The Democrats of 1968 and 1972," *American Journal of Political Science* 19 (August 1975): 501–517; and David E. Price, *Bringing Back the Parties* (Washington, D.C.: Congressional Quarterly Press, 1984), chap. 7.

10. James W. Ceaser, *Reforming the Reforms: A Critical Analysis of the Presidential Selection Process* (Cambridge, Mass.: Ballinger, 1982), 1. A good deal of the remainder of this volume elaborates the major consequences of these reforms; see his discussion in Chapter 4 especially. For other material discussing the reform movement and detailing the range of the consequences of party reform over the past two decades, see Nelson W. Polsby, *Consequences of Party Reform* (Oxford: Oxford University Press, 1983); William Crotty, *Party Reform* (New York: Longman, 1983); William Crotty, *Decision for the Democrats* (Baltimore: Johns Hopkins University Press, 1978); Austin Ranney, *Curing the Mischiefs of Faction* (Berkeley: University of California Press, 1975); Thomas R. Marshall, *Presidential Nominations in a Reform Age* (New York: Praeger, 1981); James I. Lengle, *Representation and Presidential Primaries: The Democratic Party in the Post-Reform Era* (Westport, Conn.: Greenwood, 1981); James I. Lengle and Byron E. Shafer, "Primary Rules, Political Power, and Social Change," in *Presidential Politics: Readings on Nominations and Elections* (2d ed.), ed. James I. Lengle and Byron E. Shafer (New York: St. Martin's, 1983), 176–196; David C. Paris and Richard D. Shingles, "Preference Representation and the Limits of Reform," *Journal of Politics* 44 (February 1982): 201–211; and Price, *Bringing Back the Parties*, esp. chaps. 6–7.

11. There are a number of useful, detailed discussions of these reforms (for example, see the references in the preceding note). The brief summary presented here, intended only to sketch the general contours of these reforms and to catalog their major consequences in order to set the context for the identification of possible contact points between party reform and southern political change, draws heavily from the materials in Price, *Bringing Back the Parties*, chaps. 6–7; Polsby, *Consequences of Party Reform*; Ceaser, *Reforming the Reforms*; and Crotty, *Party Reform*.

12. The Republican party has undertaken some reform, but this reform has been rather mild in comparison with that of the Democratic party. Moreover, in most instances, Republican reform efforts have been required by changes in state laws necessitated by the Democratic party reforms rather than the products of Republican initiatives. See, for example, Crotty, *Party Reform*, chaps. 17–18, esp. 206–207; and Price, *Bringing Back the Parties*, 156–159.

13. The exact count depends on whether all party commissions, including compliance review commissions and commissions having little to do with delegate selection, are included or whether the count is limited only to those commissions dealing directly and mainly with the central issues of delegate selection and behavior. Compare, for example, the slightly different lists of reform commissions in Crotty, *Party Reform*, 38–43, and Price, *Bringing Back the Parties*, 147.

14. Commission on Party Structure and Delegate Selection, *Mandate for Reform* (Washington, D.C.: Democratic National Committee, 1970), 38–48. A good summary listing of these guidelines may be found in Crotty, *Party Reform*, 50–51.

15. Crotty, *Party Reform*, 59.

16. Crotty, *Party Reform*, 52–55.

17. Commission on Party Structure and Delegate Selection, *The Party Reformed* (Washington, D.C.: Democratic National Committee, 1972), 2–3; Crotty provides a summary in *Party Reform*, 61–62.

18. Crotty, *Party Reform*, 63. See also, Byron E. Shafer, *Quiet Revolution* (New York: Russell Sage Foundation, 1983).

19. For more detailed summaries see Crotty, *Party Reform*, 68–71, and Ceaser, *Reforming the Reforms*, 43.

20. Price, *Bringing Back the Parties*, 183. Price's account of the work of these commissions, especially the Hunt Commission, is extremely useful; see the discussion in Chapter 6 in particular.

21. Charles D. Hadley, "The Capture of the American Presidential Selection Process: National Party Rules, Democratization, and Political Participation" (unpublished paper manuscript), 7–19.

22. Jeane Kirkpatrick, *Dismantling the Parties* (Washington, D.C.: American Enterprise Institute, 1978), 2.

23. Price, *Bringing Back the Parties*, 218.

24. Richard Rose, "Governments against Sub-Governments," in *Presidents and Prime Ministers*, ed. Richard Rose and Ezra Suleiman (Washington, D.C.: American Enterprise Institute, 1980), 316. See also the discussion in Polsby, *Consequences of Party Reform*, chap. 3.

25. Polsby, *Consequences of Party Reform*, 152–156.

26. Black and Black, *Politics and Society in the South*, chap. 5, esp. 120–125.

27. Black, *Southern Governors and Civil Rights*; see also Black and Black, *Politics and Society in the South*, esp. 302.

28. Juan Williams, *Eyes on the Prize: America's Civil Rights Years, 1954–1965* (New York: Viking, 1987), 226–249; also, Crotty, *Party Reform*, 55–58.

29. This was part of a larger study of state convention delegates in 11 states directed by Alan I. Abramowitz, John McGlennon, and Ronald Rapoport. Some of the findings relevant to this point about racial involvement are reported in Laurence W. Moreland, Robert P. Steed, and Tod A. Baker, "A Profile of Contemporary Black Party Activists in South Carolina" (paper delivered at the Third Citadel Conference on the South, Charleston, S.C., 23–25 April 1983); Steed, Moreland, and Baker, "In-Migration and Southern State Party Elites"; and Steed, Moreland, and Baker, "The Civil Rights Movement and Southern State Party Elites."

30. Additional discussion of relevant data on blacks in the 1984 southern state conventions may be found in Laurence W. Moreland, Robert P. Steed, and Tod A. Baker, "Black Party Activists: A Profile," in *Blacks in Southern Politics*, ed. Moreland, Steed, and Baker, chap. 6; and Laurence W. Moreland, Robert P. Steed, and Tod A. Baker, "Indicators of Political Differences among Black Party Activists" (paper delivered at the 1988 annual meeting of the Western Political Science Association, San Francisco, California, 10–12 March 1988).

31. A number of accounts document the South's historical opposition, if not outright hostility, toward the extension of various political rights to women. See, for example, Anne Firor Scott, *The Southern Lady from Pedestal to Politics: 1830–1930* (Chicago: University of Chicago Press, 1970); Diane L. Fowlkes, Jerry Perkins, and Sue Tolleson Rinehart, "Women in Southern Party Politics: Roles, Activities, and Futures," in *Party Politics in the South*, ed. Steed, Moreland, and Baker, chap. 10; and Florence King, *Southern Ladies and Gentlemen* (New York: Stein and Day, 1975).

32. For example, the survey of 1980 state convention delegates revealed a sharp distinction between Democratic activists and Republican activists across a number of economic, social, and foreign policy issues. The contrasts applied to each of the 11 states

included in the study, *including* the three southern states (with almost no differences in response patterns across regions). Analyses of data from an expanded set of policy and issue questions used in a survey of the 1984 state conventions in South Carolina reveal a similarly sharp interparty distinction; these data are part of the larger dataset from the 1984 delegate survey, which forms the basis of the present volume. Relevant material on the 1980 study is presented in Abramowitz, McGlennon, and Rapoport, "Presidential Activists and the Nationalization of Politics in Virginia"; Tod A. Baker, Robert P. Steed, and Laurence W. Moreland, "Southern Distinctiveness and the Emergence of Party Competition: The Case of a Deep South State," in *Contemporary Southern Political Attitudes and Behavior*, ed. Moreland, Baker, and Steed, chap. 10; and Steed, Moreland, and Baker, "In-Migration and Southern State Party Elites." The data on the 1984 survey in South Carolina are presented in Laurence W. Moreland, Robert P. Steed, and Tod A. Baker, "Ideological and Issue Orientations among South Carolina Party Activists at the 1984 State Party Conventions" (paper delivered at the 1985 annual meeting of the South Carolina Political Science Association, Clinton, South Carolina, 13 April 1985).

33. Charles D. Hadley and Susan Howell, "The Southern Split Ticket Voter 1952–1976: Republican Conversion or Democratic Decline?" in *Party Politics in the South*, ed. Steed, Moreland, and Baker, chap. 6; Jerry Perkins and Randall Guynes, "Federalism and Partisanship: Southern Orientations to National and State Parties" (paper presented at the 1975 annual meeting of the Southwestern Political Science Association, San Antonio, Texas, April 1975); Jerry Perkins and Randall Guynes, "Partisanship in National and State Politics," *Public Opinion Quarterly* 40 (1976): 376–378; Charles D. Hadley, "Dual Partisan Identification in the South," *Journal of Politics* 47 (1985): 254–268; and Harold W. Stanley, "Southern Partisan Changes: Dealignment, Realignment, or Both?" *Journal of Politics* 50 (1988): 64–88.

34. For useful discussions of southern political culture related to this point see W. J. Cash, *The Mind of the South* (New York: Knopf, 1941), esp. 31; William J. Havard, "The South: A Shifting Perspective," in *The Changing Politics of the South*, ed. Havard, esp. 5–6; Reed, *One South*, esp. chap. 13; John Shelton Reed, *The Enduring South: Subcultural Persistence in Mass Society* (Chapel Hill: University of North Carolina Press, 1974), esp. chap. 7; Robert P. Steed, Laurence W. Moreland, and Tod A. Baker, *The Disappearing South? Studies in Regional Change and Continuity* (Tuscaloosa: University of Alabama Press, forthcoming 1989); and Michael L. Mezey, "The Minds of the South," in *Religion and Politics in the South*, ed. Baker, Steed, and Moreland, chap. 1.

35. Democratic identification in the South declined slowly but steadily between 1952 and 1984, falling from 76 percent of the total electorate to 40 percent during this period; the decline among white southerners was even more dramatic, falling to roughly one-third identifying themselves as Democrats by 1984. While the identification category marking the largest gains during this period was that of independent (increasing from 14 percent in 1952 to 35 percent in 1984—and to roughly 40 percent among whites by 1984), the proportion of the southern electorate identifying themselves as Republicans also rose significantly, from 10 percent to 25 percent (and to 29 percent among whites). Somewhat different data on state party activists in the South in 1980 and in South Carolina in 1984 also show evidence of greater party switching among Republican delegates than among Democratic delegates (roughly two to one); moreover, approximately 75 percent of the Republican switchers said that they switched because of the parties' respective issue positions, a point that is at least indirectly related to party image. The data on the electorate are from Black and Black, *Politics and Society in the South*, 237–238, Tables

11.1 and 11.2; the data on state party activists are from the 1980 state convention survey and the 1984 survey of the South Carolina state conventions. Additional data on party identification in the southern electorate may be found in Harold W. Stanley, "The 1984 Presidential Election in the South: Race and Realignment," in *The 1984 Presidential Election in the South: Patterns of Southern Party Politics*, ed. Steed, Moreland, and Baker; additional material on party switching among the 1984 convention delegates in the South may be found in the chapter by Charles Prysby in the present volume.

36. The isolation of the southern political system added to the distinctive sense of southern consciousness long considered a salient demographic and experiential characteristic of the region. See Ralph McGill, *The South and the Southerner* (Boston: Little, Brown, and Co., 1964), 213–240; Dewey W. Grantham, "The South and the Politics of Sectionalism," in *The Regional Imagination: The South and Recent American History*, ed. Dewey W. Grantham (Nashville: Vanderbilt University Press, 1979), 1–22; and Kathy B. Smith and Craig Allen Smith, "Presidential Attention to the South" (paper delivered at the 1982 Citadel Symposium on Southern Politics, Charleston, South Carolina, 25–27 March 1982).

37. Smith and Smith, "Presidential Attention to the South."

38. While some states in the South were treated to an occasional visit from a candidate, the region as a whole was certainly not considered a key battleground during presidential campaigns. For example, when Dwight Eisenhower made a campaign trip to South Carolina in 1952 (after having received the endorsement of Jimmy Byrnes, the state's Democratic governor), the press proclaimed the event as the first campaign visit to the state in modern times by either party's nominee; see Lamis, *The Two-Party South*, 12–13.

39. See, for example, the discussion of the nomination contests in the relevant states in Steed, Moreland, and Baker, *The 1984 Presidential Election in the South*.

40. For an analysis of Super Tuesday, see Charles D. Hadley and Harold W. Stanley, "An Analysis of Super Tuesday: Intentions, Results and Implications" (paper delivered at the 1988 annual meeting of the Midwest Political Science Association, Chicago, Illinois, April 1988).

41. Smith and Smith, "Presidential Attention to the South," 18.

42. Key, *Southern Politics*, chap. 14.

Part II
Party Reform and Southern Convention Delegates

2

Blacks, the Biracial Coalition, and Political Change

Charles D. Hadley and Harold W. Stanley

Samples suitable for sustained analysis of black partisan activists are scarce: "The literature on black convention behavior is nearly nonexistent."[1] While subsamples of black activists totaling only a hundred or so can be useful for descriptive purposes,[2] so few respondents cannot support analyses probing the dynamics of partisan divisions and cohesion. The 1984 Comparative State Party Activist Survey offers an opportunity to explore characteristics of party activists, both within each party and among black delegates. This chapter analyzes the differences and similarities between state convention delegates in order to shed light on the viability and vulnerability, the promise and problems of the biracial coalition within the Democratic party in the South.

Simply comparing the characteristics and views of black and white Democratic delegates does not suffice to evaluate the strengths and weaknesses of the biracial coalition. Such comparisons need supplementing through contrasts with Republican delegates to gauge the relative degrees of cohesion and conflict within and between parties. Moreover, for black Democrats, comparisons of delegates supporting Jackson with those supporting other candidates highlight a source of possible division. Consequently, in the following analysis the southern state party delegates were split into three groups: black Democrats (n = 796), white Democrats (n = 2,040), and white Republicans (n = 1,846).[3] Black Democratic delegates were further subdivided into those who supported Jackson's presidential candidacy at the time of the state convention (n = 425) and those who supported other candidates (n = 305).

An earlier version of this chapter was presented at the American Political Science Association Annual Convention in 1986.

Table 2.1
Demographics

| | Blacks | | | Whites | |
| | Supported | | | | |
	Jackson	Other	All	Dem.	Rep.
Age (mean)	43	46	45	45	48
Age 18-44	59	45	52	52	41
Age 45+	41	55	48	48	59
Native Southerner	93	94	93	83	67
Rural Residence	53	51	53	50	45
Male	44	45	45	51	57
Mean Years in State	36	39	38	35	30

Note: Table entries are percentages of delegates surveyed except for years in the cases of mean age and mean years in state.

DEMOGRAPHICS

As regards demographic characteristics, did delegates of the two parties differ or did they exhibit striking similarities? Among Democrats, were black and white delegates demographically similar? The following discussion ranges across age, residence, native or migrant status, gender, educational attainment, occupation, income, and religion to portray the demographic composition of these delegates. To preview the findings: relative to Republicans, more white and black Democratic delegates were young, rural residents, females, and native southerners. Some differences in socioeconomic status distinguished the delegates along racial and partisan lines but high socioeconomic status, relative to the general population, characterized all racial and partisan delegate groups. In religious practice, black Democrats and Republicans showed stronger commitments than did white Democrats.

Relative youth characterized black delegates supporting Jackson, while black delegates as a whole matched the age profile of white Democratic delegates (Table 2.1). The average white Republican tended to be older. For instance, 59 percent of Republican delegates were over age 45, in contrast to 48 percent of white and black Democrats and 41 percent of the Jackson supporters. Rural residences were claimed by a majority of black delegates (53 percent). Fifty percent of Democratic and 45 percent of Republican state convention delegates also claimed rural roots. Among Democrats but not Republicans, these rural roots were reinforced by a high percentage of native southerners—93 percent of black and 83 percent of white Democrats, but only 67 percent of the Republicans.[4]

Two forces affected the relative composition of the delegations by gender: the

Table 2.2
Education, Occupation, and Income (in percent)

	Blacks			Whites		U.S.
	Supported					
	Jackson	Other	All	Dem.	Rep.	
Education:						
less than college	17	18	18	17	15	65
some college	21	22	22	25	29	18
college graduate	21	21	20	18	26	10
post college	41	39	40	40	31	7
Occupation:						
Bus. - Prof.	62	65	63	55	58	
(Teacher)	(29)	(38)	(33)	(17)	(10)	
Sales	7	5	6	8	10	
Laborer	10	14	11	6	3	
Farmer	1	0	1	3	3	
Housewife	3	4	4	7	14	
Official	8	7	7	10	9	
Income:						
Under $15,000	22	19	22	8	8	31
$15,000-$24,999	27	27	26	19	16	23
$25,000-$34,999	20	23	21	24	19	19
$35,000-$44,999	14	18	15	20	19	|
$45,000-$59,999	11	10	10	15	17	27
$60,000 or over	7	4	5	15	22	|

Sources: Educational figures for the nation in 1984 are from Bureau of the Census, Current Population Reports, P-20, Number 405, Voting and Registration in the Election of November 1984 (Washington, D.C.: Government Printing Office, 1986), 57. Income figures for 1984 are from the same source, 71.

national rules of the Democrats that stimulated the opening up of the party and Republican efforts to neutralize the "gender gap" issue. Among blacks, females actually constituted a majority (55 percent). White Democrats split evenly while 43 percent of the Republican delegates were female. The occupations of these females differed by party and race. Among blacks, only 6 percent of the females were housewives in contrast to 31 percent of the Republican females. White Democratic female housewives made up an intermediate 13 percent.

The educations, occupations, and incomes of state party convention delegates reveal their very high socioeconomic status (Table 2.2). Nearly equal proportions (three of every five) of the Republicans, white Democrats, and black Democrats have graduated from college. Two-thirds of each Democratic group had postcollege training in contrast to half of the Republicans.[5] For the sake of comparison, the 1984 national distribution of educational attainment for the U.S. population is presented in Table 2.2 to portray the very high educational attainment of southern convention delegates attending state party conventions.[6] Only 17 percent of the U.S. population holds a college degree or more. Among southern state convention delegates, regardless of party and preference, the percentage is over three-and-a-half times that.

By occupation, a majority of delegates were associated with business and the professions. Blacks, moreover, tended to have a slightly larger proportion in the professions. A major part of the explanation for the greater presence of black professionals turns on teachers. Teachers account for 33 percent of the black delegates in contrast to 17 percent of the white Democrats and 10 percent of the Republicans. Black teachers, moreover, proved to be less likely to support Jesse Jackson's candidacy. Their proportion was only 29 percent of the black delegates supporting Jackson but 38 percent of those supporting other candidates. The traditional role of teachers in the black community (forged in segregationist times when few professional occupations were open to blacks beyond teacher, minister, and funeral home director), in combination with the political activity of teachers' unions within the Democratic party, helps account for the large presence of teachers among black delegates. The support Mondale enjoyed from teachers' unions probably contributed to the lesser willingness of black teachers to back Jackson.

Income distributions among delegates reveal marked racial and partisan differences. Only 16 percent of blacks had incomes over $45,000.[7] For white Democrats 30 percent had such incomes. The figure was higher still among Republicans at 38 percent. Jackson delegates had slightly higher incomes than other black delegates; 18 percent of the former as compared to 14 percent of the latter had incomes over $45,000. The paradox of the lower incomes of black delegates who had slightly more postgraduate education and somewhat greater presence in business and professional occupations can be explained in part by the preponderance of teachers, an occupation with relatively limited financial rewards compared to other professions.

Education, occupation, and income reveal the very high socioeconomic status of these state convention delegates. Despite party reforms, the same overrepresentation of educated, affluent professionals has characterized recent national party conventions. Party reforms that sought to open the presidential nomination process to varied socioeconomic groups failed to attain political "representation" in a descriptive sense.[8] However, opening up the nomination process has allowed those with the resources to participate to do so. And the educationally, occupationally, and financially better-off individuals have done so.[9]

Religious denominations differentiate the delegates by race. Over three-quarters of the black delegates claimed affiliation with one of the pietistic Protestant denominations (primarily Baptist and Methodist). Among whites—Democrats and Republicans—about 50 percent claimed a similar religious affiliation, while nearly one-quarter claimed membership in a reformed Protestant denomination. In religious devotion, black delegates are closer to Republican delegates than to white Democrats (Table 2.3). In terms of regular church attendance and professing to having been "born again," black Democrats and Republicans showed a stronger religious commitment than did white Democrats. Fifty-six

Table 2.3
Religion (in percent)

| | Blacks | | | Whites | |
| | Supported | | | | |
	Jackson	Other	All	Dem.	Rep.
Religious Denomination					
Reformed Protestant	7	9	8	22	30
Pietistic	79	76	78	52	50
Catholic	7	7	7	12	7
Church Attendance:					
Every week	56	58	56	35	48
Almost each week	22	24	23	21	18
1 or 2 a month	14	9	12	12	11
Few times yearly	8	9	8	22	18
Never	1	1	1	10	4
"Born Again"	51	46	49	32	43

percent of the blacks, 48 percent of the Republicans, but only 35 percent of the white Democrats claimed to attend church every week. Forty-nine percent of the blacks, 43 percent of the Republicans but only 32 percent of the white Democrats claimed to be "born again."[10] (These differences have issue consequences that will be discussed later.)

GROUP ASSOCIATIONS

Group associations of the delegates differentiated the races, the parties, and Jackson supporters (Table 2.4). More Republicans were active in business groups (43 percent) than in labor unions (3 percent), which was hardly surprising. But the same was also true of white Democrats and black Jackson supporters. However, the business-union gap was narrower among these two Democratic groups (33 percent to 16 percent for whites, 30 percent to 14 percent for black Jackson supporters). Black delegates backing someone other than Jackson had nearly equal levels of involvement with unions (22 percent) and business (21 percent). Black delegates who supported Jackson were more active in religious organizations (57 percent) than were white Republicans (53 percent). Black delegates who supported other candidates trailed slightly (48 percent). White Democrats lagged considerably with only 33 percent claiming such involvement. Two-thirds of the black delegates but only 15 percent of white Democrats and 2 percent of Republicans were active in civil rights organizations. Among blacks, Jackson supporters were more active by 10 percentage points.[11]

Overall, Jackson delegates showed greater group involvement in civil rights, religious, and business organizations, and markedly less involvement in teacher organizations and labor unions. White Democrats showed somewhat more active

Table 2.4
Group Activity (in percent)*

| | Blacks | | | Whites | |
| | Supported | | | | |
	Jackson	Other	All	Dem.	Rep.
Civil Rights	72	60	66	14	2
Religious Orgs.	57	48	53	33	53
Public Interest	48	43	45	38	29
Teachers, Adminis.	37	47	41	21	14
Business Orgs.	30	21	25	33	43
Women's Rights	22	24	22	25	4
Labor Unions	14	22	17	16	3
Farm Groups	8	10	9	12	10
Conser., Ecology	6	5	5	19	9
Antiabortion	4	2	3	3	14

*Percentages of delegates indicating membership in the listed groups.

membership in business organizations and conservation groups than did black Democrats, but much less involvement in groups working in the areas of civil rights, religion, public interest, and teaching. Among white Republicans, memberships in the specified groups were less frequent. A majority were active in religious organizations. Slightly fewer were involved in business groups, and over a quarter were active in general public interest groups. Otherwise, involvement in any specific category of group was limited to less than 15 percent of the Republican delegates.

ISSUES

One potent image of political parties in the South views blacks as the anchor of the liberal wing of the Democratic party. The rise of Republicans has helped pull some formerly Democratic conservatives and moderates into Republican ranks. A critical question for the future of the parties in the South is whether additional conversions to the Republicans by moderate and conservative whites can be expected. According to James L. Sundquist, partisan changes that have characterized presidential politics in the South

appeared certain [to penetrate] steadily downward through the political levels—from presidential voting to statewide voting to local voting. . . . For as the Republican party grew through the gradual accretion of conservatives, the Democratic party would automatically come under control of its liberal wing—strengthened in any case by the rapid growth in the number of black voters—and more liberals and neo-Populists would be among its candidates. And as that occurred, party lines would be sharpened and more and more moderates and conservatives would find their home among the Republicans, placing the Democratic party under even firmer liberal control. The cycle would continue until the realignment was complete at every level.[12]

While Sundquist's predictions are based on behavior by voters as well as party elites, his view of the inevitable slide of the Democratic party into politically questionable liberalism and the migration of conservative Democrats to the Republican party can be tested with this data on state convention delegates. If this slide is ongoing, one should be able to use cross-sectional data to detect activists who are "ripe" for party switching in order to bring personal ideology into line with the relative liberal-conservative positions of the parties.[13]

Prominent examples of such switching are not hard to find. In Texas, Democratic U.S. Representative Kent Hance, defeated in the 1984 Texas Democratic senatorial primary by a more liberal candidate, switched to the Republicans. In doing so, he noted: "I have seen the conservative Democrats getting smaller and smaller each year, and I think a lot of conservative Democrats are going to be faced with making the same decision that I made."[14] In Louisiana, Democratic State Representative Quentin Dastugue, irritated over political maneuvering within the state delegation at the 1984 national Democratic convention complained, "It's becoming increasingly obvious that the Democrats don't want me in their party. They can cater to gays and everybody else, but there's no place in it that fiscal conservatives can get a hearing." Dastugue switched and attended the national Republican convention the next month as a special guest.[15]

Despite such well-publicized switches, their number remains below the level required to raise Republicans to an equal plane with the Democrats. Were Democratic state convention delegates, particularly whites, closer to the Republicans than to black Democrats on the issues? The State Delegate Survey included 21 issues: civil rights, spending priorities, military policy, social issues, and the like. Although the issues do not give exhaustive coverage of the political agenda, they do include principal topics of that agenda. On each issue, delegates could check one of five responses: strongly agree (or favor), agree, undecided, disagree, strongly disagree (or oppose).[16] The average positions on each issue for black and white Democratic delegates showed very few differences. In fact, the average white Democratic state convention delegate was closer to the average black Democratic delegate than to the average Republican on all but one of the 21 issues (Tables 2.5 and 2.6). For the average white Democratic activist, the pull of the Republican party on issues was very limited.[17]

To be sure, the exceptional issue is affirmative action, but on this issue the average white Democratic delegate was equidistant from the average Republican and average black Democratic delegate. Insofar as this one issue of affirmative action was emblematic of other issues touching civil rights and race relations (whether it was cannot be determined with this data), the significance should be considered far greater than the frequency of one out of 21 issues would suggest.

Were Jackson supporters ideologically distinctive? Apparently not, for black delegates supporting Jackson did not take issue positions at odds with those taken

Table 2.5
Issue Positions I*

(Averages)	Blacks			Whites	
	Supported				
	Jackson	Other	All	Dem.	Rep.
Equal Rights Amendment	1.5	1.4	1.4	2.0	4.1
Increase in Def. Spending	4.3	4.2	4.3	3.9	1.9
Nat. Health Insurance	1.8	1.9	1.9	2.7	4.2
More Nuc. Power Development	4.0	3.9	3.9	3.7	2.3
Spending Cuts to Balance Bud.	3.1	3.0	3.0	2.7	1.8
Affirmative Action Progs.	1.2	1.2	1.2	2.6	4.0
Nuclear Freeze	1.7	1.8	1.7	1.8	3.2
Handgun Control Leg.	2.0	2.1	2.1	2.6	3.8
Public Works Program	2.4	2.5	2.5	2.9	4.2
Ed. Funding Tax Increase	1.8	1.8	1.8	2.2	3.6
Food Stamp Reduction	3.5	3.2	3.4	2.8	1.7

*Responses ranged from one to five: (1) strongly agree/favor;
(2) agree/favor; (3) undecided; (4) disagree/oppose; (5) strongly
disagree/oppose. On these issues the average black Democrat anchors
one "extreme," the average Republican the other.

by blacks supporting other candidates. The average positions of Jackson supporters on the 21 issues differed very little if at all from the average positions
of other black delegates. On only three issues did the averages diverge by more
than two-tenths of a point. This divergence was limited to three-tenths of a point
on all three issues: raising taxes to lower the federal deficit, reducing food stamp
coverage, and increasing the U.S. military presence in the Middle East. On each
issue, the average Jackson delegate was more firmly opposed to the proposed
policy.

The general view of blacks being on one side of an issue, Republicans on the
other and white Democrats somewhere in the middle was only partially accurate
for these party activists. On 11 issues, the average white Democrat did occupy
an intermediate position between the average black Democrat and white Republican (Table 2.5). Yet for eight of the 21 issues, the average white Democrat
and Republican anchored the extremes with the average black taking a middle
position. On two others black and white Democrats shared the same average.
Hence, on almost half of the issues examined (Table 2.6), the average white
Democrat was the same distance or farther from the Republican position than
was the average black Democrat. Such results are not symptomatic of a racially

Table 2.6
Issue Positions II*

| | Blacks | | | Whites | |
| | Supported | | | | |
(Averages)	Jackson	Other	All	Dem.	Rep.
Antiabortion Amendment	2.9	2.8	2.9	3.8	2.7
More Arms Control Neg.	1.9	1.9	1.9	1.7	2.5
Tax Increase to Cut Bud. Def.	3.5	3.2	3.3	2.9	4.0
Increase Energy/Hurt Env.	3.4	3.5	3.4	3.7	3.0
Use of Marijuana Immoral	2.4	2.3	2.4	2.8	1.8
Excessive Environmental Reg.	3.4	3.3	3.4	3.6	2.4
Homosexual Behavior Immoral	2.2	2.2	2.2	2.6	1.5
School Prayer Amendment	2.6	2.7	2.7	3.4	2.0
U.S. Military in Mid. East	4.1	3.8	3.9	3.9	2.9
U.S. Military in Lat. Am.	4.0	3.8	3.9	3.9	2.4

*For the range of responses, see the note to Table 2.5. On eight of
these issues the average white Democratic delegate anchors one
"extreme," the average Republican delegate anchors the other. On two
issues black and white Democratic delegates occupy the same average
position.

divided Democratic party pulling itself apart on the issues, whites leaving the
party to liberals and blacks and opting for a more philosophically compatible
Republican alternative.

Three observations qualify the implications of these findings on issues. First,
the results are for party activists, not voters, and a lengthy literature leads us to
expect sharper differences on issues among party activists than voters.[18] Second,
this cross-sectional count of the number of 1984 delegates still "ripe" for party
switching on ideological grounds needs supplementing through consideration of
those delegates who have already switched parties—a topic that will be considered later. Third, concentrating on the average position on the issues downplays
the extent of overlap across the groups on issue attitudes. The average position
has merits as a summary statement of central tendency, but a number of Republicans and Democrats, both white and black, share similar outlooks on particular issues. Increasing Republican strength can result from issue positions
pulling only a fraction of Democrats away from the biracial coalition. For instance, only 38 percent of black Democrats, but 52 percent of white Democrats
and 85 percent of white Republicans favor spending cuts to balance the federal
budget (admittedly, agreement on this still masks disagreement about which cuts
to make). Some 27 percent of white Democrats and 75 percent of white Re-

publicans (but only one percent of black Democrats) share opposition to affirmative action programs. Such overlap serves as a potent reminder that some Democratic state convention delegates would have found activists in the opposite party more congenial on some issues even though average positions showed common white and black Democratic outlooks.

Rather than chart the partisan overlap on each issue, a special case of that overlap—the shared outlook of black Democrats and Republicans on moral matters—and then, in the next section, the cross-party similarities in liberal-conservative orientations will be considered. Reflective of strong religious ties, Republicans and black Democrats took similar stances on matters such as abortion and school prayer. However, the religious conservatism of blacks seems unlikely to spill over into a more broadly based political conservatism. The religious right had a very strong presence among Republican delegates as 63 percent claimed to be a member of or sympathizer with "conservative Christian organizations." Yet only 12 percent of black Democratic delegates made the same claim. Moreover, the great divide between liberal blacks and conservative Republicans on most other issues makes improbable the development and extension of a common conservative outlook on moral issues. Yet prospects for black Democratic and white Republican collaboration across party lines may be brighter in particular localities for specific purposes. As Baker, Steed, and Moreland note, although "it appears unlikely that on the national level moral issues will supplant economic, military, or foreign policy issues as topics of dominant concern, it may well be that in southern states and communities issues such as abortion, pornography, school prayer, gambling and legalization of liquor might occupy the center ring of political discourse."[19] Even here, however, given the currently high levels of black attachment to the Democratic party, the presence of Republican partisan cues would work to inhibit a biracial coalition centered on religious and moral conservatism.[20]

LIBERALISM AND CONSERVATISM

In addition to the 21 issues surveyed, insight into ideological similarities and divisions among the delegates is possible through analysis of liberal-conservative ratings.[21] Delegates ranked themselves, voters, the parties, and candidates on this dimension.[22] Delegates placed themselves in distinctive ways by party and by race (Table 2.7). As expected, the average black delegate's self-placement was more liberal than that of the white Democratic delegate, but both were far from the very conservative self-ranking of white Republican delegates. These three groups had general agreement on the liberal or conservative positions of Reagan, the average national or state voter, and the Republican party in the nation and in the state. Moreover, the average black and white Democrats ranked almost all items similarly. Contrasted with this Democratic like-mindedness, the average Republican delegate ranked Democratic candidates and the Democratic party, both in the nation and in the state, as being far more liberal.

Table 2.7
Liberal-Conservative Placements of Delegates, Candidates, Parties, and Voters*

	Blacks			Whites	
	Supported				
	Jackson	Other	All	Dem.	Rep.
Respondent	2.6	2.5	2.5	3.3	5.9
Reagan	6.2	6.4	6.3	6.2	6.0
Mondale	3.1	2.6	2.9	2.6	1.3
Jackson	2.2	2.1	2.1	1.9	1.3
Hart	3.8	3.6	3.7	2.9	1.7
Glenn	4.6	4.4	4.5	4.4	3.1
Avg. U.S. Voter	3.9	3.7	3.9	4.2	4.4
Nat. Dem. Party	3.3	3.1	3.3	2.9	1.5
Nat. Rep. Party	6.2	6.2	6.2	5.8	5.6
Avg. State Voter	4.4	4.2	4.3	4.8	4.8
State Dem. Party	3.9	3.6	3.8	3.8	2.3
State Rep. Party	6.2	6.2	6.2	6.1	5.9

*Table entries are the mean ratings given by the indicated groups of
delegates on the following scale: 1) "extremely liberal," 2)
"liberal," 3) "slightly liberal," 4) "middle-of-road," 5) "slightly
conservative," 6) "conservative," and 7) "extremely conservative."

Table 2.8
Southern Delegates Rating Other Party Closer (in percent)*

	Other National Party		Other State Party	
	Average		Average	
	U.S. Voter	Self	State Voter	Self
Black Democrats	11	5	14	5
Jackson Backers	12	5	15	6
Others	11	5	14	5
White Democrats	28	18	27	12
White Republicans	13	2	19	4

*Table entries are the percentages of delegates rating the opposite
party in the nation (or in the state) closer to the delegate's ranking
of the average voter (or himself) on the liberal-conservative scale.

Partisan distinctiveness can be brought into focus much more tellingly by
assuming that ideological proximity implies potential political support. The delegates' liberal-conservative rankings permit determination of how many delegates
saw the opposite party as being closer to the average voter and to themselves
(Table 2.8). Over one-quarter of the white Democratic delegates ranked the

Republican party in the nation and in the state closer than the Democratic party to the relevant average voter. At the national level 18 percent considered the Republican party closer than the Democratic party to their own individual ideological outlook. At the state level 12 percent thought this to be so. White Republicans only rarely thought the national or state Democratic party was closer than the Republican party to their personal ideological outlook (2 percent and 4 percent, respectively), but 13 percent placed the Democrats closer to the average national voter and 19 percent closer to the average state voter. Blacks were least likely to consider the opposite party closer to the typical voter. Twelve percent did so for the national level and 14 percent for the state level. Only 5 percent of blacks thought the Republicans were closer to their own ideological outlook at either level.

These figures suggest that on the basis of personal ideological proximity 12 to 18 percent of the white Democratic activists—but almost no black Democrats or Republicans—could have been considered likely candidates to convert to the opposite party. Black Democratic and white Republican delegates have a far firmer commitment to their current party attachment.

The figures for those thinking the opposite party is closer to the average state or national voter reflect an appreciation among these activists of the attractiveness of the opposite party and serve to emphasize the importance of the choice of candidate for winning elections.[23] The party is not a single entity presented to the voter at one fixed point on the ideological spectrum. Rather, the party appears, certainly in presidential elections, wearing the human face of the nominee. The perceived liberal nature of the 1984 Democratic choices for president are borne out firmly in the state delegate data, but vulnerabilities that might result from such a liberal stance are not carried over in most instances to Democratic candidates for state and local offices.

DELEGATE PERCEPTIONS OF LIKELY PRESIDENTIAL ELECTION OUTCOMES IN 1984

Southern delegates differed dramatically on their assessment of the likely outcome of the presidential election. Delegates were asked to reveal how good a chance Reagan, Hart, Mondale, Jackson, and Glenn would have of winning the November election if nominated by their respective parties (Table 2.9). Of the white Republican delegates, 98 percent thought Reagan would definitely or probably win the general election. Less than a third of the white Democratic delegates thought the same about Mondale. Two-thirds of the black delegates thought Mondale would definitely or probably win, only one-third thought Reagan would. The delegate data do not support the notion that most Jackson supporters thought Mondale had little chance of winning. Even among Jackson backers, optimism about Democratic chances prevailed as over half thought Mondale would definitely or probably win.

Table 2.9
Rating the Candidates on Chances to Win the Presidential Election (in percent)*

| | Blacks | | | Whites | |
| | Supported | | | | |
	Jackson	Other	All	Dem.	Rep.
Reagan	33	30	33	56	98
Mondale	56	77	66	30	5
Jackson	28	11	21	2	0
Hart	18	21	19	21	2
Glenn	3	4	3	5	2

*Table entries are the percentages of the delegates in each group who think the candidate will "definitely" or "probably" win the presidential general election in 1984, if the candidate secures the party nomination. The other choices were "might win," "probably would lose," and "definitely would lose."

PARTY ORGANIZATION

Southern state convention delegates in 1984 had, on average, over a decade of involvement in the party. The typical black and white Democratic delegate had 14 to 15 years, the Republican less than 12 years. Jackson supporters had slightly less lengthy involvement in the party than other black delegates (Table 2.10). Over one-third of black Democrats, just under one-half of white Democrats, and slightly less than one-third of Republicans had attended a state party convention in the past eight years as a delegate.

Although black Democratic delegates shared some appreciation of strong parties with white Republican delegates, some sharp differences existed as well. Black delegates professed much less tolerance for ticket splitting.[24] The greater Republican acceptance of ticket splitting (Table 2.10) could have reflected the absence of choice down the ticket where Republican candidates seldom contest seats in parts of the South. The quality of choice, not just the absence of choice, could also account for some of the difference. Some Republican loyalists at the national level seem to find conservative Democrats compatible choices for state and local office.[25]

One survey question directly measured the delegate's willingness to subordinate personal preferences on issues to the electoral advancement of the party. If the continuance and cohesion of a party coalition was vulnerable on issue grounds, a substantial share of coalition members would presumably be willing to "take a walk" if the party took a major stand that differed significantly with the views of those members. Yet southern Republican delegates, not Democratic delegates, professed a stronger willingness to walk out on the party. A delegate

Table 2.10
Involvement in the Party (in percent)

	Blacks			Whites	
	Supported				
	Jackson	Other	All	Dem.	Rep.
Years Active in Party					
0-4	26	19	23	27	31
5-10	25	25	25	24	29
Over 10	49	57	53	48	40
(Mean no. of yrs.)	13	15	14	15	12
1976-1984 Campaign Activity*					
Local elections	64	70	66	59	51
State elections	42	57	49	49	45
National elections	36	42	40	34	44
Broad Party Appeal**	76	79	77	68	62
No Split Ballots***	62	67	63	50	32
Cand. Selection Criteria					
Loyalty, service	23	28	25	15	5
Issues, ideology	66	60	64	77	85
Chance to win	4	6	5	5	7
Not sure	7	6	7	3	2

*Entries are the percentages of delegates indicating they worked "very actively" in the type of campaign listed.

**Entries are the percentages of delegates agreeing with the following statement: "It is more important to me that my party make a broad electoral appeal than for my party to take stands on issues that I personally agree with."

***Entries indicate the percentages of delegates opposing the practice of splitting the ballot between Democratic and Republican candidates.

was given an opportunity to indicate the one statement that more clearly expressed his opinion: (1) "If I disagreed with a major stand of my party that was important to me, I would stop working for the party" or (2) "It is more important to me that my party make a broad electoral appeal than for my party to take stands on issues I personally agree with." Among the delegates, 77 percent of black Democrats, 68 percent of white Democrats, and 62 percent of white Republicans placed broad electoral appeal ahead of personal agreement.[26]

The local focus of the Democratic delegates is clear from their self-reports of campaign involvement in 1976 to 1984 (Table 2.10). Among Republicans, more were involved in local campaigns (51 percent) than in state (45 percent) or national ones (44 percent), but this gap is small compared to the differences among Democratic delegates. Fifty-nine percent of the white Democrats were very actively involved at the local level, 49 percent at the state level, but only 34 percent at the national level. Among blacks, the corresponding figures were 66, 49, and 40.

Table 2.11
Party and Public Office: Experience and Ambition (in percent)

	Blacks			Whites	
	Supported				
	Jackson	Other	All	Dem.	Rep.
'76 or '80 State Party Conven. Delegate	33	42	37	47	63
Local Party Committee					
Now	54	53	55	54	68
Past	16	15	15	22	31
Future	22	18	19	21	16
Local Party Officer					
Now	20	26	23	27	38
Past	7	6	7	14	21
Future	29	22	25	24	17
State Party Officer					
Now	7	11	9	11	11
Past	3	2	3	7	9
Future	36	29	32	29	24
National Conven. Del.					
Now	6	8	6	4	6
Past	2	4	2	5	6
Future	45	43	43	39	34
Elected Pub. Official					
Now	9	8	8	8	7
Past	2	2	2	6	5
Future	36	30	32	24	21
App. Pub. Official					
Now	8	10	9	8	6
Past	5	3	4	6	6
Future	32	31	31	24	18
Experience (Now or Past)					
None	28	28	28	25	15
At least 1 (>=1)	72	72	72	76	85
Ambition (Future)					
None	39	43	40	43	53
At least 1 (>=1)	61	58	60	57	48
Experience/Ambition					
None/None	8	9	8	9	9
>=1/None	31	34	32	34	44
None/>=1	20	19	20	15	7
>=1/>=1	41	39	40	42	41

Roughly three-quarters of the delegates—somewhat less among black Democrats, somewhat more among white Republicans—had been elected or appointed to public office or had held state or local party office (Table 2.11). Over half of the Democratic delegates had ambitions to stay in such a position in the future (60 percent among blacks, 57 percent among whites). Only 48 percent of the Republicans had such ambitions. Jackson supporters had similar overall expe-

Table 2.12
Partisanship (in percent)

	Blacks			Whites	
	Supported				
	Jackson	Other	All	Dem.	Rep.
Strong Party ID					
State	79	84	81	81	83
Nation	78	79	78	72	89
Switched Parties	5	3	4	15	31
Mixed Partisanship					
Consistent	81	86	83	77	85
Inconsistent	10	8	10	10	6
Mixed	9	6	7	13	9

rience in these positions but slightly more ambition to hold such positions in the future. Just under ten percent of the delegates in each group had never held one of these positions and had no desire to do so in the future. About one-third of each Democratic group had held (or was holding) such a position and did not want to do so again. For Republicans the figure for those experienced but unambitious delegates was even higher—44 percent.

In general, both in identification and in the role envisioned for the party, black delegates showed stronger support for their party than did white delegates. At the state level, 81 percent of both black and white Democrats showed strong identification with the party (Table 2.12). At the national level, however, blacks claiming strong identification were slightly fewer at 78 percent, but whites fell even further to 72 percent.[27] Taken together, national and state partisanship—in both direction and strength—were exactly the same for 83 percent of black Democratic, 77 percent of white Democratic, and 85 percent of white Republican delegates.

One major source of Republican party growth in supporters—voters, activists, and candidates—has been individuals who switched from the Democrats to the Republicans. Prominent individuals who switch—U.S. Senator Phil Gramm in Texas is one recent example—give this source of Republican growth great visibility.[28] Indeed, 31 percent of Republican delegates to southern state conventions in 1984 claim to have switched parties. Such switches among southern party activists supply the Republican party with candidates and leaders capable of exploiting the increased Republican constituency among voters.[29] While current emphasis frequently is given to those switching from the Democrats to the Republicans,[30] a neglected but nontrivial facet of this general phenomenon is Democrats who have switched from prior Republican identification. In Alabama in 1978, two top Democratic officeholders—the governor and the attorney general—were former Republicans who realized that securing statewide office required running as a Democrat. Although less prominent, this crossing of party lines from Republican to Democrat is a significant qualification to the ultimate Republican gain from party switching. In fact, some 15 percent of white Democratic delegates stated that they switched parties. So even in the recent South, the crossing of party lines has been a two-way street among whites.[31] Yet because of the solid attachment of southern blacks to the Democratic party since 1964, black convention delegates, including Jackson supporters, have no comparable frequency of party switching.

The importance of party switchers to the activists of each party can be gauged by comparing the percentages of delegates who claim to have switched parties. Plotting the percentage of switchers against the time of that switch (Figure 2.1) reveals the importance of presidential election years and, by inference, of presidential politics. Figure 2.1 and the fact that twice as many Republican delegates as Democrats had switched parties, suggests the long-term erosion such switching has inflicted on the Democrats. However, the figures for 1980 (the last full presidential election year) show similar percentages of Republican and Democratic state convention delegates claim to have switched parties that year. If such offsetting gains prevail in the future, the Republican advantage from party switching will be slim indeed.[32]

REFLECTIONS ON THE VIABILITY OF THE BIRACIAL DEMOCRATIC COALITION IN THE SOUTH

The preceding analysis of Republican and Democratic delegates to state party conventions in the South documents the different outlooks and characteristics of the activists in the two parties. Black and white Democratic delegates both had some elements in common with the Republican delegates; however, the elements they had in common with each other far outweighed what either shared with Republican activists. Blacks, like Republicans, had a firm devotion to religion that helped foster kindred outlooks on moral issues such as abortion. As a group, white Democratic delegates attached far less importance to religion than did black Democrats or Republicans. Generally, on issue positions and on liberal-conservative placements, the average Democrat, white or black, was far closer to his fellow Democrat than to the average Republican.

Those who see the racial tension within the state Democratic parties of the South as beyond repair and a reason for an inevitable decline in that party's fortunes point to a cycle of ideological "purification" in which the liberals drive more moderate and conservative Democrats over to the Republicans. Yet surveys of state convention delegates produced little evidence of ideological misfit promising greater Democratic decline. On the issues examined here, the average positions of black and white Democratic delegates had strong similarities and little in common with the average Republican position. However, more than one out of every four white Democratic delegates placed the Republican party closer in general liberal-conservative terms than the Democratic party to the average voter in the nation and in the state. On the other hand, similar appreciation for

Figure 2.1
Percentage of Democratic and Republican 1984 Southern State Convention Delegates Who Switched Parties, by Year of Switch

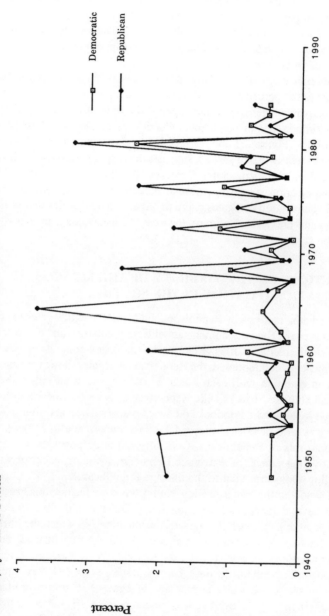

the Democratic party held true for Republican delegates: 19 percent thought the Democratic party closer to the average state voter, 13 percent thought so for the average national voter. About one of every seven white Democrats saw the Republican party as closer to their own ideological outlook. Party switchers figured prominently among Republican delegates. Yet, while the largest flow of party switchers among whites was from Democratic to Republican, a not insignificant stream flowed in the opposite direction.

One might argue that in 1984, the year the national Democrats nominated Mondale, a state Democratic convention even in the South would be chiefly composed of liberal elements likely to minimize the Democratic party infighting that typically stems from the clash between whites and blacks. These white Democratic delegates, the majority of whom favored the presidential candidacy of Walter Mondale, no doubt differed politically from those who would have turned out to support John Glenn, had his 1984 presidential candidacy remained viable longer.[33] Yet these state party conventions were not all subordinated to the task of picking the presidential nominee. At one extreme (Arkansas and Louisiana), no selection of national convention delegates occurred at the state conventions; at the other extreme (Texas), all national convention delegates were selected at the state convention. At most of the state party conventions surveyed, only the state's at-large delegates were selected. To suggest that moderate and conservative white Democratic party activists sat home in order to give more liberal elements a free run due to the restricted range of the presidential nominees ignores the truth that these conventions carried out normal state party business as well. Consequently, while a moderate candidate with strong southern appeal could have altered a composition somewhat, to consider these southern state party delegations as aberrations goes beyond the facts.

On balance, the evidence presented highlights the strengths and weaknesses of the biracial coalition among southern Democratic state party activists. However, attitudes and orientations of black and white Democratic activists might well be lagging behind the partisan change among voters. One has firm reasons to suspect that state party convention delegates would be one of the major bastions of partisanship, even in times of change.[34] Data from surveys of state convention delegates in 1984 indicate that while the biracial Democratic coalition in the South was far from the rock-solid, neither was that coalition on the verge of collapse.

NOTES

1. Hanes Walton, Jr., *Invisible Politics: Black Political Behavior* (Albany: State University of New York Press, 1985), 134, 161.

2. For example, Jeanne Kirkpatrick, "Representation in the American National Conventions: The Case of 1972," *British Journal of Political Science* 5 (July 1975): 310–312; and *The New Presidential Elite: Men and Women in National Politics* (New York: Russell Sage Foundation and Twentieth Century Fund, 1976), 320–326. Ronald W.

Walters with Diane R. Brown, "Black Presidential Politics in 1976: A Study of Black Delegates to the Democratic and Republican National Conventions in 1976" (Washington, D.C.: Institute for Urban Affairs and Research, 1980).

3. The 29 black Republican delegates are too few for analysis, so this group has been omitted. Consequently, all references to Republican delegates refer only to whites.

4. The difference between Jackson backers and other blacks on absolute number of years lived in state (Table 2.1) reflects the younger average age of Jackson delegates.

5. The low Republican percentage claiming some postcollege work does not arise from the larger presence of housewives among these delegates. Even after omitting housewives from the calculations, 9 percentage points fewer Republicans than Democrats have had some postcollege education.

6. Of course, 1984 data for these southern convention states by race would support even greater contrasts than do the national figures.

7. The income distribution for the U.S. population in 1984 approximates that for southern black delegates. However, these income distributors appreciably exceed that of the black population. For 1984 among black households in the nation, the following income distribution prevailed: 54 percent below $15,000; 21 percent $15,000–24,999; 12 percent $25,000–34,999; and 14 percent over $35,000 (U.S. Bureau of the Census, *Statistical Abstract of the United States: 1986*, 106th edition [Washington, D.C.: Government Printing Office, 1985], 446).

8. For a discussion of descriptive representation, see Hanna Fenichel Pitkin, *The Concept of Representation* (Berkeley: University of California Press, 1967), 60–91.

9. Kirkpatrick, "Representation in the American National Conventions," 273–285; Nelson W. Polsby, *Consequences of Party Reform*, (New York: Oxford University Press, 1983), 161–162; and William Crotty and John S. Jackson III, *Presidential Primaries and Nominations* (Washington, D.C.: Congressional Quarterly Press, 1985): 111–137.

10. For a discussion of fundamentalism and its connection to politics in the South and non-South among white state party convention delegates in 1980, see Robert P. Steed, Laurence W. Moreland, and Tod A. Baker, "Religion and Party Activists: Fundamentalism and Politics in Regional Perspective," in *Religion and Politics in the South: Mass and Elite Perspectives* (New York: Praeger, 1983), Tod A. Baker, Robert P. Steed, and Laurence W. Moreland, eds., 105–132.

11. See John G. Francis and Robert C. Benedict, "Issue Group Activists at the Conventions," in *The Life of the Parties* (Lexington, Ky., University of Kentucky Press, 1986), Ronald B. Rapoport, Alan I. Abramowitz, and John McGlennon, eds., 105–113.

12. James L. Sundquist, *Dynamics of the Party System: Alignment and Realignment of Political Parties in the United States*, revised edition (Washington, D.C.: Brookings Institution, 1983), 375.

13. Mary Grisez Kweit, "Ideological Congruence of Party Switchers and Nonswitchers: The Case of Party Activists," *American Journal of Political Science* 30 (February 1986): 184–196.

14. Quoted in Raymond Wolfinger and Michael Hagen, "Republican Prospects: Southern Comfort," *Public Opinion* 8 (October/November 1985): 13.

15. Charles D. Hadley, "Louisiana," in *The 1984 Presidential Election in the South: Patterns of Southern Party Politics* (New York: Praeger, 1986), Robert P. Steed, Lawrence W. Moreland, and Tod A. Baker, eds., 36.

16. The analyses of positions on these issues treats the "undecided" response as a middle position between "agree" and "disagree."

17. Kweit, "Ideological Congruence," 192; Robert W. Kweit and Mary Grisez Kweit, "The Permeability of Parties," *The Life of the Parties*, 202–213.

18. Herbert McClosky, Paul J. Hoffman, and Rosemary O'Hara, "Issue Conflict and Consensus among Party Leaders and Followers," *American Political Science Review* 54 (June 1960): 406–429; Kirkpatrick, "Representation in the American National Conventions," 285–307; John S. Jackson III, Barbara L. Brown, and David Bositis, "Herbert McClosky and Friends Revisited," *American Politics Quarterly* 10 (April 1982): 158–180.

19. Tod A. Baker, Robert P. Steed, and Laurence W. Moreland, "Fundamentalist Beliefs and Southern Distinctiveness: A Study of the Political Attitudes of State Party Activists," in *Religion and Politics in the South: Mass and Elite Perspectives* (New York: Praeger, 1983), Tod A. Baker, Robert P. Steed, and Laurence W. Moreland, eds., 140.

20. Linda F. Williams, "Blacks and the Religious Right Have Few Common Interests: Polls, History Show That Alliance Is Unlikely," *Focus* (September 1986): 6–7.

21. For a complementary assessment of recent regional change among voters on liberalism and conservatism, see Edward G. Carmines and Harold W. Stanley, "Ideological Realignment in the Contemporary South: Where Have All the Conservatives Gone?" in Robert P. Steed, Laurence W. Moreland, and Tod A. Baker, eds., *The Disappearing South? Studies in Regional Change and Continuity* (Tuscaloosa: University of Alabama Press, forthcoming 1989).

22. For a more limited analysis, see Walter J. Stone and Alan I. Abramowitz, "Ideology, Electability, and Candidate Choice," in *The Life of the Parties*, 75–95.

23. On this point see Walter J. Stone and Alan I. Abramowitz, "Winning May Not Be Everything, But It's More Than We Thought: Presidential Party Activists in 1980," *American Political Science Review* 77 (December 1983): 945–956; and their *Nomination Politics: Party Activists and Presidential Choice* (New York: Praeger, 1984), Chapters 5 and 6. For a relevant but only suggestive methodological caution, see Larry M. Bartels, "Expectations and Preferences in Presidential Nominating Campaigns," *American Political Science Review* 79 (September 1985): 804–815.

24. For an analysis of ticket splitting in the South, see Charles D. Hadley and Susan E. Howell, "The Southern Split Ticket Voter, 1952–1976: Republican Conversion or Democratic Decline?" in *Party Politics in the South* (New York: Praeger, 1980), Robert P. Steed, Laurence W. Moreland, and Tod A. Baker, eds., 127–151.

25. See Harold W. Stanley, "Southern Partisan Changes: Dealignment or Realignment?", *Journal of Politics* 50 (February 1988): 64–88, for an evaluation of partisanship and voting loyalty (for president, U.S. senator, U.S. House, and governor), among whites in the recent South. See Harold W. Stanley, "The 1984 Presidential Election in the South: Race and Realignment," in *The 1984 Presidential Election in the South: Patterns of Southern Party Politics* (New York: Praeger, 1986), Robert P. Steed, Lawrence W. Moreland, and Tod A. Baker, eds., 303–335 for a discussion of partisan change from the perspective of the 1984 election.

26. Stone and Abramowitz, "Winning May Not Be Everything, But It's More Than We Thought," 945–956, and *Nomination Politics*.

27. Republicans show the reverse tendency, more having stronger identification at the national level than at the state, but even at the state level the percentage (83 percent) compares favorably with those for the Democrats. Interestingly, white Democrats were not the only group exhibiting mixed partisanship at the national and state levels. ("Mixed

partisanship'' entails being partisan at one level, independent or a partisan of the opposite party at the other level. Independent includes those who profess independence but claim to be close to one party.) To be sure, 13 percent of the white Democrats had mixed partisanships, but so did nine percent of the Republicans and 7 percent of the black Democrats. For a discussion of multiple partisanship at different levels of government, see M. Kent Jennings and Richard G. Niemi, ''Party Identification at Multiple Levels of Government,'' *American Journal of Sociology* (1966): 86–101; and Charles D. Hadley, ''Dual Partisan Identification in the South,'' *Journal of Politics* 47 (February 1985): 254–268.

28. See ''Republicans Launch Operation Open Door,'' *First Monday: The Republican Newsmagazine* (Spring 1985): 10–18. In Louisiana, the open elections system means that Democratic incumbents who switch to the Republican party do not run for reelection on a Republican ''line.'' Consequently, Republicans there have successfully courted and converted sitting Democratic elected officials. In 1984 and 1985, eleven state house members and two senators switched to the Republicans, bringing the Republican totals to 22 of 105 House seats and 3 of 39 Senate seats (Charles D. Hadley, ''The Impact of the Louisiana Open Elections System Reform,'' *State Government* 58, No. 4 (1986): 153–154).

29. Wolfinger and Hagen, ''Republican Prospects,'' 13.

30. For example, Kweit, ''Ideological Congruence and Party Switchers.''

31. Alan I. Abramowitz, John McGlennon, and Ronald Rapoport, ''Party Activists in the United States,'' *International Political Science Review* 4, No. 1 (1983): 17.

32. The 1984 figure is undoubtedly far too low. In hindsight, many more activists will have switched parties in 1984 than this figure indicates. The election year had not run its course at the time of these conventions. The general election and its aftermath undoubtedly spurred additional crossing of party lines. Also, even for those who did switch parties early in 1984 the prospects for showing up soon thereafter as a delegate at the new party's state convention were limited.

33. Very few of these delegates admit to having backed Glenn in January of 1984. Perhaps early Glenn backers sat out the nomination process once Glenn dropped out. Perhaps, but even before January, Glenn's campaign was troubled and unlikely to make inroads. Hart's finish in the Iowa caucuses and the New Hampshire primary in February put him on the map, even in the South. The substantial minority of delegates in this survey claiming to have backed Hart in January suggests either political precociousness or that many of the earlier Glenn backers switched to other candidates once Glenn's campaign appeared unlikely to gather momentum.

34. Alan I. Abramowitz, John McGlennon, and Ronald B. Rapoport, ''The Party Isn't Over: Incentives for Activism in the 1980 Presidential Nominating Campaign,'' *Journal of Politics* 45 (November 1983): 1014.

3

Civil Rights Activists: Contributions to Party Transformation

Robert P. Steed

In 1928 the distinguished southern historian Ulrich B. Phillips maintained that southern white solidarity was based primarily on a common resolve that the region should be a white man's country.[1] Approximately two decades later, V. O. Key, Jr., identified race as the central ingredient in the region's politics. He went on to argue that the Jim Crow system of racial segregation was one of four essential institutions that formed the foundation of the South's political and social sectionalism.[2]

Other factors such as distinctive patterns of settlement, military defeat, and unusual poverty contributed to southern regionalism; but none had the impact of the race issue. Concern with white supremacy underlay the Jim Crow laws that segregated and disenfranchised blacks in the South and contributed significantly to the establishment of a one-party system in the region in the 1890s.[3] Given the centrality of race to the southern political, social, and economic systems, it is not surprising that efforts to extend basic citizenship rights to southern blacks ultimately paralleled and contributed to the sweeping changes in the region following World War II.

The civil rights movement had its roots in the early twentieth-century activities of such leaders as W. E. B. DuBois and Marcus Garvey as well as organizations such as the Niagara Movement and the National Association for the Advancement of Colored People.[4] However, prior to World War II progress was limited and uneven. Despite an occasional Supreme Court ruling in favor of extending black rights (e.g., the 1944 decision in *Smith* v. *Allwright* against the continuation of the white primary), black disenfranchisement and racial segregation remained the rule.

Following the end of World War II, pressure to change the Jim Crow system increased. In the mid–1950s, a new era of activity was launched with the Court's school desegregation decision in *Brown* v. *Board of Education* and with the Montgomery bus boycott. New leaders and new organizations appeared and intensified the effort. By the 1960s confrontational strategies—boycotts, sit-ins, freedom rides, and marches—shook the traditional southern political and social systems to their foundations. The federal judiciary was joined by the executive and the legislative branches as powerful external allies of the movement. The passage of important civil rights legislation in 1964 and 1965 was especially significant. The 1964 Civil Rights Act was an omnibus bill that attacked discrimination in a wide range of activities (e.g., access to public accommodations, employment opportunities and practices, and voting rights), and the 1965 Voting Rights Act paved the way for judicial action against the continued use of the poll tax in state and local elections, suspended the literacy test in areas where voting registration fell below 50 percent of the voting age population, and required the listing of voters.

Without question, then, the civil rights movement was a central ingredient in the political history of the South during the 1950s and 1960s. Not only was the movement itself at the heart of much of southern politics, its effects reverberated throughout the region's political system and contributed importantly to regional change.

Some of the ways in which the civil rights movement affected southern party politics are fairly obvious. For example, the movement's success in eliminating legal barriers to black voting, especially with passage of the 1965 Voting Rights Act, changed the face of the southern electorate. It introduced new constraints on the traditional functions of state and local parties. Nominations, election campaign strategies, and political rhetoric all changed to accommodate the new realities of the polling booth.[5] Moreover, pressures for fuller participation by blacks in the political process contributed significantly to the rules changes undertaken by the national Democratic party after 1968 to include them meaningfully in the presidential nominating process. Southern state delegations to subsequent Democratic National Conventions (as well as caucuses and conventions at the state and local levels) were altered to reflect black political support.[6] In a similar vein, these changes are linked to increased opportunities for blacks to participate at other party organizational levels in the region (e.g., as county committee members).

Beyond such obvious consequences, there is also evidence that the civil rights movement contributed to the sharpening of interparty differences in the South. Not only were Democratic party organizations opened to blacks but also less conservative whites were brought into the ranks of the party elite. For example, data on delegates to state party conventions in Texas, South Carolina, and Virginia in 1980 revealed that both black and white delegates with histories of civil rights organization involvement constituted a liberalizing element within the Democratic party.[7] Such data are suggestive, but they are also limited. Inasmuch as the civil rights movement was such a crucial ingredient in the contemporary transformation of southern politics, additional attention to the party activist-civil rights linkage is desirable. Such an examination should help clarify the nature of changing party coalitions in the region.

This chapter updates and expands the 1980 analysis cited above by exploring (1) the extent to which civil rights activists have penetrated the southern party system, and (2) their impact on that system in terms of such matters as ideological and issue orientations, candidate orientations, and party perspectives. The initial discussion analyzes all southern delegates included in the Comparative State Party Activists Survey without the introduction of race controls. This is followed by an examination of white activists with a history of ties to civil rights organizations. Controlling for race in this manner should be particularly interesting since this subgroup constitutes an intriguing departure from the traditional image of most southern whites with regard to the issue of race.

SOUTHERN STATE PARTY ELITES AND CIVIL RIGHTS ACTIVISM: DATA AND ANALYSIS

Until fairly recently an investigator looking for party activists who were also active in the civil rights movement would have been hard-pressed to find any at any organizational level; to find enough to sustain statistical analysis would have been miraculous. That such a search can now succeed illustrates, perhaps as well as any other single piece of evidence, the changes in southern politics over the past three decades.

The state convention delegate data clearly indicate that civil rights activists have penetrated the southern party system. Overall, in response to a set of questions on activity in a variety of types of organizations, over 900 (19 percent) of the delegates surveyed indicated past or present involvement in civil rights organizations. Not surprisingly, civil rights activists are more heavily involved in the southern Democratic party than in its Republican counterpart. In the six states surveyed, approximately 29 percent of the Democratic delegates indicated civil rights organizational activity as compared to only three percent of the Republican delegates. Also as might be expected, a greater percentage of these delegates are black than white. Even so, over a third (36 percent) of the civil rights activists are white. Beyond party and race, there are few background differences between the delegates who have been active in civil rights organizations and those who have not. (See Tables 3.10 and 3.11 in the appendix at the end of this chapter for descriptive data.)

Not only are civil rights activists of both races now active in southern party organizations, they also bring a relatively distinct set of ideological and issue orientations to the parties. The initial evidence on this point is presented in Table 3.1. For all southern state party convention delegates, civil rights activism is associated with greater liberalism on general political philosophy and on each of the nineteen specific issues included in the survey. Although the correlation coefficients are relatively small on a number of the issues (e.g., tax increase, more intensive arms control negotiations), the consistency of the pattern is im-

Table 3.1
Ideological and Issue Orientations of State Party Convention Delegates by Civil Rights Activism

Item*	Simple Correlations
Ideology	.47
Social Issues	
Equal Rights Amendment	.38
Affirmative Action Programs	.46
Food Stamp Reduction	-.41
Handgun Control Legislation	.32
School Prayer Amendment	-.23
Excessive Environmental Reg.	-.27
Use of Marijuana Immoral	-.23
Homosexual Behavior Immoral	-.27
Antiabortion Amendment	-.18
Defense/Foreign Policy Issues	
Increase in Defense Spending	-.36
U.S. Military in Mid East	-.23
U.S. Military in Lat. Am.	-.34
Nuclear Freeze	.24
More Arms Control Neg.	.16
Economic Issues	
Tax Increase to Cut Bud. Def.	.14
Nat. Health Insurance	.42
Spending Cuts to Balance Bud.	-.28
Public Works Program	.42
Increase Energy/Hurt Env.	-.17

*See Appendix for question wording

pressive; and on some issues (e.g., affirmative action, national health insurance, public works programs), the correlation coefficients themselves are rather strong.

Since there are sharp interparty differences on these issues, as illustrated elsewhere in this volume,[8] a logical refinement of the analysis is to examine the delegates' ideological and issue orientations within each party.[9] Here the data support the conclusion that civil rights activists do indeed bring distinctive perspectives and positions into their respective parties. Among the Democrats, for example, 70 percent of the civil rights activists consider themselves to be liberal or extremely liberal as compared to only 35 percent of the non–civil rights activists who placed themselves in these categories (Table 3.2). Similarly, in the Republican party, the few civil rights activists tend to be more liberal and less conservative than their overwhelmingly conservative colleagues.

These broad ideological predispositions in both parties are reflected in their delegates' positions on a wide range of specific issues important during the 1984 election year. Among Democratic delegates, for example, on 16 of the 19 issues included in the analysis (Table 3.3), the civil rights activists were more liberal in the aggregate than their partisan colleagues who have no history of organized

Table 3.2

Ideological Positions of State Party Convention Delegates by Civil Rights Activism (in percent)

Ideology	Democrats		Republicans	
	CR Dels.	NCR Dels.	CR Dels.	NCR Dels.
Extremely liberal	19	7	4	0
Liberal	51	28	8	1
Slightly liberal	14	20	6	1
Middle-of-the-road	9	22	10	3
Slightly conservative	4	14	14	11
Conservative	2	8	46	66
Extremely conservative	1	1	12	18
	100	100	100	100
(N=)	(858)	(2058)	(50)	(1607)

CR = civil rights delegates
NCR = non-civil rights delegates

civil rights involvement. The Democratic civil rights activists are less liberal than the non–civil rights activists on only one issue: increasing taxes to cut the federal deficit. The proportionate differences are greatest among the social and economic issues, exceeding 20 percentage points on five of the fourteen issues in these categories (affirmative action, food stamps, handgun legislation, national health insurance, and spending cuts). On nine of these issues, the differences are over 10 percent. This pattern is confirmed by the simple correlations reported in Table 3.3. Only on defense and foreign policy issues are the group differences relatively small; but even here the general pattern of greater liberalism among civil rights activists holds.

For the Republican delegates, the patterns are similar. While these party leaders are considerably less liberal on all issues than their Democratic counterparts, the Republican civil rights activists are, without exception, more liberal than their Republican counterparts who have not been involved in civil rights organizations (Table 3.4). The largest differences appear on affirmative action, the Equal Rights Amendment, increasing defense spending, handgun control, national health insurance, and food stamps.

To some extent, civil rights activism also is associated with candidate preferences within the Democratic party. Jesse Jackson's support in 1984 is linked especially tightly to the civil rights movement. Among civil rights activists, he was their first choice for the party's presidential nomination (44 percent) followed closely by Walter Mondale (42 percent). Gary Hart trailed far behind with only 13 percent. For non–civil rights activists, Walter Mondale was the clear first choice with 59 percent support, followed distantly by Gary Hart (27 percent) and even more distantly by Jesse Jackson (8 percent). In the Republican state

Table 3.3
Issue Positions of Southern Democratic State Convention Delegates by Civil Rights Activism

Issue*	Percentage Liberal		Simple Correlations
	CR Dels.	NCR Dels.	
Social Issues			
Equal Rights Amendment	96	80	.72
Affirmative Action Programs	97	68	.89
Food Stamp Reduction	71	41	-.55
Handgun Control Legislation	86	62	.59
School Prayer Amendment	61	54	-.14
Excessive Environmental Reg.	79	70	-.24
Use of Marijuana Immoral	50	38	-.22
Homosexual Behavior Immoral	46	31	-.32
Antiabortion Amendment	67	67	.00
Defense/Foreign Policy Issues			
Increase in Defense Spending	94	82	-.59
U.S. Military in Mid. East	95	89	-.38
U.S. Military in Lat. Am.	92	84	-.37
Nuclear Freeze	94	91	.19
More Arms Control Neg.	94	94	.00
Economic Issues			
Tax Increase to Cut Bud. Def.	45	53	-.16
Nat. Health Insurance	92	66	.71
Spending Cuts to Balance Bud.	59	35	-.46
Public Works Program	78	54	.50
Increase Energy/Hurt Env.	81	77	-.14

*See Appendix for question wording

conventions the near unanimity of delegate support for Ronald Reagan precluded any such division among civil rights and non–civil rights activists.

Not only are activists' issue and ideological positions important for the party system, their orientations toward the party and its activities are also important. Much of the literature on party leadership has examined the implications of amateur-professional (or purist-pragmatist) divisions within the ranks of party elites.[10] It is possible that civil rights activists, with their history of involvement in an intense issue-related cause, have brought a perspective into party work different from that of their non–civil rights colleagues.

Tables 3.5 and 3.6 report party leaders' responses on a series of questions that broadly tap their views toward their respective parties. For the Democrats (Table 3.5), there are virtually no differences between delegates who have been active in civil rights organizations and those who have not. For example, almost identical proportions of both groups gave "party support" as their main reason for becoming involved in party politics in 1984 (indeed, for both groups that is the motivation most frequently mentioned as most important). The patterns of group responses regarding the other motivations listed in Table 3.5 are also

Table 3.4
Issue Positions of Southern Republican State Convention Delegates by Civil Rights Activism

Issue*	Percentage Liberal		Simple Correlations
	CR Dels.	NCR Dels.	
Social Issues			
Equal Rights Amendment	40	15	.58
Affirmative Action Programs	52	14	.75
Food Stamp Reduction	23	6	-.66
Handgun Control Legislation	45	24	.44
School Prayer Amendment	33	18	-.37
Excessive Environmental Reg.	36	26	-.22
Use of Marijuana Immoral	22	15	-.24
Homosexual Behavior Immoral	16	8	-.40
Antiabortion Amendment	49	42	-.13
Defense/Foreign Policy Issues			
Increase in Defense Spending	35	8	-.70
U.S. Military in Mid. East	52	48	-.07
U.S. Military in Lat. Am.	37	22	-.34
Nuclear Freeze	57	47	.20
More Arms Control Neg.	84	72	.34
Economic Issues			
Tax Increase to Cut Bud. Def.	22	16	.20
Nat. Health Insurance	26	9	.57
Spending Cuts to Balance Bud.	14	8	-.27
Public Works Program	13	6	.40
Increase Energy/Hurt Env.	58	49	-.16

*See Appendix for question wording

remarkably similar. Moreover, both groups of Democratic delegates are quite close in their views on what activities the state party organization should be doing, the most important factors in candidate selection, the acceptability of ticket splitting, and the nature of recent changes in their party. In fact, the only item on which there is even a slight difference is the 1980 presidential vote of these delegates. The civil rights activists were slightly more loyal to their party's ticket than the non–civil rights activists. Perhaps most striking is their general agreement on their personal orientation toward the party. Significant majorities (72 percent and 69 percent respectively) of civil rights activists and non–civil rights activists alike indicate that it is more important to make a broad electoral appeal than to take positions on issues with which they personally agree. This, in conjunction with the other data reported in Table 3.5, suggests strongly that the involvement of civil rights activists in the southern state Democratic parties has not introduced a strong amateur orientation with a potential for internal disruption.

The picture within the Republican party is different. While similarities between civil rights activists and non–civil rights activists outweigh their differences, the

Table 3.5
Party Orientations of State Democratic Convention Delegates by Civil Rights Activism (in percent)

Item	Civil Rights Delegates	Non-Civil Rights Delegates
Reason for Pol. Involvement		
To support party	40	43
To help political career	2	4
To enjoy campaign excitement	1	2
To meet people	1	2
To support particular candidate	24	20
To work for issues	23	17
To enjoy delegate visibility	0	0
To fulfill civic duty	7	9
To make business contacts	1	2
	99	99
(N=)	(876)	(2117)
Most Important State Party Role		
Provide campaign assistance	26	29
Take positions on issues	25	18
Provide services/information	21	22
Recruit candidates	4	4
Inform electorate about party goals and positions	24	27
	100	100
(N=)	(819)	(1956)
Most Important Factor in Candidate Selection		
Party loyalty and prior service	17	18
Positions on issues/ideology	74	72
Chance for victory	5	5
Not sure; no opinion	4	4
	100	99
(N=)	(822)	(1985)
Splitting Ballots Justified?		
Yes, national elections only	4	11
Yes, state/local elections only	10	8
Yes, all election levels	18	21
No	58	52
Not sure; no opinion	9	8
	99	100
(N=)	(826)	(2000)
1980 Presidential Vote		
Jimmy Carter	92	83
Ronald Reagan	2	10
John Anderson	3	4
Other	2	3
	99	100
(N=)	(871)	(2102)
Party Switcher?		
Yes	11	13
No	89	87
	100	100
(N=)	(865)	(2092)

Table 3.5 (continued)

Item	Civil Rights Delegates	Non-Civil Rights Delegates
Opinions on Proper Party Role		
Would stop working for party if it took disagreeable issue stands	13	14
Party's broad electoral appeal is more important than its taking personally agreeable issue positions	72	69
No opinion	15	17
	100	100
(N=)	(816)	(1967)
Party Organization Changed?		
Yes, improved	59	55
Yes, deteriorated	16	20
No change	25	25
	100	100
(N=)	(791)	(1901)

few Republican civil rights activists do demonstrate some slight deviations from the party mainstream on a number of points listed in Table 3.6. For example, although party support is mentioned by slightly over one-third of each group, both differ rather sharply on the importance of working for issues as a major motivation for party work. The percentage of non–civil rights activists mentioning issues as a motivation is double that of civil rights activists. It is reasonable to speculate that, for the civil rights activists, the Republican party is not viewed as the appropriate mechanism for promoting civil rights; other factors draw them into Republican party activity. This speculation receives mild support in the data that show that a slightly larger percentage of the civil rights activists than of the non–civil rights activists see broad electoral appeal as more important than issue positions.

In the same vein, although a larger percentage of civil rights activists switched parties, only ten (roughly half of those who switched) said that the Republican party's positions on issues prompted their decision as compared to almost 80 percent of the non–civil rights switchers. Finally, these two groups of delegates differ somewhat with regard to their perceptions of recent party change and to their views on party activities. The civil rights activists are less likely to feel that Republican party organizations have improved (66 percent to 80 percent). They are also more likely to stress campaign assistance as the party's most important role (41 percent to 31 percent). We must remember, however, that any potential consequences these differences may have for the party are muted by the scarcity of civil rights activists within Republican state party ranks.

Table 3.6
Party Orientations of State Republican Convention Delegates by Civil Rights Activism (in percent)

Item	Civil Rights Delegates	Non-Civil Rights Delegates
Reason for Pol. Involvement		
To support party	36	35
To help political career	8	1
To enjoy campaign excitement	8	1
To meet people	4	1
To support particular candidate	16	22
To work for issues	14	28
To enjoy delegate visibility	2	0
To fulfill civic duty	12	9
To make business contacts	0	2
	100	99
(N=)	(50)	(1693)
Most Important State Party Role		
Provide campaign assistance	41	31
Take positions on issues	13	16
Provide services/information	22	20
Recruit candidates	6	12
Inform electorate about party goals and positions	18	21
	100	100
(N=)	(46)	(1602)
Most Important Factor in Candidate Selection		
Party loyalty and prior service	11	5
Positions on issues/ideology	83	85
Chance for victory	2	7
Not sure; no opinion	4	2
	100	99
(N=)	(46)	(1640)
Splitting Ballots Justified?		
Yes, national elections only	0	3
Yes, state/local elections only	17	29
Yes, all election levels	40	27
No	28	32
Not sure; no opinion	15	9
	100	100
(N=)	(47)	(1635)
1980 Presidential Vote		
Jimmy Carter	6	1
Ronald Reagan	90	97
John Anderson	4	0
Other	0	2
	100	100
(N=)	(50)	(1703)
Party Switcher?		
Yes	40	31
No	60	69
	100	100
(N=)	(50)	(1685)

Table 3.6 (continued)

Item	Civil Rights Delegates	Non-Civil Rights Delegates
Opinions on Proper Party Role		
Would stop working for party if it took disagreeable issue stands	16	25
Party's broad electoral appeal is more important than its taking personally agreeable issue positions	70	61
No opinion	14	14
	100	100
(N=)	(50)	(1573)
Party Organization Changed?		
Yes, improved	66	80
Yes, deteriorated	12	7
No change	21	13
	99	100
(N=)	(47)	(1585)

On the basis of these data, the participation of civil rights activists in the southern party system is most significant with respect to ideological, issue, and, to a lesser degree, candidate orientation. Moreover, it is clear that this significance is greatest in the state Democratic parties where nearly all civil rights activists are located. Since a majority of these civil rights activists are black, the greater liberalism evident in the data on ideologies, issues, and candidate orientations is not too surprising inasmuch as black delegates in general tend to be more liberal on most of these points than their white copartisans.[11]

Differences between Black and White Democratic Delegates

Still, when we introduce controls for race and focus on white Democrats, we find that civil rights activism remains a distinguishing variable. For example, over three-fourths (77 percent) of the white civil rights activists said that they consider themselves to be "very liberal" or "liberal" as compared to less than one-third (31 percent) of the white Democratic delegates who have not been active in civil rights organizations (Table 3.7). Conversely, only 10 percent of the white civil rights activists consider themselves middle-of-the-road or conservative as compared to 48 percent of the non-civil rights activists. There are small differences between the respective groups of black delegates categorized by civil rights organization activity, but such activity is not nearly as important a differentiating variable for black activists as it is for whites. Perhaps even more striking are the data showing white civil rights activists to be somewhat more

Table 3.7
Ideological Positions of Southern Democratic State Convention Delegates by Civil Rights Activism and Race (in percent)

Ideology	White Delegates		Black Delegates	
	CR	NCR	CR	NCR
Extremely liberal	24	5	15	18
Liberal	53	26	52	44
Slightly liberal	12	22	15	14
Middle-of-the-road	6	23	10	14
Slightly conservative	3	15	4	6
Conservative	1	9	3	4
Extremely conservative	0	1	2	1
	99	101	101	101
(N=)	(287)	(1667)	(501)	(255)

liberal in the aggregate than black civil rights activists (77 percent "extremely liberal" or "liberal" for whites compared to 67 percent for blacks).

The same sharp intraparty differences exist with respect to the stands of these delegates on the issues. White civil rights activists again demonstrate greater liberalism than their white non–civil rights counterparts (Table 3.8). These differences are especially dramatic on most of the social issues and on two of the economic issues (national health insurance and budget spending cuts). They are present, though much less significantly, on the defense/foreign policy issues. Indeed, with regard to issues and ideology, white civil rights activists constitute as much of a liberalizing influence on the southern Democratic party as do civil rights activists in general. While the white non–civil rights activists tend to be liberal on 15 of the 19 issues under analysis, the proportional strength of the support for the liberal position consistently lags far behind that of white civil rights activists.

Civil rights activity is much less important in distinguishing among the black Democratic state party delegates, all of whom are generally in agreement on these issues regardless of their civil rights organization involvement. This is consistent with the analyses of Hadley and Stanley (Chapter 2) and Baker (Chapter 9) in this volume, which demonstrate high issue homogeneity among black delegates when other types of controls are introduced. However, it is again noteworthy that white civil rights activists demonstrate a greater level of liberalism on a number of the issues than their black counterparts (or, for that matter, black non–civil rights activists). On approximately half of the issues examined, white civil rights activists take positions considerably more liberal than their black colleagues. These variations are particularly pronounced with regard to five of the social issues: a school prayer/Bible reading amendment, environmental regulation, marijuana use, homosexual behavior, and an antiabortion amendment. Differences also surface on the questions of a tax increase and spending

Table 3.8

Issue Positions of Southern Democratic State Convention Delegates by Civil Rights Activism and Race (percent liberal)

Issues*	White Delegates		Black Delegates	
	CR	NCR	CR	NCR
Social Issues				
Equal Rights Amendment	95	78	97	97
Affirmative Action Programs	92	62	99	98
Food Stamp Reduction	77	38	67	60
Handgun Control Legislation	89	59	85	82
School Prayer Amendment	89	57	43	37
Excessive Environmental Reg.	92	70	71	63
Use of Marijuana Immoral	79	39	31	34
Homosexual Behavior Immoral	80	32	24	24
Antiabortion Amendment	93	71	51	46
Defense/Foreign Policy Issues				
Increase in Defense Spending	96	80	94	92
U.S. Military in Mid East	96	89	94	88
U.S. Military in Lat. Am.	95	84	91	89
Nuclear Freeze	96	91	93	90
More Arms Control Neg.	98	95	92	88
Economic Issues				
Tax Increase to Cut Bud. Def.	60	55	35	41
Nat. Health Insurance	92	61	92	93
Spending Cuts to Balance Bud.	65	33	45	54
Public Works Program	79	53	76	66
Increase Energy/Hurt Env.	91	77	74	71

*See Appendix for question wording

cuts to balance the federal budget. Additionally, while black civil rights activists take more liberal than conservative positions on 14 of the 19 issues listed in Table 3.8, the white civil rights activists assume majority liberal positions on all 19 issues.

Another major difference between black and white Democratic civil rights activists is the latter's relative lack of enthusiasm for Jesse Jackson's presidential candidacy. Even though considerably more white civil rights than non–civil rights activists favored Jackson, only 11 percent identified Jackson as their first choice for the party's presidential nomination as compared to 62 percent of their black counterparts. Among whites, with the slight exception of differing levels of Jackson support, civil rights activism differentiates little among candidate preferences. For both groups, the first choice for the Democratic nomination was Walter Mondale (58 percent and 61 percent of the civil rights and non–civil rights activists, respectively) followed by Gary Hart (28 percent and 32 percent respectively). For the black delegates, Jackson was much more popular with civil rights than with non–civil rights activists (62 percent to 50 percent) while Mondale was significantly less popular (34 percent to 44 percent). Clearly,

Jackson's support was based more on racial considerations than on civil rights involvement.

Finally, the white civil rights activists generally demonstrate a greater concern for issues (and a smaller concern with party regularity) than their white non–civil rights brethren within the state Democratic parties. As shown in Table 3.9, white civil rights activists' main reason for becoming involved in party work is their concern with working for issues, a motivation listed as most important by a considerably smaller percentage of the white non–civil rights activists (40 percent to 19 percent). Conversely, 43 percent of the white non–civil rights activists identified party support as their main motivation for party involvement compared to 33 percent of the white civil rights activists. These data are consistent with those on the delegates' feelings about the party organization's most important role, about the most important factor in selecting a candidate, and about the proper party role in balancing issue positions and broad electoral appeals. In each case, white civil rights activists demonstrate greater concern with issues than do their white non–civil rights counterparts (although the central tendencies of each group on these points are quite similar). Although the other data in Table 3.9 reveal practically no group differences among white delegates, that above suggests the involvement of white civil rights activists in Democratic state conventions has brought a mildly different party/issue orientation into the arena.

This observation is underscored when we compare white and black civil rights activists on the questions considered in Table 3.9. While the differences between the two groups of black delegates are negligible, civil rights activists themselves differ sharply across racial lines. For example, white civil rights activists are considerably more motivated to party work by issue concerns than are black civil rights activists (40 percent to 15 percent). They are somewhat less motivated by their desire to support the party (33 percent to 45 percent). Similarly, the white civil rights delegates are much more supportive of selecting candidates based on issue and ideological positions, more likely to be party switchers, and less likely to feel that the party should emphasize broad electoral appeals rather than issue positions. Moreover, they are less supportive of the party's 1980 presidential candidate, more supportive of ballot splitting, and less likely to believe that the party organization has improved in recent years. Only on the question of the state party organization's most important role do the civil rights activists come together. In short, white civil rights activists demonstrate a clear potential for bringing a significant amateur orientation into the southern Democratic party, much more so than it appeared when civil rights activism was considered without the introduction of controls for race. The potential for intra-party disruption along these lines is more the product of white civil rights activist involvement than of general civil rights involvement.

CONCLUSION

The civil rights movement, perhaps more than any other single factor, helped to undermine and transform the mid-twentieth century patterns of southern pol-

Table 3.9
Party Orientations of Southern Democratic State Convention Delegates by Civil Rights Activism and Race (in percent)

Item	White Delegates		Black Delegates	
	CR	NCR	CR	NCR
Reason for Pol. Involvement				
To support party	33	43	45	45
To help political career	2	4	2	3
To enjoy campaign excitement	2	2	1	2
To meet people	1	2	1	1
To support particular candidate	19	19	25	25
To work for issues	40	19	15	10
To enjoy delegate visibility	0	0	1	1
To fulfill civic duty	2	9	9	10
To make business contacts	1	2	1	3
	100	100	99	100
(N=)	(288)	(1706)	(516)	(262)
Most Important State Party Role				
Provide campaign assistance	25	29	25	29
Take positions on issues	25	17	25	23
Provide services/information	17	21	24	26
Recruit candidates	7	4	2	3
Inform electorate about party goals and positions	27	29	23	19
	101	100	99	100
(N=)	(276)	(1625)	(496)	(256)
Most Important Factor in Candidate Selection				
Party loyalty and prior service	6	17	23	27
Positions on issues/ideology	89	75	66	58
Chance for victory	3	5	5	4
Not sure; no opinion	1	3	5	10
	99	100	99	99
(N=)	(283)	(1650)	(495)	(259)
Splitting Ballots Justified?				
Yes, national elections only	4	12	4	5
Yes, state/local elections only	13	8	8	7
Yes, all election levels	24	23	15	13
No	50	50	63	61
Not sure; no opinion	8	7	10	14
	99	100	100	100
(N=)	(285)	(1663)	(497)	(258)
1980 Presidential Vote				
Jimmy Carter	84	81	97	94
Ronald Reagan	5	11	1	1
John Anderson	8	5	1	1
Other	2	2	1	3
	99	99	100	99
(N=)	(287)	(1683)	(511)	(270)
Party Switcher?				
Yes	22	14	4	4
No	78	86	96	96
	100	100	100	100
(N=)	(285)	(1685)	(511)	(265)

Table 3.9 (continued)

Item	White Delegates		Black Delegates	
	CR	NCR	CR	NCR
Opinions on Proper Party Role				
Would stop working for party if it took disagreeable issue stands	25	14	5	6
Party's broad electoral appeal is more important than its taking personally agreeable issue positions	60	70	80	71
No opinion	14	16	15	23
	99	100	100	100
(N=)	(273)	(1606)	(479)	(240)
Party Organization Changed?				
Yes, improved	53	54	64	67
Yes, deteriorated	19	20	14	15
No change	29	26	22	18
	101	100	100	100
(N=)	(270)	(1577)	(479)	(248)

itics. It touched the region's educational, social, and legal systems. It helped to open the doors of the southern political parties (especially the Democratic) to blacks and paved the way for increased black participation in the South's electoral processes.

The data presented here indicate that some of those who have been involved in the movement have also touched the region's party system through their penetration of the party elite. Those state party activists involved in civil rights organizations are clearly different with respect to ideology and issue positions from their colleagues who have no such record of involvement. In general, these activities represent a liberalizing influence within the party system. While the presence of a significant portion of blacks within the ranks of civil rights activists undoubtedly contributes to this group's liberalism, it remains strong even when racial controls are introduced. A sizeable percentage of white Democratic delegates were involved in civil rights activities. On almost all points considered here—ideology, issue orientations, party perspectives, and, to a lesser degree, candidate preferences—this group is clearly and consistently differentiated from the remainder of their white state-party brethren. They also differ in numerous ways from black convention delegates who have a history of involvement in civil rights organizations. There is strong evidence that this group constitutes a liberalizing element in the region's Democratic party and introduces a type of internal diversity not significantly present in the southern party system before the civil rights movement.

It is well established that the southern party system has changed. The Republican party has become increasingly competitive electorally and increasingly viable organizationally in the South.[12] In many respects southern Republican parties have come to be most closely identified with ideological views, issue positions, and compositional characteristics associated with traditional southern politics.[13] It is not surprising, then, to find that the Republican state parties remain largely untouched in any direct sense by party activists' involvement in civil rights organizations. In sharp contrast, the southern Democratic parties have lost much of their uniquely regional character. Other research indicates that southern state Democratic parties have become more heterogeneous and more liberal as a result of such things as increased black participation and increased involvement of people moving into the South from outside the region. The analysis presented here is consistent with this picture; it points to another aspect of the diversity and liberalism of the contemporary southern Democratic parties. Even though vestiges of the old party remain, largely in the persons of white non–civil rights activists, southern Democratic parties are being transformed as white civil rights activists join blacks moving into the organizational structure. It strongly suggests that the presence of civil rights activists in party ranks is neither transitory nor inconsequential for the party's future.

APPENDIX

Table 3.10
Backgrounds of Southern State Democratic Convention Delegates by Civil Rights Activism (in percent)

Background Variable	Civil Rights Delegates	Non-Civil Rights Delegates
Age		
18–25	3	5
26–30	9	8
31–40	31	28
41–50	21	20
51–60	16	19
60+	20	20
	100	100
(N=)	(878)	(2149)
Race		
White	35	85
Black	62	13
Other	3	2
	100	100
(N=)	(839)	(2049)
Education		
Less than high school	3	3
High school graduate	7	12
Some college	24	30
College graduate	18	18
Post-college	48	37
	100	100
(N=)	(846)	(2041)

Table 3.10 (continued)

Background Variable	Civil Rights Delegates	Non-Civil Rights Delegates
Occupation		
Professional	50	38
Business	15	19
Sales/Clerical	6	8
Blue Collar/Service	8	8
Public officials	8	10
Housewife	4	7
Student	2	3
Other	6	6
Unemployed	2	2
	101	101
(N=)	(827)	(2006)
Income		
$0 - $24,999	40	30
$25,000 - $44,999	37	43
$45,000 - $59,999	13	14
$60,000+	11	13
	101	100
(N=)	(820)	(1961)
"Born-again" Experience?		
Yes	40	36
No	60	64
	100	100
(N=)	(829)	(1977)
Church Attendance		
Every week	45	39
Almost every week	19	22
Once or twice a month	12	13
Few times a year	16	20
Never	8	7
	100	101
(N=)	(842)	(2031)
State of Childhood		
South	80	81
Non-South	20	19
	100	100
(N=)	(882)	(2158)
Type of Community		
Urban/Suburban	56	46
Small town/Rural	44	54
	100	100
(N=)	(867)	(2114)
Length of Residence		
5 years or less	6	4
6-10 years	5	5
11-20 years	11	11
Over 20 years	77	80
	99	100
(N=)	(881)	(2156)

Table 3.11
Backgrounds of Southern State Republican Convention Delegates by Civil Rights Activism (in percent)

Background Variable	Civil Rights Delegates	Non-Civil Rights Delegates
Age		
18-25	6	5
26-30	10	8
31-40	22	18
41-50	20	22
51-60	12	24
60+	30	24
	100	101
(N=)	(50)	(1713)
Race		
White	62	98
Black	31	0
Other	7	2
	100	100
(N=)	(45)	(1667)
Education		
Less than high school	4	2
High school graduate	2	8
Some college	27	33
College graduate	19	26
Post-college	48	31
	100	100
(N=)	(48)	(1653)
Occupation		
Professional	42	32
Business	17	30
Sales/Clerical	6	10
Blue Collar/Service	0	4
Public officials	6	3
Housewife	13	13
Student	0	3
Other	15	5
Unemployed	0	0
	99	100
(N=)	(47)	(1632)
Income		
$0 - $24,999	24	25
$25,000 - $44,999	47	39
$45,000 - $59,999	17	17
$60,000+	13	20
	101	101
(N=)	(46)	(1603)
"Born-again" Experience?		
Yes	38	42
No	62	58
	100	100
(N=)	(50)	(1621)

Table 3.11 (continued)

Background Variable	Civil Rights Delegates	Non-Civil Rights Delegates
Church Attendance		
Every week	52	48
Almost every week	21	18
Once or twice a month	8	11
Few times a year	17	19
Never	2	4
	100	100
(N=)	(48)	(1670)
State of Childhood		
South	59	62
Non-South	41	38
	100	100
(N=)	(51)	(1720)
Type of Community		
Urban/Suburban	54	57
Small town/Rural	46	43
	100	100
(N=)	(50)	(1689)
Length of Residence		
5 years or less	14	7
6-10 years	16	12
11-20 years	16	19
Over 20 years	55	62
	100	100
(N=)	(51)	(1719)

NOTES

1. Ulrich B. Phillips, "The Central Theme of Southern History," *American Historical Review* 34 (October 1928): 31.

2. V. O. Key, Jr., *Southern Politics in State and Nation* (New York: Alfred A. Knopf, 1949), esp. chap. 1.

3. See, for example, J. Morgan Kousser, *The Shaping of Southern Politics: Suffrage Restriction and the Establishment of the One-Party South, 1880–1910* (New Haven: Yale University Press, 1974), esp. chap. 1; Key, *Southern Politics*, chap. 1; Dewey Grantham, *The Democratic South* (New York: W. W. Norton, 1963), chap. 2; and Frederick D. Wright, "The History of Black Political Participation to 1965," in *Blacks in Southern Politics*, ed. Laurence W. Moreland, Robert P. Steed, and Tod A. Baker (New York: Praeger, 1987), 9–30.

4. There are a number of detailed discussions of blacks, politics, and the civil rights movement. See, for example, H. D. Price, *The Negro in Southern Politics* (New York: New York University Press, 1957); Everett Carll Ladd, Jr., *Negro Political Leadership in the South* (Ithaca: Cornell University Press, 1966); Harry Holloway, *The Politics of the Southern Negro: From Exclusion to Big City Organization* (New York: Random House, 1969); Hanes Walton, Jr., *Black Politics: A Theoretical and Structural Analysis*

(Philadelphia: J. B. Lippincott, 1972); Donald R. Matthews and James W. Prothro, *Negroes and the New Southern Politics* (New York: Harcourt, Brace and World, 1966); Aldon D. Morris, *The Origins of the Civil Rights Movement* (New York: Free Press, 1984); Doug McAdam, *Political Process and the Development of Black Insurgency, 1930–1970* (Chicago: University of Chicago Press, 1982); Steven F. Lawson, *Black Ballots: Voting in the South 1944–1969* (New York: Columbia University Press, 1976); Clayborne Carson, *In Struggle: SNCC and the Black Awakening of the 1960s* (Cambridge, Mass.: Harvard University Press, 1981); David J. Garrow, *Protest at Selma: Martin Luther King, Jr., and the Voting Rights Act of 1965* (New Haven: Yale University Press, 1978); Howell Raines, *My Soul is Rested: The Story of the Civil Rights Movement in the Deep South* (New York: Putnam, 1977); Numan V. Bartley, *The Rise of Massive Resistance: Race and Politics in the South in the 1950s* (Baton Rouge: Louisiana State University Press, 1969); William C. Berman, *The Politics of Civil Rights in the Truman Administration* (Columbus: Ohio State University Press, 1970); William Brink and Louis Harris, *The Negro Revolution in America* (New York: Simon and Schuster, 1963); Robert Frederick Burk, *The Eisenhower Administration and Black Rights* (Knoxville: University of Tennessee Press, 1984); John H. Fenton and Kenneth N. Vines, "Negro Registration in Louisiana," *American Political Science Review* 51 (September 1957): 704–713; Thurgood Marshall, "The Rise and Collapse of the 'White Democratic Party'," *Journal of Negro Education* 36 (Summer 1957): 249–254; U.S. Commission on Civil Rights, *The Voting Rights Act: Ten Years After* (Washington, D.C.: 1975); James Q. Wilson, *Negro Politics: The Search for Leadership* (Glencoe, Ill.: Free Press, 1960); James Q. Wilson, "The Negro in Politics," *Daedalus* 94 (Fall 1965): 949–973; Hanes Walton, Jr., *Black Political Parties* (New York: Free Press, 1972); Lester M. Salamon, "Leadership and Modernization: The Emerging Political Elite in the American South," *Journal of Politics* 35 (August 1973): 615–646; Lucius J. Barker and Jesse J. McCorry, Jr., *Black Americans and the Political System* (Cambridge, Mass.: Winthrop, 1976); Mack H. Jones, "The 1965 Voting Rights Act and Political Symbolism" (paper presented at the 1979 annual meeting of the Southern Political Science Association, Gatlinburg, Tennessee, November 1–3, 1979); Richard Murray and Arnold Vedlitz, "Racial Voting Patterns in the South: An Analysis of Major Elections in Five Cities," *Annals of the American Academy of Political and Social Science* 439 (September 1978): 29–39; Robert P. Steed, Laurence W. Moreland, and Tod A. Baker, eds., *Party Politics in the South* (New York: Praeger, 1980), esp. chaps. 8–9; Hanes Walton, Jr., *Invisible Politics: Black Political Behavior* (Albany: State University of New York Press, 1985); Hanes Walton, Jr., "The Recent Literature on Black Politics," *PS* 18 (Fall 1985): 769–780; and Moreland, Steed, and Baker, *Blacks in Southern Politics*, esp. chaps. 1–7.

5. Although Earl and Merle Black argue that, in spite of striking differences from the past, blacks are still in a tangential position in the southern political system, they also note that southern politics reflects a new concern with avoiding the racism of the past; see Black and Black, *Politics and Society in the South*, esp. chap. 14. See also Earl Black, *Southern Governors and Civil Rights* (Cambridge, Mass.: Harvard University Press, 1976); and Alexander P. Lamis, *The Two-Party South* (New York: Oxford University Press, 1984), esp. chap. 15.

6. See the discussion in William Crotty, *Party Reform* (New York: Longman, 1983); and Robert P. Steed, "Party Reform, the Nationalization of American Politics, and Party Change in the South," in the present volume.

7. Robert P. Steed, Laurence W. Moreland, and Tod A. Baker, "The Civil Rights

Movement and Southern State Party Elites'' (paper presented at the 1982 annual meeting of the Southern Political Science Association, Atlanta, Georgia, October 28–30, 1982).

8. See the discussion by Laurence W. Moreland in Chapter 9 of the present volume.

9. The Republicans are included in the analysis even though there are very few civil rights activists within that party (only 3 percent totaling approximately 50 delegates). It is useful to look at this subgroup for comparative purposes, but quite clearly the major significance of civil rights activity for the state conventions is within the Democratic party.

10. See, for example, James Q. Wilson, *The Amateur Democrat* (Chicago: University of Chicago Press, 1962); and Aaron Wildavsky, ''The Goldwater Phenomenon: Purists, Politicians and the Two-Party System,'' *Review of Politics* 27 (1965): 386–413. For the view that this distinction is not as significant for the parties as traditionally argued, see Walter J. Stone and Alan I. Abramowitz, ''Ideology, Electability, and Candidate Choice,'' in Ronald B. Rapoport, Alan I. Abramowitz, and John McGlennon (eds.), *The Life of the Parties: Activists in Presidential Politics* (Lexington, Ky.: University Press of Kentucky, 1986), 75–95.

11. The main exception to this may be found in social issues with religious overtones (e.g., abortion, school prayer); for elaboration of this point, see Moreland, Steed, and Baker, ''Black Party Activists''; and Laurence W. Moreland, Robert P. Steed, and Tod A. Baker, ''Black Party Activists: A Profile,'' in Moreland, Steed, and Baker (eds.), *Blacks in Southern Politics*, chap. 6.

12. See, for example, Charles L. Prysby, ''Electoral Behavior in the U.S. South: Recent and Emerging Trends,'' in Steed, Moreland, and Baker, *Party Politics in the South*, chap. 5; Charles D. Hadley and Susan E. Howell, ''The Southern Split Ticket Voter, 1952–1976: Republican Conversion or Democratic Decline?'' in Steed, Moreland, and Baker, *Party Politics in the South*, chap. 6; Malcolm E. Jewell, ''Participation in Southern Primaries,'' in Steed, Moreland, and Baker, *Party Politics in the South*, chap. 1; Merle Black and Earl Black, ''The Growth of Contested Republican Primaries in the American South, 1960–1980,'' in Moreland, Baker, and Steed, *Contemporary Southern Political Attitudes and Behavior*, chap. 6; Paul Allen Beck and Paul Lopatto, ''The End of Southern Distinctiveness,'' in Moreland, Baker, and Steed, *Contemporary Southern Political Attitudes and Behavior*, chap. 8; Alexander P. Lamis, ''The 1980 Elections in the South: Two-Party Development in Perspective'' (paper presented at the 1982 Citadel Symposium on Southern Politics, March 25–27, 1982, Charleston, South Carolina); Seagull, *Southern Republicanism*; Black and Black, *Politics and Society in the South*; Lamis, *The Two-Party South*; Steed, Moreland, and Baker, *The 1984 Presidential Election in the South*; Robert P. Steed, Laurence W. Moreland, and Tod A. Baker, ''The Nature of Contemporary Party Organization in South Carolina'' (paper presented at the 1987 Annual Meeting of the American Political Science Association, September 3–6, 1987, Chicago, Illinois); and Lewis Bowman, William E. Hulbary, and Anne E. Kelley, ''Party Sorting at the Grassroots: Stable Partisans and Party Changers among Florida's Precinct Officials'' (paper presented at the 1986 Citadel Symposium on Southern Politics, March 1986, Charleston, South Carolina).

13. See the discussion in Tod A. Baker, Robert P. Steed, and Laurence W. Moreland, ''Southern Distinctiveness and the Emergence of Party Competition: The Case of a Deep South State,'' in Moreland, Baker, and Steed, *Contemporary Southern Political Attitudes and Behavior*, chap. 10. See also John C. Green and James L. Guth, ''The Transformation

of Southern Political Elites: Regionalism among Party and PAC Contributors,'' in *The Disappearing South? Studies in Regional Change and Continuity*, ed. Robert P. Steed, Laurence W. Moreland, and Tod A. Baker (Tuscaloosa: University of Alabama Press, 1989), chap. 3.

4

The Changing Roles of Women in Southern State Party Politics

Robert Darcy, Janet M. Clark, and Charles D. Hadley

For quite some time the South has lagged behind the rest of the nation in integrating women into political life. The simplest political activity is voting. While women traditionally voted at lower rates than men all over the country, the difference was most pronounced in the South.[1] Recently this national trend was reversed. Women now vote at greater rates than men. An analysis of the 1984 American National Election Study found 77 percent of the women outside the South voting in comparison with 75 percent of the men.[2] In contrast, men still reported outvoting women 68 to 63 percent in the South, the states of the former Confederacy. While the survey results exaggerate actual voter turnout, it remains likely that southern men and women are still behind the rest of the nation in this regard.[3]

Southern women also lag behind those of other regions in other aspects of political life. They are less likely than others, for example, to run for and be elected to political office. Consider state legislatures. In 1975, on the average, the percentage of women among state legislators was half that of the rest of the country (4 versus 9 percent). The regional disparity persisted in 1985 despite the doubling of their number (8 versus 16 percent).[4]

The South lags in other ways. There were two attempts through constitutional amendment in this century to advance the political rights of women: the Nineteenth Amendment extending suffrage to women and, more recently, the Equal Rights Amendment (ERA). In both cases the major opposition came from southern states. Eight of the ten states that failed to ratify the Nineteenth Amendment

This research was supported in part by a grant from the College of Liberal Arts, University of New Orleans, and by the Computer Research Centers, University of New Orleans and Oklahoma State University.

were in the region: Alabama, Florida, Georgia, Louisiana, Mississippi, North Carolina, South Carolina, and Virginia.[5] The ERA ratification pattern was remarkably similar. Of the fifteen states in which ratification failed, nine were southern: Alabama, Arkansas, Florida, Georgia, Louisiana, Mississippi, North Carolina, South Carolina, and Virginia. A tenth, Tennessee, rescinded its ratification.[6]

There are several explanations for the distinctive political role of women in the South. The first is the region's traditionalistic political culture, a culture in which society is viewed as hierarchical with a clear economic, social, and political elite.[7] The role of politics is to maintain the existing social arrangements and control. New groups, such as women, seeking political influence are resisted because they pose a threat both to the wider social and economic system and to the political establishment itself. Seen as a new group challenging political power, women are resisted by the political structure.[8]

One problem with the application of the political culture concept to an entire state or region of states is that it implies more uniformity than may actually exist. Daniel J. Elazar, for example, found important strains of moralistic and individualistic political culture in the South.[9] Joan Carver, moreover, found regional variation within Florida to account for a large share of the difference in female political representation.[10]

Another problem with political culture as an explanatory variable is the establishment of mechanisms by which the culture enforces its ethos. In the case of women, several studies failed to document prejudice against female candidates by either voters or political elites even where it was expected given the dominant political culture.[11] The traditionalistic political culture, then, has serious weaknesses as an explanation for the diminished role of women in southern political life.

The traditionalistic political culture in the South, arguably, is maintained through the dominant one-party Democratic political system.[12] In the absence of political challenge, political interest was minimized and the possibility of challenge to the existing order limited. This explanation, too, has its weaknesses. That dominant political system began to crumble at the presidential level with the Dixiecratic revolt against the national Democratic party over the civil rights plank adopted at its 1948 national convention. Republicans subsequently became increasingly competitive with and came to dominate the Democrats in presidential elections.[13]

The political setting itself changed dramatically over the last several decades. The South moved from an economy based on agriculture to one based on industry. That industrial base moved to the South from other parts of the nation due to the availability of a large pool of inexpensive nonunion labor. While its people moved from the country to the city and to the continuously expanding suburbs, large numbers of people moved into the region. With significant advances in higher education attainment, its population joined the ranks of the affluent society.[14]

Table 4.1

Backgrounds of Southern State Party Activists by Political Party and Gender (in percent)

	Democrats		Republicans	
	Men	Women	Men	Women
Sex	49	51	43	57
Race				
White	73	68	98	97
Black	25	30	1	2
Other	2	3	1	2
Age				
18-29	11	11	8	12
30-39	30	30	15	23
40-49	22	24	27	20
50-59	18	21	29	21
60+	19	15	21	24
Native Born	86	86	65	69
College Graduate	60	56	44	67
Family Income $25,000+	73	62	73	78

Moreover, the politics of race moved from exclusion to inclusion. The Voting Rights Act of 1965 was responsible for the reintegration of blacks (and poor whites) into the political life of the region. With massive black voter registration came both black political organization and the systematic election of blacks to public and party office. The national Democratic party, the champion of the civil rights cause, became their natural political home. This, in turn, led to the systematic erosion of the state Democratic party as racially conservative whites moved to the ranks of its growing Republican rival.[15] The politics of race, then, was responsible for the emergent southern two-party system.[16] By the end of the 1970s the South lost its political distinctiveness, including the lack of participation by women in its political parties.[17]

The political parties themselves were opened to meaningful participation by both women and blacks. The national Democratic party, through successive presidential candidate selection rules reforms, forced the individual states to rewrite the laws that governed that process for both Democrats *and* Republicans. Democrats were required to include *women* and blacks in that process.[18] Political parties were opened to their activist members into the foreseeable future.[19] The South, then, became but another collection of states in a nationalized political process.[20]

A direct consequence of the process described above was a significant increase in the numbers of women active in the Democratic *and* Republican parties of the South (Table 4.1). In direct contrast to the Republican women, nearly 30 percent of the Democratic women are black, a figure five percentage points higher than that for their male colleagues. Other meaningful differences between the Democratic and Republican women state party activists exist. A larger proportion of Democratic women is substantially younger (41 percent in contrast to 23 percent of the Republican women), native-born southerners and college educated. On the other hand, a larger proportion of Republican women have annual family incomes in excess of $25,000, a figure comparable to the politically active men in both political parties. How meaningful that female participation is and whether or not it can be projected into a changed role for women in southern politics remains to be explored.

GENDER ROLES AMONG STATE PARTY ACTIVISTS

Talcott Parsons and Robert Bales distinguished male and female roles within the traditional family arrangement.[21] The male role, characterized as *instrumental*, involves dealing with the outside world. Thus the male engages in a series of activities aimed at enhancing or maintaining his own status and that of his family. The female role, characterized as *expressive* in contrast, involves harmonizing the activities of the several family members and providing a support environment within the family itself.

If Parsons and Bales are correct and men and women do have distinct societal roles, it is not unreasonable to expect a similar division of labor when men and women join together in political activity. Such male-female party role differences were documented by Edmond Costantini and Kenneth H. Craik in their 1964–65 survey of California party activists.[22] Subsequent studies of California party leaders, both Democratic and Republican, found these differences to persist into the 1980s.[23] Similar gender patterns were found in Michigan and Georgia.[24]

In political parties, instrumental and expressive roles manifest themselves in two ways: in incentives or motives for party activity and in the kinds of activities engaged in by men and women. From this perspective, being active out of party loyalty, for the excitement of the campaign, to meet people, or to fulfill civic responsibilities is to be active for expressive motives. All involve loyalty and service or personal pleasure. The party is viewed as an end in itself. On the other hand, those who are active for personal political advancement, to make business and professional contacts, or to further a candidate or specific issues are motivated by instrumental ends. Their party activity is viewed as a means to a more remote goal.

The activities of party leaders, then, are differentiated into expressive and instrumental depending on the meaning of the activity to either the individual or organization. Thus, getting out the vote and building the party organization involve the party activist in supporting others and, typically, in working behind the scenes within the party itself. In contrast, communicating with the public, representing a group, and recruiting candidates are typically instrumental activities. They place the party activists in positions of personal visibility and bring them into contact with individuals outside the party organization.

If men and women bring the traditional gender roles described earlier into their party activities, then the mere presence of large numbers of women in the party organizations will not mean the beginnings of change in the political role of women. Instead, it may simply satisfy demands for increased female visibility and, at the same time, limit the real opportunities for women. The fact that Diane L. Fowlkes, Jerry Perkins, and Sue Tolleson Rinehart clearly documented such divisions among Atlanta, Georgia, Democratic and Republican party activists strengthens the concern that the influx of women into the southern political parties may not constitute a meaningful change in their gender roles.[25]

The survey of state party convention delegates included two questions providing the basis for measuring expressive and instrumental activities and motives. These are:

During the past 8 years, which of the following activities, if any, have you performed for your party? (Check as many as apply).

1. Getting out the vote
2. Communicating with the public about issues
3. Representing a particular group (such as business, women, teachers, etc.)
4. Recruiting candidates for party or public office
5. Building party organization (such as maintaining lists of party voters, doing clerical work, etc.)

Look at the reasons listed below for becoming involved in politics this year. Please indicate how important each of them was for you. [Very important, somewhat important, not important.]

1. To support my party
2. To help my political career
3. To enjoy the excitement of the campaign
4. To meet other people with similar interests
5. To support a particular candidate I believe in
6. To work for issues
7. To enjoy the visibility of being a delegate
8. To fulfill my civic responsibility
9. To make business or professional contacts.

Responses 1 and 5 to the first question were considered indications of expressive activities and the remaining responses instrumental. The second question measured motives for political activity. Responses 1, 3, 4, 7, and 8 were considered indications of expressive motives and the remaining responses instrumental. Two scales were constructed by counting the number of expressive and instrumental responses for each individual for both their motives and activities.

From the results in Table 4.2, there is very little difference between men and women in their expressive and instrumental orientations. Women, on the average,

Table 4.2
Role Orientations of Southern State Party Activists by Political Party and Gender (in percent)

	Democrats		Republicans	
	Men	Women	Men	Women
Most Imp. Party Activity				
Getting out the vote	61	64	60	47
Communicating with public	20	21	18	25
Representing a group	3	4	1	1
Recruiting candidates	3	2	5	8
Building party organization	13	9	16	19
	100	100	100	100
(N=)	(1302)	(1327)	(726)	(963)
Very Important Reasons for 1984 Political Involvement				
Support party	76	79	83	70
Help political career	19	15	7	10
Campaign excitement	28	29	20	14
Meet like-minded people	41	43	32	26
Support specific cand.	77	85	88	80
Work for issues	72	82	81	80
Delegate visibility	17	19	11	7
Civic responsibility	57	64	60	55
Make business contacts	11	14	4	5
Summary Political Role (Mean Scores)				
Expressive	4.6	4.7	4.4	4.5
Instrumental	3.5	3.4	3.1	2.9

are slightly more likely than men to indicate expressive activities and motives and slightly less likely to indicate instrumental activities and motives. These differences are very small, however, and provide no basis for characterizing male and female political party activities and motives as distinct or as originating in traditional gender roles.

Fowlkes, Perkins, and Rinehart found distinctions in the roles of men and women in the two political parties.[26] Here, too, we find some distinctions but not nearly enough to conclude there are major gender role differences among female and male activists in the two parties. Republican women are less likely to indicate instrumental motives or activities than their Democratic counterparts. There are slight differences in expressive responses as well. However, expressive and instrumental roles are distributed very similarly among these state party activists in the two parties.

Finally, there are some surprising findings with respect to the differences between southern party activists and those in other states (not shown). There are no regional differences among Republicans. Southern Democratic women, on the other hand, are slightly more expressive than those outside the region. Moreover, they are more likely to indicate instrumental activities and motives. Again, however, the differences among women Democratic activists are quite small and only of interest because they are opposite the hypothesized direction in contrast to those for Republican women.

Breaking down the responses by activities considered most important and motives considered very important, fails to find any differences in excess of those already noted with respect to activities performed. Motives, on the other hand, provide more of a contrast. Democratic women were found consistently more involved than Republican women in *both* expressive and instrumental activities. For example, Democrats, regardless of sex, were more involved in politics than Republicans to meet like-minded people and to help their political careers, the percentage difference being about 10 in both instances for both sexes.

From the responses given by men and women who attended the 1984 state party conventions in the southern states, gender roles no longer seem to be playing a significant structuring function among male and female activists within their state political parties. The hypothesized difference between southern men and women, furthermore, failed to materialize. Strength of motivation for political involvement, in contrast, indicates that there is a continued importance of gender roles between political parties.

AMBITION

The presence of significant numbers of women among party activists can enhance the chances of women being nominated for public office in two ways. Female voters might be more likely to favor the nomination of women or, at least, not be as opposed as men to such recruitment and nomination.[27] They themselves are a source of future candidates for government office. While party activity in the United States is not the kind of prerequisite it is to gaining the party nomination in Europe, party activists long were considered an important source of office-holders.[28] Studies consistently found women party activists less likely to indicate ambition to run for elective office. Consistent with the women officeholding lag noted earlier, southern female party activists might be expected to exhibit less personal political ambition than their counterparts in the rest of the country.

This was explored with the following question asked state party convention delegates:

Please indicate which, if any, of the following positions you now hold, have held in the past, or would like to hold in the future.

1. Member of local (precinct, city, county, or town) party committee
2. Local party officer (chairperson or other office)
3. State party officer or member of state-level committee
4. Delegate to national party convention
5. Elected public office (local, state, or national)
6. Appointed public office (local, state, or national)

Table 4.3
Ambition of Southern State Party Activists by Political Party and Gender
(in percent)

	Democrats		Republicans	
	Men	Women	Men	Women
Those Who Would Like To Be:				
Member of local party comm.	19	23	13	29
Officer of local party comm.	24	25	14	20
Officer of state party	30	30	21	28
National convention del.	40	42	30	39
Elected public official	30	23	13	29
Appointed public official	27	25	14	23

The responses for those presently not holding the position are presented in Table 4.3. First, the ambition of men exceeds that of women for Republicans for all positions. With the single exception of the ambition of southern Democratic men to hold elected public office (30 percent versus 23 for Democratic women), there is a very slight difference favoring women rather than men for four of the five remaining positions among Democrats. The second point of note is that the differences between men and women generally are greater among the Republicans than among the Democrats. Third, Democratic women exhibit a great deal more ambition than those active in the southern Republican parties.

Southern women were hypothesized to have less ambition than their counterparts in the rest of the country. This proved not to be the case at all. The level of ambition for southern Democratic women, regardless of race,[29] exceeds that of their nonsouthern counterparts in every instance. Their ambition for all of the party and government positions is almost half again the rate for those outside the region. Among the Republicans the differences in levels of political ambition are generally less than among Democrats regardless of region. Republican women outside the South, however, were slightly more likely to aspire to public office than those in the South. In contrast, southern Republican women are more likely to aspire to state party office. In any event, the image of less politically ambitious southern women is not borne out.

AMATEURS AND PROFESSIONALS

One final aspect of the political participation of women was examined. James Q. Wilson suggested, and others have since confirmed, two distinct groups of party activists: amateurs and professionals.[30] The professionals are motivated by winning elections because of the power and resources brought by election victory. They are also motivated by loyalty to the party organization itself. The amateurs, in contrast, are concerned with issues and causes, causes likely connected with specific candidates. They are more concerned with being ideologically or issue

Table 4.4
Orientations of Southern State Party Activists by Political Party and Gender (in percent)

	Democrats		Republicans	
	Men	Women	Men	Women
Most Important Factor in Selecting Candidates for Public Office				
Party loyalty, prior service	19	18	3	4
Ideology, issue positions	75	78	86	88
Chance for electoral victory	6	4	8	7
Summary Professional Orientation Toward Politics by Region				
South	25	23	14	12
Other	18	13	17	16

correct then with winning elections. For them, the party organization and political power itself are viewed as a means to some further goal rather than an end in itself as it is with the professional.

That women tend toward the amateur rather than professional viewpoint is well established.[31] As a consequence women do not seek power for themselves. They remain outside the political organization and can only exert influence as part of a larger movement. The fact that women active in the two political parties hold amateur orientations compared with the orientations held by men serves to limit the personal benefits possible through their political activity.

The following question included in the survey administered to state party convention delegates serves to distinguish between amateur and professional orientations:

Which one of the following statements most closely expresses your own opinion? (Check only one.)

1. The most important factor in selecting candidates for public office is their party loyalty and prior service to the party.

2. The most important factor in selecting candidates for public office is their positions on issues and ideology.

3. The most important factor in selecting candidates for public office is their chance for electoral victory.

4. Not sure, no opinion.

Responses 1 and 3 are taken to indicate a professional orientation. The results are presented in Table 4.4.

Generally there are only small differences in professional orientations between men and women state political party activists. What differences there are have men holding slightly more professional orientations then women.[32] Southern Republicans are an exception; women here are slightly more professional than men. Interestingly, there is an interaction between region and political party. Among Democrats, it is the southern activists who are more professional. Republican party activists in the rest of the country, in contrast, show the greater professionalism. Generally, there is little basis for the contention that southern women are less professional in political party orientation than men. And in the South the differences in this regard between men and women are less than those for state party activists in the other states.

DISCUSSION: WOMEN IN THE SOUTHERN POLITICAL PARTIES

In several dimensions relating to the nature of, and motives for, political party activity, southern men and women activists are similar to those in the rest of the country. On the other hand, women are ahead in other characteristics, such as instrumental role orientation, ambition, and professionalism. At this point there are two tenable contrasting conclusions. First, the characteristics of party activity eventually will be projected into greater numbers of females elected to public office in the southern states. Second, there may be difficulties in translating these characteristic advantages into actual political power, especially effective political power. It is to this relationship we now turn.

California women party activists were found less centrist than the men in both political parties.[33] Democratic women were further left and Republican women further right of their male counterparts. If this is the case in the South, women are expected to be found at the ideological fringes of their respective political parties and out of step with the party itself and its broader electorate, especially for the Democrats. Thus, the electoral influence of women would be limited. Table 4.5 presents the ideological self-identification of activists in state Democratic and Republican parties by gender.[34]

First, unlike in California, in the South women of both political parties are more liberal than men. Only the Democratic women are at the fringe of their political party. Next, while the differences between male and female Republican activists are somewhat fewer in the South than in the rest of the country, Republican activists remain substantially conservative regardless of gender or region.[35] Among Democrats, in contrast, almost 10 percent more women than men can be identified as liberals. It is about the same for both the South and the rest of the country. In each case, however, the men and women of each political party express the same modal ideology. Women as a group, while more liberal philosophically, are not isolated within their respective political parties with their liberalism.

On the other hand, southern Democratic women may have a problem with their greater liberalism. The electorate in the region is considerably more conservative. While liberal Democratic women party activists form a substantial

Table 4.5
Ideological Self-identification of Southern State Party Activists and the General Population by Political Party and Gender (in percent)

| | Democrats | | Republicans | |
	Men	Women	Men	Women
Party Activists				
Liberal	59	69	4	2
Middle-of-the-road	20	16	5	3
Conservative	21	16	91	95
	100	101	100	100
(N=)	(1384)	(1411)	(782)	(1009)
General Population				
Liberal	34	27	15	14
Middle-of-the-road	37	41	20	17
Conservative	29	32	65	69
	100	100	100	100
(N=)	(84)	(106)	(81)	(61)

majority within the South, they do not have the same relationship with the southern electorate. A problem women party activists in the South face, then, especially among the Democrats, is to translate their party organizational strength into electoral and office holding strength.

Differences in political philosophy are explored further with comparable data from the 1984 CPS American National Election Study. The orientation of the potential southern electorate is decisively conservative (45 percent) as opposed to liberal (22 percent) or moderate (33 percent).[36] Respondents from the rest of the country are slightly less conservative/more liberal, the respective percentages being 40, 26, and 34. Broken down by partisan affiliation,[37] the patterns for the general electorate are the reverse of those for state party activists. Men in the South with Democratic partisan identifications are more liberal than similarly identified women and are about 15 to 20 percent more liberal than those in the general population, both regardless of region. Democratic men and women outside the South, moreover, remain about 12 to 15 percent more liberal than their southern counterparts. The modal political philosophy of southern Democrats is moderate while that for those in the rest of the country is liberal, *both regardless of gender.*[38]

Republican state party activists and those with Republican partisan identifications among the general electorate, on the other hand, are more compatibly conservative. There is little variation either by gender or by region with one exception. Republican women outside the South are 13 percentage points less conservative than their male counterparts regardless of region and 10 percentage points less conservative than southern Republican women. Though less conservative than their party activists, Republican identifiers fall into the same conservative pattern.

In this context, southern Democratic women who are state party activists stand out. Why? One common element likely to have played a role in the selection of delegates to the Democratic state party conventions is the ability to mobilize enough supporters to attend local meetings or to vote in low turnout primary elections. Here we know that those who attend meetings or vote in primary elections are already somewhat of a political elite atypical of the ordinary participant. It certainly is possible that an organized group, even a relatively small group, can exercise disproportionate influence when compared to their influence in the electorate at large.

The state delegate survey asked respondents to indicate groups in which they were active.[39] The one response on which Democratic women stood alone was "women's rights groups."[40] Among Democrats, over a third of the women indicate such affiliations regardless of region and race. Strikingly, more southern Democratic men (almost 10 percent) also indicate such affiliations, slightly more than the Republican women. Only a very small proportion of the Republican state convention delegates did so, in contrast.

This suggests a possible explanation for the exaggerated liberalism among women who are state Democratic party activists, especially among those in the South. The women's rights groups (and others) were able to mobilize their memberships to take advantage of favorable national convention delegate selection rules. Once mobilized, as a direct consequence of these advantageous rules put in place by the national Democratic party, women (and blacks) remained mobilized in state party politics, especially in the weakened southern Democratic parties.

Another problem is the translation of their influence by force of numbers within the several state political parties into elective political office. The problem they face, especially in the Democratic parties of the southern states, is how to bring into the party more moderate and conservative women who are more compatible with the general electorate. Unless this can be done, there is the danger that the Democrats, especially the women activists, will be outside the regional political mainstream. This will diminish their ability for political influence and election potential.

NOTES

1. Angus Campbell, Philip E. Converse, Warren E. Miller, and Donald E. Stokes, *The American Voter* (New York: Wiley, 1960), Chapter 17; Gerald M. Pomper, *Voters' Choice* (New York: Dodd, Mead, 1975); Sandra Baxter and Marjorie Lansing, *Women and Politics: The Invisible Majority* (Ann Arbor: University of Michigan Press, 1981).

2. The 1984 American National Election Study data, originally collected by the Center for Political Studies, Institute for Social Research, University of Michigan, under the direction of Warren E. Miller, were made available through institutional membership in the Inter-university Consortium for Political and Social Research. The South is defined as the CPS states classified Solid South and includes Tennessee.

3. Aage R. Clausen, "Response Validity: Vote Report," *Public Opinion Quarterly* 32 (Winter 1968): 588–606.

4. R. Darcy, Susan Welch, and Janet Clark, *Women, Elections, and Representation* (New York: Longman, 1987), Chapter 3.

5. Ida Husted Harper, ed., *The History of Women Suffrage* (Volume 6; New York: National American Woman Suffrage Association, 1922), 628.

6. Janet Boles, *The Politics of the Equal Rights Amendment* (New York: Longman, 1979); Mark Daniels and R. Darcy, "As Time Goes By: The Arrested Diffusion of the Equal Rights Amendment," *Publius* 15 (Fall 1985): 51–60.

7. Daniel J. Elazar, *American Federalism: A View from the States* (2nd ed.; New York: Harper and Row, 1972), 86–126. Cf. Charles Johnson, "Political Culture in the American States: Elazar's Formulation Examined," *American Journal of Political Science* 20 (August 1976): 491–509; Joan Carver, "Women in Florida," *The Journal of Politics* 41 (August 1979): 941–955.

8. Jeane Kirkpatrick, *Political Woman* (New York: Basic Books, 1974); Irene Diamond, *Sex Roles in the State House* (New Haven: Yale University Press, 1977); Wilma Rule, "Why Women Don't Run: The Critical Contextual Factors in Women's Legislative Recruitment," *Western Political Quarterly* 34 (March 1981): 60–77; David Hill, "Political Culture and Female Political Representation," *The Journal of Politics* 43 (February 1981): 159–168; Carol Nechemias, "Women's Success in Capturing State Legislative Seats: Stability and Instability of Empirical Relationships Over Time." Paper presented at the annual meeting of the Midwest Political Science Association, Chicago, April 1985; Carver, "Women." Cf. Woodrow Jones and Albert Nelson, "Correlates of Women's Representation in Lower State Legislative Chambers," *Social Behavior and Personality* 9 (#1 1981): 9–15.

9. Elazar, *American Federalism*, 97.

10. Carver, "Women."

11. R. Darcy, Margaret Brewer, and Judy Clay, "Women in the Oklahoma Political System: State Legislative Elections." *Social Science Journal* 21 (January 1984): 67–78.

12. Diamond, *Sex Roles*; Rule, "Why Women Don't Run"; Nechemias, "Women's Success."

13. E.g., Everett Carll Ladd, Jr. and Charles D. Hadley, *Transformation of the American Party System: Political Coalitions from the New Deal to the 1970s* (New York: W. W. Norton, 1975), 129–177; Alexander P. Lamis, *The Two-Party South* (New York: Oxford University Press, 1984); Harold W. Stanley, "Southern Partisan Changes: Dealignment, Realignment, or Both?" *Journal of Politics* 50 (February 1988): 64–88.

14. Ladd and Hadley, *Transformations*.

15. Charles D. Hadley, "The Continuing Transformation of Southern Politics," in *Political Ideas and Institutions*, ed. Edward V. Heck and Alan T. Leonhard (Dubuque, IA: Kendall/Hunt), 93–103.

16. James L. Sundquist, *Dynamics of the Party System: Alignment and Realignment of Political Parties in the United States* (Rev. ed.; Washington, D.C.: Brookings Institute, 1983), 352–375; Harold W. Stanley, "The 1984 Presidential Election in the South: Race and Realignment," in *The 1984 Presidential Election in the South: Patterns of Southern Party Politics*, eds., Robert P. Steed, Laurence W. Moreland, and Tod A. Baker (New York: Praeger, 1986), 303–335; Lamis, *The Two-Party South*.

17. Paul Allen Beck and Paul Lopatto, "The End of Southern Distinctiveness," *Contemporary Southern Political Attitudes and Behavior*, eds., Laurence W. Moreland, Tod

A. Baker, and Robert P. Steed (New York: Praeger, 1982), 160–182; Diane L. Fowlkes, "Ambitious Political Women: Countersocialization and Political Party Context," *Women and Politics* 4 (Winter 1984): 5–32.

18. Austin Ranney, "Changing the Rules of the Nominating Game," *Choosing the President*, ed., James David Barber (Englewood Cliffs: Prentice-Hall, 1974), 71–93.

19. Thomas R. Marshall, *Presidential Nominations in a Reform Age* (New York: Praeger, 1981), 170.

20. Charles D. Hadley, "The Nationalization of American Politics: Congress, the Supreme Court, and the National Political Parties," *The Journal of Social and Political Studies* 4 (Winter 1979): 359–380. On this and the other points examined, see Earl Black and Merle Black, *Politics and Society in the South* (Cambridge, MA: Harvard University Press, 1987).

21. T. Parsons and R. Bales, *Family: Socialization and Interaction Process* (Glencoe, IL: The Free Press, 1955).

22. Edmond Costantini and Kenneth H. Craik, "Women as Politicians: The Social Background, Personality, and Political Careers of Female Party Leaders," *Journal of Social Issues* 28 (#2 1972): 217–236.

23. Edmond Costantini and Julie Davis Bell, "Women in Political Parties: Gender Differences in Motives among California Party Activists," *Political Women: Current Roles in State and Local Government*, ed., Janet Flammang (Beverly Hills: SAGE, 1984), 114–138.

24. M. Kent Jennings and Norman Thomas, "Men and Women in Party Elites: Social Roles and Political Resources," *Midwest Journal of Political Science* 12 (November 1966): 469–492; Diane L. Fowlkes, Jerry Perkins, and Sue Tolleson Rinehart, "Gender Roles and Party Roles," *American Political Science Review* 73 (September 1979): 772–780.

25. Fowlkes, Perkins and Rinehart, "Gender Roles."

26. Fowlkes, Perkins, and Rinehart, "Gender Roles."

27. Diane Sainsbury, "Women's Routes to National Legislatures: A Comparison of Eligibility and Nomination in the United States, Britain, and Sweden." Paper presented at the ECPR Workshop on Candidate Selection in Comparative Perspective, Barcelona, Spain, March 25–30, 1985.

28. Sainsbury, "Women's Routes to National Legislatures"; Jennings and Thomas, "Men and Women"; M. Fiedler, "Congressional Ambitions of Female Party Elites." Paper presented at the annual meeting of the Capital Area Political Science Association, Washington, D.C., April 1975; Fowlkes, Perkins, and Rinehart, "Gender Roles"; Fowlkes, "Ambitious Political Women."

29. Among Democrats, black men and women are equally ambitious to attain party and political positions; black women, on the other hand, are somewhat more ambitious than their white counterparts in their desire to attain the position of national convention delegate (+6 percent) and to be appointed (+7 percent) or elected (+11 percent) to public office.

30. James Q. Wilson, *The Amateur Democrat* (Chicago: University of Chicago Press, 1962); John W. Soule and James W. Clarke, "Amateurs and Professionals: A Study of Delegates to the 1968 Democratic National Convention," *American Political Science Review* 64 (September 1970): 888–898. Cf. Alan I. Abramowitz, John McGlennon, and Ronald Rapoport, "The Party Isn't Over: Incentives for Activism in the 1980 Presidential Nominating Campaign," *The Journal of Politics* 45 (November 1983): 1,006–1,015;

Walter J. Stone and Alan I. Abramowitz, "Winning May Not Be Everything But It's More Than We Thought: Presidential Party Activists in 1980," *American Political Science Review* 77 (December 1983): 945–956.

31. Mary C. Porter and Ann B. Matasar, "The Role and Status of Women in the Daley Organization," in *Women in Politics*, ed., Jane Jaquette (New York: Wiley, 1974); Diamond, *Sex Roles*; Costantini and Bell, "Women in Political Parties."

32. Cf. Alan I. Abramowitz and Walter J. Stone, *Nomination Politics* (New York: Praeger, 1984), 31.

33. Costantini and Bell, "Women in Political Parties."

34. Respondents were asked "How would you describe your own political philosophy?" Responses were coded on a seven-point scale from "extremely liberal" to "extremely conservative" with "middle-of-the-road" in the middle position. The respective liberal (1–3) and conservative (5–7) codes were collapsed for the analysis. Among Democrats, while 80 percent of the black women considered themselves liberal in contrast to 63 percent of their white counterparts, together their percentage is 69; there are comparable distinctions among Democratic men. Southern blacks, then, push Democratic state party activists to assume a slightly more liberal posture.

35. Outside the South 89 percent of the men consider themselves conservative in contrast to 82 percent of the women.

36. The question is: "We hear a lot of talk these days about liberals and conservatives. Here is a seven-point scale on which the political views that people might hold are arranged from extremely liberal to extremely conservative. Where would you place yourself on this scale, or haven't you thought much about this?" The reported data are for the respective collapsed liberal (1–3) and conservative (5–7) response categories. Moderates (4) are the balance.

37. The analysis was run excluding and including independents leaning toward a political party with strong and weak partisans. The variation was only 1–2 percentage points. The figures shown in Table 4.5 and reported in the text include the learners with partisans. (Cf. Stanley, "Southern Partisan Changes.")

38. Controlling for race depresses the liberalism of Democratic state party activists by only 6 percent regardless of gender.

39. The question asked was: "You may have been active in some of the following groups. If so, check those groups to which you belong. (Check as many as apply.)"

40. Democratic women, also, are twice as likely as men and Republican women to be active in teacher or academic administrator groups (34%), black women at a level about twice that of whites. In two other groups—civil rights and religious—Democratic women and men are nearly equally active but differentiated from their Republican counterparts. Black women, moreover, remain far more active than white women in these two groups (61 percent versus 16 percent in civil rights groups; 56 percent versus 33 percent in religious groups). While, among Democrats, black and white women are closer together in their activity in women's rights organizations, they are uniquely participant given Democratic men and both women and male Republicans.

5

Southern State Party Convention Delegates: The Role of Age

Stephen D. Shaffer

A time-honored pursuit of political scientists has been the study of the demographic correlates of the political behavior of mass publics. One major demographic characteristic often examined has been the role of age. In the study of political attitudes, Everett Carll Ladd, Jr., and Charles D. Hadley found that by the 1960s newer, well-educated political generations were more Democratic in partisanship than were their older counterparts.[1] They also discovered a life-cycle effect, in that older Americans were more Republican than younger people. Lamis also stresses the importance of age in political change; he points out that younger southerners in the 1980s were much more Republican in partisanship and voting behavior than were older southerners.[2]

Age is also found to be an important variable in explaining the political activities of the masses. Using longitudinal data to disentangle the life-cycle, generational, and period effects of age on voter turnout, Michael Hout and David Knoke find that older generations vote at higher rates than younger generations, presumably because of differing political contexts and socialization experiences.[3] They also discern life-cycle effects reflected in a curvilinear relationship between age and voter turnout, as middle-aged Americans have higher turnout rates than either the young or the old. Shaffer argues that the increased numbers of both younger and older Americans in the potential electorate since 1960 helps explain the corresponding decline in voter turnout beginning in 1972.[4] While young people may be less active in conventional modes of participation, they may compensate for this by being more active in nonconventional forms of political activity. For example D. D. Sears and J. B. McConahay point out that young people were disproportionately represented among those participating in the urban riots of the 1960s.[5]

Most studies of the effects of age on political orientations have focused on the mass public rather than on political elite groups, so there is a need to examine a more specialized group of political activists. This need is especially great given the national Democratic party effort beginning in 1972 to increase the presence of young adults on national convention delegations.[6] It is especially important to focus on activists in the southern region of the United States, because of the expectation that major political changes such as partisan realignment are occurring in that geographic area.[7] Hence this paper examines the role of age in shaping the political orientations of delegates to the 1984 state party conventions in six southern states.

Some political scientists have discerned a rise at national party conventions since the 1960s in the numbers and influence of political "amateurs," who were more oriented toward intraparty democracy and ideological purity than were other delegates.[8] A concomitant decline in the influence of political "professionals," who are more oriented toward compromise in order to achieve electoral victories, is viewed by many political scientists as a threat to the existing party system and its ability to offer the electorate centrist and experienced political leadership.[9] Age becomes central for analysis because of the belief that young people are more likely to be amateurs in their political orientation than are older national convention delegates.[10] Some have also argued that younger delegates may be more liberal on political issues than older delegates, as James W. Soule and Wilma E. McGrath discovered in their study of the 1968 and 1972 national Democratic conventions.[11]

Recent "revisionist" studies have cast doubt on the utility of an abstract examination of political styles. In *Nomination Politics: Party Activists and Presidential Choice*, Alan I. Abramowitz and Walter J. Stone argued that activists attending state party conventions in 1980 wanted to win, and employed an "Expected Utility Model" in which they considered candidates' electability primarily and ideological proximity only secondarily in deciding whom to support for the presidential nomination.[12] Stone and Abramowitz also found that amateurs as well as professionals were motivated to support presidential nominees more by electability than ideological concerns.[13] *The Life of the Parties: Activists in Presidential Politics* refutes other aspects of the conventional wisdom of the rise of amateurs in party politics and their detrimental effects on the political parties.[14] And despite reforms opening up the national parties to more blacks, women, and young people, convention delegates are still drawn primarily from the higher socioeconomic status segment of society, minimizing the effects of reform on transforming delegates' attitudes or orientations.[15] Because of the complexity of this subject, this paper examines possible age differences in the correlates of candidate support, as well as age differences in numerous political perceptions, attitudes, and orientations.

METHODOLOGY

There is some debate in the literature as to how the age variable should be disaggregated.[16] Many regard the age period surrounding eighteen to be critical in one's political socialization, since it involves such critical events as graduation, leaving home, and becoming eligible to vote. One might also classify presidential nomination and general election politics into three major eras: (1) The Early New Deal Era prior to 1951, in which party alignments were based on issues arising out of an industrialized society, but the seeds of realignment were evident in the Dixiecrat movement. (2) The Late New Deal Era from 1952 to 1967, characterized first by Republican party presidential victories and then by growing independence in partisan ties among the public in the face of political upheaval occasioned by events such as the civil rights movement and the Vietnam protests. But Democratic party leaders remained in control of the southern political process and presidential nomination machinery. (3) The Dealignment-Reform Era from 1968 on, characterized by continued dealignment but also by the "opening up" of the presidential nomination process beginning with the effects of the reen-franchisement of blacks with the Voting Rights Act and with the 1968 Democratic convention's call for party reform. For these and other reasons, age is tricho-tomized into the categories: 18 to 34; 35 to 50; and 51 and over.

The first portion of results are based on bivariate cross-tabulations showing the relationships between age and various political factors. The next portion examines the multivariate relationships between ideological proximity, perceived electability, and candidate support for different age groups of Democratic del-egates. That analysis is based only on those Democratic delegates who perceived one of the three presidential hopefuls (Hart, Mondale, Jackson) as ideologically closer to them or as more electable than either of the other two. Delegates equidistant to two or all three candidates in these two attributes were eliminated from the analysis. The group of delegates perceiving Jackson as the most electable candidate was also too small to analyze.[17]

FINDINGS

Demographics, Officeholding, and Political Activity

Consistent with patterns existing at national party conventions, we find that state party convention delegates continue to be drawn from a higher socioeco-nomic status stratum, despite party reform efforts.[18] Fifty-six percent of Repub-lican delegates and 57 percent of Democratic delegates had completed at least four years of college, compared to only 19 percent of the national population in 1984. Delegates also had higher incomes and more prestigious occupations than the general citizenry. These patterns also existed across all age groups, with younger delegates especially well educated (among delegates under 35, 68 per-cent of Republicans and 66 percent of Democrats had college degrees).

The literature suggests that younger delegates are more likely to be political amateurs than are older delegates, and that amateurs are less experienced and active in party affairs and governmental officeholding than are professionals. One must also consider an "opportunity" hypothesis—that younger delegates have had less time and therefore less opportunity to be elected to a party or

Table 5.1
Age, Party, and Public Officeholding (in percent)

	Democrats			Republicans		
	18-34	35-50	51+	18-34	35-50	51+
Local Party Comm.						
Current	44	53	52*	73	72	68*
Previous	12	17	21*	24	35	34*
Future	31	21	16*	24	20	10*
Local Party Officer						
Current	20	21	28*	41	45	39
Previous	8	10	12*	13	25	25*
Future	37	26	15*	33	21	9*
State Party Officer						
Current	9	9	13*	11	14	15
Previous	3	6	7*	6	11	11*
Future	44	30	21*	46	30	17*
National Convention Delegate						
Current	3	5	6*	8	6	9
Previous	3	4	7*	4	5	10*
Future	59	45	28*	60	41	24*
Elected Pub. Office						
Current	4	10	12*	5	9	6
Previous	1	5	8*	4	5	8*
Future	43	27	14*	46	26	11*
Appointed Pub. Off.						
Current	5	8	10*	3	11	6
Previous	2	6	8*	5	6	7
Future	40	26	16*	35	23	12*

*indicates statistical significance at the .05 level

public office than have older delegates. We therefore expect that older delegates will be more likely to have held or to be currently holding party and public offices than younger delegates.

Our expectations are generally upheld by data, especially for Democrats. Older Democratic delegates in the South compared to younger Democratic delegates are more likely to have been and to currently be local party committee members, local party officers, state party officers, national convention delegates, elected public officials, and appointed public officials (Table 5.1). Among Republican delegates, these patterns exist only for those who have held positions in the past. It suggests that the Republican party is more successful than the Democratic party in incorporating younger elements into their party structure, which may also relate to their contemporary success at attracting the youth vote in the 1984 presidential election.[19] It should also be noted that Republican delegates regardless of age were currently and previously more active in the party organization than were Democratic delegates, suggesting that the more intense competition for the presidential nomination in the Democratic party made that party's state conventions more permeable to activists less involved in party politics on a day-to-day basis.

Some may argue that these data reflect the greater amateur orientation of younger delegates, and their distaste for partisan politics. If this were so, one would not necessarily expect them to desire partisan positions in the future. Yet our data indicate that younger delegates in both parties had a greater desire to hold positions in their party and public office than any other age group. Reflecting the literature on initiating and sustaining motivations for partisan activity, one may speculate that younger delegates are more naive and idealistic than more experienced delegates, and that they may overestimate the policy relevance and importance of partisan offices. In any event, younger delegates are as interested as their elders in the political parties, though one should ask whether their motivations for wanting to be active in the parties may differ from those of their elders.

The literature on participation of the mass public finds that younger people are less politically active than older ones, owing to problem of "starting up" participation.[20] In contrast, after taking into account factors such as socioeconomic status and length of residence in the local community, Verba and Nie have found older Americans to be equally as active as middle-aged Americans. Our expectation based on the opportunity and start-up theses is that older delegates in the South will have been more active in political campaigns and will have engaged in a greater range of political activities than younger delegates.

These expectations are also upheld by the data. A greater percentage of older Democratic and Republican delegates were very or moderately active in local, state, and national campaigns than were younger delegates (Table 5.2). While younger delegates in both parties were more likely to have never attended a state party convention, older delegates were the most likely age group to have attended two or more state party conventions. Also within both the Democratic and Republican parties, older delegates were more likely to have been active in get-out-the vote drives, recruiting candidates, and building the party organization than younger delegates, though these age-related differences were modest. No significant differences emerged in communicating with the public or representing a group among Democrats, though younger Republican delegates were slightly more likely to engage in these activities than older delegates. These data may also reflect a more amateur orientation among the young.

Partisan and Amateur-Professional Orientations

The literature on the mass public also finds that young people are more independent in their partisan attachments, reflecting generational and period effects as well as possible life-cycle effects.[21] For this reason as well as the expectation of a greater amateuristic orientation among younger national convention delegates, one expects older southern delegates to be more partisan than their younger counterparts. For instance, we expect older delegates to be more likely to have

Table 5.2
Past Political Activities by Age and Party, 1976–1984 (in percent)

	Democrats			Republicans		
	18-34	35-50	51+	18-34	35-50	51+
Very or Moderately						
Active in:						
Local Election Campaigns	63	81	87	56	75	83*
State Campaigns	55	73	85*	63	72	83*
National Campaigns	42	58	73*	60	69	80*
Number of State Party						
Conventions Attended						
None	74	56	42*	61	41	29*
One	13	19	21	20	23	23
Two	13	25	37	19	36	48
	100	100	100	100	100	100
Party Activities Performed						
Getting Out Vote	78	83	83*	74	83	82*
Communicating w/ Public	59	66	61	70	69	62*
Representing a Group	32	40	29	24	28	21*
Recruiting Candidates	19	29	27*	29	42	34*
Building Party Org.	43	46	44	58	69	67*

*indicates statistical significance at the .05 level

intense partisan identifications and to have parents with more intense partisan-ships than younger delegates, as well as to appreciate the important role of the state party and to behave in a more partisan manner than younger delegates.

Many of our expectations are upheld by the data. Older delegates are more likely to be intense partisans at the national and state levels than younger del-egates, though the strength of this relationship is weaker for Republicans (Table 5.3). It is also important to note that a significant majority of all age groups including the young are intense identifiers with their party, supporting the ar-guments offered in *The Life of the Parties*.[22] Regarding parental partisanship, only among Democrats do the parents of older delegates have more intense partisanship than the parents of younger delegates. The intense partisanship of older Democratic delegates' parents is especially interesting and noteworthy and may reflect the greater historical strength of that party. Among Republicans there is a weak pattern in the opposite direction: younger delegates have more partisan parents than older delegates, suggesting an embryonic development in the po-litical environment of the South that could eventually favor the Republican party.

In terms of consistent partisan behavior the results are mixed. Older delegates of both parties are more likely to oppose the practice of ballot splitting than are younger delegates. Republican delegates in the South regardless of age are more likely to have switched parties than Democratic delegates, demonstrating that the Republican party has gained activists through the process of conversion. Older Republicans are especially likely to have switched parties that may again reflect the opportunity thesis, as older Republican delegates have had more time

Table 5.3
Partisan Orientations by Age and Party (in percent)

	Democrats			Republicans		
	18-34	35-50	51+	18-34	35-50	51+
Strong State Party ID	74	78	87*	76	84	86*
Strong Nat. Party ID	67	70	80*	87	89	90*
Strong Identifiers						
Father's State Party	47	54	69*	31	17	27*
Father's Nat. Party	40	48	63*	38	22	31*
Mother's State Party	45	49	59*	30	14	24*
Mother's Nat. Party	41	43	55*	34	18	29*
Opposed to Ballot Splitting	50	57	64*	32	32	39*
Party Switchers	12	13	12	22	33	39*
Perception of Current State Party Role**						
Provide Campaign Help	37	42	56*	52	51	58*
Take Issue Positions	29	33	43*	31	34	43*
Provide Service/Info	36	45	50*	45	50	53*
Recruit Candidates	31	33	39*	45	49	58*
Inform Electorate	34	46	57*	48	46	57*
1980 Presidential Vote						
Carter	80	87	92*	2	2	1
Reagan	11	10	6	97	97	99
Anderson	9	3	2	1	1	0
	100	100	100	100	100	100

*indicates statistical significance at the .05 level

**percent reporting role as "very important"

to have switched their parties than younger delegates. Older delegates of both parties clearly believe that the state political party does play a more important role in the political arena than do younger delegates, suggesting that their greater psychological support for their parties is linked to their perceptions of the importance of their parties. Finally, older Democratic delegates were more loyal to their party's candidate in the 1980 presidential election than were younger delegates who were somewhat more likely to have voted for Reagan or Anderson. Regardless of age, Republican delegates voted overwhelmingly for Reagan, suggesting a greater homogeneity of ideological views in the Republican party than in the Democratic party.

The literature stresses that the major differences between amateurs and professionals are their style and their approach to politics. Amateurs stress intraparty democracy and issue positions in the selection of nominees and the party platform. In contrast, professionals are more oriented toward compromise because of their desire for their party to win the general election. We therefore expect the same patterns to emerge in this study of southern state party convention delegates.

Our expectations receive some evidential support, suggesting that younger

Table 5.4

Amateur-Professional Orientation by Age and Party (in percent)

	Democrats			Republicans		
	18-34	35-50	51+	18-34	35-50	51+
Party Orientation						
Stop Work for Party if						
Disagree on Imp. Issue	18	15	8*	28	23	20*
More Imp. for Party to Make						
Broad Electoral Appeal	58	70	80	52	61	70
No Opinion	24	15	12	20	16	10
	100	100	100	100	100	100
Most Important Factor in Selecting Candidates for Office Is in your Opinion:						
Party Loyalty/Service	11	16	26*	5	4	6*
Issues/Ideology Position	85	78	69	90	88	85
Chance for Victory	4	6	5	5	8	9
	100	100	100	100	100	100
Most Important State Party Activity in Your Opinion of Activities Engaged in:						
Getting Out Vote	58	61	67*	51	50	52*
Communicating with Public	26	21	18	31	23	18
Build Party Organ.	9	12	10	12	20	22
Other Activities	7	6	5	6	7	8
	100	100	100	100	100	100
Reasons for Political Involvement in 1984 (% very important):						
To Support My Party	67	73	89*	70	74	84*
To Help My Pol. Career	22	15	16*	15	9	4*
Enjoy Campaign Excitement	35	25	27*	28	15	12*
Fulfill Civic Responsib.	50	56	69*	52	52	62*

*indicates statistical significance at .05 level

delegates are somewhat more likely to be amateurs than older delegates, who are more likely to be professionals. Older delegates of both parties were more likely to urge that their party make a broad electoral appeal than were younger delegates, while younger delegates were somewhat more likely to say they would stop working for their party if they disagreed with a major stand of their party (Table 5.4). In choosing candidates for the party's nomination, younger delegates placed a greater stress on issue positions while older delegates stressed other factors. Older Democrats stressed party loyalty more than younger delegates. On the other hand, older Republicans stressed electoral victory slightly more than younger Republicans.

Other data also bear on the utility of the amateur-professional perspective. Younger delegates were more oriented toward communicating with the public than were older delegates, while older delegates stressed other activities that differed from the two parties: older Democrats stressed getting out the vote activities, while older Republicans stressed building the party organization. In terms of reasons for political involvement in 1984, older delegates of both parties were more likely to cite support for the party and civic duty reasons, while younger delegates were more likely to talk about the excitement of the campaign and helping their political career, two factors that may reflect life-cycle "start up" effects.

One should not overstate the magnitude of the age differences in these political orientations. Despite statistical relationships, majorities of all age groups cited party loyalty as a very important reason for their involvement in 1984, and cited the need for the party to make a broad electoral appeal, substantiating the "revisionist" argument.[23] Yet it should also be noted that majorities of all age groups said that the most important factor in selecting a party nominee should be issue positions rather than party loyalty or electoral victory reasons.

Policy and Candidate Preferences and Group Involvement

Moving to specific policy preferences, the ideological homogeneity of the Republican party suggests little or no age differences in policy orientations. For the Democratic party, generational forces may be more evident. One may hypothesize that older Democrats entered and became active in the party because of the party's liberal posture on economic issues that were a part of the New Deal. With the entrance of America into the postindustrial, information age and the rise of affluence, social issues have become more salient in recent decades. From this, one may hypothesize that younger Democrats have been attracted by the party's liberal posture on these issues. We therefore expect that among southern Democratic delegates, older Democrats will be more liberal than younger Democrats on economic issues, while younger Democrats will be more liberal on social issues.

Our expectations receive the most evidential support on social issues. Older Democratic delegates were much more likely to say that marijuana and homosexuality were wrong and to support a school prayer amendment than were younger delegates (Table 5.5). Majorities of all age groups in the Republican party took these positions, with older Republicans especially opposed to marijuana. Young Democratic delegates were also somewhat more supportive of the ERA, abortion, and affirmative action than older delegates. On economic issues like national health insurance and public works jobs, older delegates rather than younger Democrats were the more liberal group, though the magnitude of the relationships are not as great as on the social issues.

Despite these patterns of age being related to policy preferences, partisanship is clearly the more important correlate of policy views. Democrats regardless of age are consistently and significantly more liberal than Republicans. The same pattern emerges on ideological self-identification. Though older delegates of both parties were more conservative than their younger counterparts, these differences were minor compared to the vast ideological differences between the parties. Democratic delegates regardless of age described themselves as liberal or mod-

Table 5.5
Issue Orientations by Age and Party (in percent)

	Democrats			Republicans		
	18-34	35-50	51+	18-34	35-50	51+
Favoring:						
ERA Amendment	81	80	74*	15	17	16
Anti-Abortion Amend.	22	28	39*	51	50	49
Nat'l Health Insurance	54	57	62*	6	8	13*
Affirmative Actions	69	65	65	12	14	15*
Public Works Program	45	45	49	6	6	7
Agreeing:						
Marijuana Use Morally Wrong	31	48	73*	68	76	86*
Homosexuality Morally Wrong	45	55	69*	85	87	89
School Prayer Amendment	36	41	47*	76	72	75
Ideological Self-Placement						
Liberal (1-2 categories)	46	47	42*	2	1	1*
Moderate (3-5)	49	46	48	20	21	13
Conservative (6-7)	5	7	10	78	78	86
	100	100	100	100	100	100

*indicates statistical significance at the .05 level

erate, while at least three-quarters of Republicans described themselves as con-servative.

Because of social and economic changes such as the declining importance of agriculture and interest in labor unions and the increased importance of social issues with respect to the quality of life, we expected that generational differences would emerge in the organizational memberships of the delegates and the types of presidential nominees they supported. Perhaps older southern Democratic delegates would be more active in labor unions and agricultural organizations than younger Democrats, while younger delegates of both parties would be more involved in organizations concerned with life-style types of issues with the nature of the organization depending on the ideological orientation of the delegate.

These expectations were generally upheld. Older Democrats were somewhat more active in agricultural and labor organizations than younger delegates (Table 5.6). Younger Republicans were more active than older Republicans in religious and antiabortion groups, while younger Democrats were slightly more active in women's rights and ecology groups. While some generational differences in group membership are found in both parties, important differences are found between the parties once again. Democratic delegates were more active in or-ganizations with more liberal policy agendas while Republicans reflected the opposite tendency. Democratic delegates were more active in labor unions, teacher, civil rights, conservation, and women's rights groups than were Re-publicans, who were more active in business, religious, and antiabortion groups. Some policy realignment may also be occurring within the parties because of generational replacement. While older Republican delegates were only modestly more active in religious and antiabortion groups than older Democrats, declining

Table 5.6
Age and Group Involvement/Candidate Preference (in percent)

	Democrats			Republicans		
	18-34	35-50	51+	18-34	35-50	51+
Active in Each Group:						
Labor Unions	14	21	17*	5	5	5
Business Organizations	30	31	31	46	54	42*
Religious Groups	34	36	43*	59	56	49*
Civil Rights Groups	27	30	25	4	4	3
Teacher Groups	19	29	27*	13	21	13
Conservation/Ecology Gr.	16	15	13	11	10	10
Anti-Abortion Groups	3	3	3	21	16	11*
Agricultural Groups	9	10	17*	13	15	12
Women's Rights Groups	25	24	20*	5	5	4
Public Interest Groups	35	39	42*	26	33	33*

	White Democrats			Black Democrats		
	18-34	35-50	51+	18-34	35-50	51+
Current First Preference Party Nomination:						
Hart	45	34	25	4	4	3
Mondale	52	63	75	28	35	46
Jackson	3	3	0	68	61	51
	100	100	100	100	100	100

*indicates statistical significance at .05 level

religious activity among younger Democrats and increased involvement among younger Republicans has resulted in much sharper differences between the parties.

With respect to southern Democratic delegates, it is clear that younger delegates compared to older delegates were more likely to be newcomers to politics, to be less partisan, to have a more amateuristic rather than professional style, to be more liberal on social issues, and to be more active in life-style, and quality of life types of organizations.[24] Hence we would hypothesize that older Democrats would be more supportive of the "old politics" candidacy of Walter Mondale, while younger Democrats would be more supportive of the insurgent Hart and Jackson candidacies.

These expectations were upheld in a different manner for white and black delegates. The insurgency candidacies of Hart and Jackson served to separate out young delegates by their race, as among whites Hart was significantly stronger among younger compared to older delegates, while among blacks Jackson was the candidate of most young delegates (Table 5.6). Neither candidate received significant support from delegates of the other race, regardless of age. Since Mondale was the only establishment-oriented candidate, he received more support among older compared to younger delegates of both races. The age cleavage within the Democratic party in candidate support is quite probably due to both life-cycle and generational factors, but the relative importance of each is difficult to ascertain. An answer to this question is nevertheless important in speculation as to whether the division that existed at the 1984 Democratic national convention will persist, and whether a "new politics" type of candidacy like Gary Hart's will be successful in 1988 or later years.

It is also interesting to note that socioeconomic status was related to candidate support even after controlling for age, as Hart's candidacy appealed to highly educated whites while Mondale was stronger among the disadvantaged. Thirty-eight percent of whites with four or more years of college supported Hart, compared to 24 percent of those with no more than a high school degree. Seventy-five percent of high school educated whites favored Mondale, compared to 59 percent of the college educated. These patterns existed within each age group, and suggest that if party reform ever extends to providing more representation for lower socioeconomic status groups at state or national conventions, it could affect the levels of support for the candidates and the actual outcome in a close contest.

Ideology Versus Electability in Candidate Choice

With the confirmation of most of our expectations, it is important to examine in greater depth why younger Democratic delegates in the South were more supportive of Gary Hart's candidacy than older delegates were. Did younger delegates feel that Gary Hart was closer to them on the issues than was Walter Mondale, or did they feel that Hart was a more electable candidate than Mondale, who was accused of being a captive of traditional special interests in the party? Given the more amateur orientation of younger Democratic delegates as well as their more liberal views on social issues, one might hypothesize that younger delegates would be more affected by concerns of ideological proximity, while older delegates would be more influenced by concerns of electability. In view of Abramowitz and Stone however, we acknowledge that electability may be so important to all of the delegates that age-related differences in the sources of candidate support may be insignificant.[25]

Our hypothesis receives no evidential support, as age did not significantly affect the magnitudes of relationships between candidate support and ideological proximity or electability (Table 5.7). Regarding ideology, delegates under thirty-five years of age were 13 percent more likely than the norm to support the candidate that they were ideologically closest to, while delegates aged 35 to 50 were 17 percent more supportive of the ideologically closest candidate, and delegates over 50 years of age were 11 percent more supportive of the ideological favorite.[26] Turning to electability, younger delegates were 22 percent more likely than the norm to support the candidate that they perceived as most electable, compared to 23 percent for middle-aged delegates and 17 percent for older delegates.[27]

Table 5.7

Electability Versus Ideology in Shaping Candidate Preference among Southern Democrats (in percent)*

	Most Proximate to Hart	Most Proximate to Mondale	Most Proximate to Jackson
18-34 Age Group			
Hart Most Electable	81 Hart 16 Mondale 3 Jackson (84)	91 Hart 0 Mondale 9 Jackson (11)	54 Hart 17 Mondale 29 Jackson (35)
Mondale Most Electable	8 Hart 82 Mondale 10 Jackson (19)	0 Hart 88 Mondale 12 Jackson (47)	1 Hart 45 Mondale 54 Jackson (40)
35-50 Age Group			
Hart Most Electable	89 Hart 10 Mondale 1 Jackson (73)	46 Hart 41 Mondale 13 Jackson (32)	46 Hart 26 Mondale 28 Jackson (16)
Mondale Most Electable	13 Hart 67 Mondale 20 Jackson (44)	1 Hart 94 Mondale 5 Jackson (86)	4 Hart 60 Mondale 36 Jackson (52)
51+ Age Group			
Hart Most Electable	83 Hart 17 Mondale 0 Jackson (56)	55 Hart 45 Mondale 0 Jackson (11)	53 Hart 19 Mondale 28 Jackson (8)
Mondale Most Electable	17 Hart 69 Mondale 14 Jackson (27)	0 Hart 92 Mondale 8 Jackson (79)	2 Hart 72 Mondale 26 Jackson (40)

*N's are indicated in parentheses

By comparing these percentages that represent the direct effects of ideology and electability on delegate preference, we find that, consistent with Stone and Abramowitz, delegates regardless of age were more motivated in their candidate preferences by their perceptions of the candidates' chances of being elected than by their perceptions of which candidate was the closest to their own ideological views.[28] Ideological proximity also plays a role in shaping candidate preferences, though a lesser role than concerns of electability.[29]

Given the primary importance of electability, it is likely that an important reason that Mondale received more support among older Democrats than among younger delegates is their perception of him as a more electable candidate. The data support this conclusion, as among Democratic delegates over 50 years of age, 47 percent felt that Mondale definitely or probably would win the general election, compared to only 25 percent of delegates under 35 who felt that Mondale definitely or probably would win. There were few age-related differences in evaluations of Hart's chances, however, as 28 percent of delegates over 50 rated him as a definite or probably winner compared to 24 percent of delegates under 35.

These findings raise some interesting questions, and continue to demonstrate the importance of an age-based analysis of political activists. Why were the younger delegates less likely to feel that Mondale was a winner? Was it perhaps because of a social similarity thesis—that Hart was viewed by younger delegates as being similar to them by being less tied to traditional, old-line constituencies of the party and was more concerned about "new issues" rather than economic New Deal types of concerns? Our data suggest an affirmative response, since generational and life-style factors were important in shaping the orientations of state party convention delegates during the 1984 presidential nomination contest.

CONCLUSIONS

This examination demonstrates the importance of age in shaping the perceptions, motivations, and actions of state political activists in the South in presidential election years. It has also demonstrated the importance of drawing upon a variety of theoretical approaches to help explain age-related differences in political orientations.

Certainly in a democratic society one would expect that representative bodies like state party conventions would represent the orientations of average citizens. While most studies focus on representation in terms of issue orientations or candidate support, we find that more basic perceptual and behavioral factors may also be represented. For instance, in the general population younger people are generally less active in politics and less partisan than are older people, and this same pattern is reflected among a more specialized group that has already demonstrated some basic level of political partisanship and activity—state party convention delegates. As generational and period forces have helped to explain why young people in the population are less partisan than older people, the same process may be reflected in our more specialized population.

Generational forces are also evident in terms of the policy orientations and organizational memberships of convention delegates. The 1960s and 1970s saw decreased emphasis on New Deal economic issues as social issues concerned with the quality of life and life-style issues like racial, women's rights, and environmental concerns became more important in the political arena. Thus younger delegates often held more liberal orientations on social issues than did older delegates. Older Democratic delegates were more active in agricultural organizations reflecting the earlier economic base of the region while younger delegates were more active in organizations concerned with more contemporary life-style issues.

The utility of the amateur versus professional theoretical orientation in explaining political behavior also was demonstrated in this analysis. The amateur versus professional framework does help to differentiate convention delegates by age, especially in their political motivations and activity level. Younger delegates were more likely to stress the importance of issues in selecting candidates, while older delegates stressed compromise and party unity. Younger delegates were also less likely to have ever held party or public offices, though another explanation for this pattern based on an opportunity thesis may be equally important.

A major purpose of this paper has been to demonstrate the utility of the time-honored factor of age in explaining political orientations of one group of political activists, and to suggest the theoretical complexity of an age-based analysis of political activists. A next step in this process is to focus more closely on explaining why younger delegates may be more supportive of a more nontraditional candidacy than older delegates are. Some insight and suggestions already offered in this paper may be tested in a more comprehensive fashion and with additional activist populations in future studies.

NOTES

1. Everett Carll Ladd, Jr., and Charles D. Hadley, *Political Parties and Political Issues: Patterns in Differentiation since the New Deal* (Beverly Hills: Sage, 1973), 40–60.

2. Alexander P. Lamis, *The Two-Party South* (New York: Oxford University Press, 1984), 215–218.

3. Michael Hout and David Knoke, "Change in Voting Turnout, 1952–1972," *Public Opinion Quarterly* 38 (Spring 1975): 52–68.

4. Stephen D. Shaffer, "A Multivariate Explanation of Decreasing Turnout in Presidential Elections, 1960–1976," *American Journal of Political Science* 25 (February 1981): 68–95.

5. D. O. Sears and J. B. McConahay, *The Politics of Violence: The New Urban Black and the Watts Riot* (Boston: University Press of America, 1973), 26.

6. William Crotty and John S. Jackson, III. *Presidential Primaries and Nominations* (Washington: Congressional Quarterly Press, 1985), 107–111.

7. Paul Allen Beck, "Realignment Begins: The Republican Surge in Florida," *American Politics Quarterly* 10 (October 1982): 421–438; Norman Nie, Sidney Verba, and John Petrocik, *The Changing American Voter*, enlarged edition (Cambridge, MA: Harvard University Press, 1979), 210–242; Tod Baker, Robert Steed, and Laurence Moreland, "The Emergence of the Religious Right and the Development of the Two-Party System in the South" (Paper presented at the annual meeting of the American Political Science Association, 1986).

8. James W. Soule and James Clarke, "Amateurs and Professionals: A Study of Delegates to the 1968 Democratic National Convention," *American Political Science Review* 64 (September 1970): 888–899; James W. Soule and Wilma E. McGrath, "A Comparative Study of Presidential Nomination Conventions: The Democrats 1968 and 1972," *American Journal of Political Science* 19 (August 1975): 501–518.

9. Jeane Kirkpatrick, *The New Presidential Elite* (New York: Russell Sage Foundation and Twentieth Century Fund, 1976); Everett Carll Ladd, Jr., and Charles D. Hadley,

Transformations of the American Party System: Political Coalitions from the New Deal to the 1970s (New York: W. W. Norton, 1978), 333–349.

10. Soule and McGrath, "Comparative Study," 501–518; Thomas Roback, "Amateurs and Professionals: Delegates to the 1972 Republican National Convention," *Journal of Politics* 37 (May 1975): 436–468; Robert Hitlin and John Jackson, "On Amateur and Professional Politicians," *Journal of Politics* 39 (August 1977): 786–793.

11. Soule and McGrath, "Comparative Study," 507.

12. Alan I. Abramowitz and Walter J. Stone, *Nomination Politics: Party Activists and Presidential Choice* (New York: Praeger Publishers, 1984), 99–124.

13. Alan I. Abramowitz and Walter J. Stone, "Winning May Not Be Everything, But It's More than We Thought," *American Political Science Review* 77 (December 1983): 945–956.

14. Ronald B. Rapoport, Alan I. Abramowitz, and John McGlennon, *The Life of the Parties: Activists in Presidential Politics* (Lexington, KY: University Press of Kentucky, 1986).

15. Crotty and Jackson, *Presidential Primaries*, 111–113.

16. Paul Allen Beck, "Young Versus Old in 1984: Generations and Life Stages in Presidential Nominating Politics," *PS* 17 (Summer 1984): 515–524; Seymour Martin Lipset, "Beyond 1984: The Anomalies of American Politics," *PS* 19 (Spring 1986): 222–236.

17. Each respondent was weighted so that the weighted N's were equal for each state party (Rapoport et al., 1986, 8).

18. Crotty and Jackson, *Presidential Primaries*, 112.

19. Michael Nelson, *The Elections of 1984* (Washington, D.C.: Congressional Quarterly Press, 1985), 106.

20. Sidney Verba and Norman Nie, *Participation in America: Political Democracy and Social Equality* (New York: Harper and Row, 1972), 138–148.

21. Nie, Verba, and Petrocik, *Changing American Voter*, 47–73.

22. Rapoport, Abramowitz, McGlennon, *Life of Parties*.

23. Stone and Abramowitz, *Winning May Not Be Everything*; Abramowitz and Stone, *Nomination Politics*; Rapoport, Abramowitz, and McGlennon, *Life of Parties*.

24. Given the importance of racial divisions in the Democratic party in the South, we repeated these analyses separately for whites, blacks, and black delegates supporting Jackson. These age-related differences were found within each of these three groups. For a thorough analysis of the role of race in the 1984 southern state party conventions, see Charles D. Hadley and Harold Stanley's "Blacks, the Biracial Coalition, and Southern Politics: 1984 State Party Convention Delegates" (Paper presented at the annual meeting of the American Political Science Association, 1986).

25. Abramowitz and Stone, *Nomination Politics*, 72–98.

26. The effect of ideological proximity may be estimated by comparing each cell in Table 5.7 with the average support provided to the candidate for each age-electability group. For example, Hart received 7 percent more support among young people who perceived him as most proximate and also most electable, compared to the support he received among all young delegates who perceived him as most electable but who had varying perceptions of ideological proximity. For young delegates who also perceived Hart as most electable: those most proximate to Jackson ideologically gave Jackson 18 percent more support than average, but those most proximate to Mondale gave Mondale 15 percent less support than average. Weighting these values by the numbers of delegates

falling in these three proximity categories, we find that the ideology effect among young delegates who perceived Hart as most electable was 8 percent. For young delegates who perceived Mondale as most electable: those most proximate to Hart gave Hart 6 percent more support; those proximate to Mondale gave Mondale 18 percent more support; those most proximate to Jackson gave him 26 percent more support than did all young delegates who saw Mondale as more electable. This results in a weighted average of 19 percent, which represents the ideology effect among young delegates who perceived Mondale as most electable. The weighted average of all young delegates is therefore 13 percent. Similar calculations were performed for the middle and older age groups.

27. The effect of electability can be estimated by comparing the values in each cell of Table 5.7 with the average support provided for each candidate by each age-proximity group. For example, Hart received 13 percent more support among those young delegates perceiving him as most electable and ideologically closest to him than he did among all young delegates ideologically closest to him. Mondale received 54 percent more support among young delegates perceiving him as most electable and who were ideologically closest to Hart than he did among all young delegates ideologically closest to Hart. The weighted average of these values is 21 percent, which reflects the electability effect among young delegates ideologically closest to Hart. The corresponding electability effects for young delegates ideologically closest to Mondale are 27 percent, and for young delegates closest to Jackson are 20 percent. The weighted average electability effect for young delegates overall is 22 percent. Similar calculations were performed for middle- and older-aged delegates.

28. Stone and Abramowitz, "Winning May Not Be Everything."

29. We have relied on an ideological proximity indicator to be consistent with previous studies (see Stone and Abramowitz, "Winning May Not Be Everything,") and because the only perceptual items in the questionnaires pertained to ideology. More disaggregated issue items would be desirable, especially in view of the findings of differential patterns for some economic and social issues. Use of such disaggregated issue proximity items may magnify the effects of issue items found in this and other studies, since some delegates may not be as ideologically sophisticated as many researchers expect.

Part III
Cultural Changes in Southern Party Coalitions

6

The Ideological and Issue Bases of Southern Parties

Laurence W. Moreland

Although the extent to which voters perceive political choice in terms of ideology or even issues[1] has been a continuing question in U.S. politics,[2] party leaders in competitive political systems are more likely than rank-and-file voters to be philosophically or ideologically oriented and more likely to take distinct positions on issues.[3] Even though research suggests that the mass electorate became more ideological in the decades of the 1960s and the 1970s,[4] differences between Democratic and Republican party leaders at all levels continued to be greater than the differences between their respective party identifiers in the general electorate.[5] These differences between party hierarchies take on significance because of the roles that party leaders play in recruiting or choosing candidates, in defining their parties through the adopting of platforms and other issue statements, and in shaping the images that each party presents to the electorate.

Differences between interparty elites occur in systems that are to some degree two-party competitive. Because partisan politics in the South was dominated nearly completely by the Democratic party from shortly after the Civil War until quite recently, interparty elite differences were not very useful in understanding the regional politics of the South. Southern politics traditionally was characterized not by interparty differences but by fluid factions operating under the all-embracing umbrella of the Democratic party.[6] Inasmuch as there was no effective Republican party, the Democratic party of necessity became the vehicle for the expression of political opinions intended to influence elections. Such an arrangement resulted in numerous shifting factions, all operating within the Democratic party. Consequently, voter choice on the basis of issues or general ideology was often difficult, if not impossible, since telling the factions apart was no easy task. Voter choice was further complicated by the movement of faction leaders around the political spectrum, moves facilitated by the fact that all candidates and nearly all voters belonged to the same party. V. O. Key, Jr., noted that South Carolina politics in the late 1940s demonstrated well the character of the South's one-party politics. In South Carolina, as elsewhere, the one-party system made it possible for a politician to change even his general philosophy or orientation with less risk to his political survival than had a two-party system been in operation. Indeed, it resulted in "no institutional obstacle to collaboration with erstwhile enemies"; both leaders and followers could freely and easily change their affiliations and loyalties.[7]

While political choice was easier in those few states (such as Louisiana) where a bifactional system emerged within the Democratic party, it still lacked the clarity of a two-party choice.[8] Moreover, bifactionalism was the exception, not the rule, as most southern party systems were characterized by multifactionalism and fragmentation based to a large extent on personal and highly localized friends-and-neighbors followings. These arrangements resulted in great voter difficulty in discerning which candidates belonged to what faction and why. Ideological and issue differences, where they existed, were largely masked. Sorting them out was difficult, if not impossible.

In the years since World War II, however, profound political, social, cultural, and economic changes have eroded the traditional domination of southern politics by the Democratic party.[9] At the presidential level, the Republican party now nearly dominates the politics of the South, and at other levels too the Republican party is, if not fully competitive, at least often a factor that the Democratic party cannot ignore.[10] An extensive literature has documented the many faces of these pervasive changes in the regional politics of the South.[11]

The consequence of these changes is the emergence of a competitive party system. Although political scientists are not wholly agreed on the precise nature of the political changes that have occurred in the South (or even on the appropriate terminology to describe such changes[12]), a fair reading of the literature suggests that at least three developments should have occurred if indeed a partisan realignment has taken place or is not underway. First, familiar voting patterns should be undergoing substantial change, generally, over a "critical election" period.[13] This disruption may be a consequence of existing voters changing their party preferences and voting behavior or, more likely, as a consequence of new voters (such as young persons, blacks, and nonsouthern immigrants) entering the electorate. Second, new issues emerge that the old party system is unable to contain or exploit; opinions may become so strongly held, as with race relations, for example, that a single party can no longer provide an umbrella large enough to shelter all who may have joined a changing electorate.[14] And, third, ideological polarization may emerge more clearly as evidence of stress within the political system, as the old electoral arrangement breaks down. Those dissatisfied with the nonideological or ideologically ambiguous stance of a fluid Democratic party might leave that party for a minority party with a clearer philosophical focus; the result is that both parties become more clearly ideolog-

Table 6.1
Political Philosophy of Delegates (in percent)

Political Philosophy	Democrats			Republicans
	Black	White	All	All
Extremely liberal	16	8	10	*
Liberal	49	30	35	1
Slightly liberal	14	20	18	1
Middle-of-the-road	12	21	18	4
Slightly conservative	5	13	11	11
Conservative	3	8	6	65
Extremely conservative	1	1	1	18
Totals	101	100	99	100
(N=)	(756)	(1956)	(2919)**	(1849)

*less than 0.5 percent

**includes not only whites and blacks but also Hispanics, Asian-
Americans, American Indians, and those who responded to the ideology
question but not to the racial identification question

ically defined. Research suggests that ideological polarization particularly char-
acterizes political elites during periods of party realignment.[15]

This chapter, by examining the extent of ideological polarization between
southern Democratic and Republican party elites, tests the third element of
political realignment noted above. As Walter Dean Burnham has observed, eras
of critical realignment are marked, in part, by an ideological polarization characterized by unusually large issue-distances between the major parties.[16] To
analyze this aspect of the party coalitions in the South, delegates to southern
state party conventions are examined in terms of their ideological polarity and
the nature of the issue concerns that drive them. This is an essentially "party
sorting" hypothesis, that is, the two parties in each state should demonstrate
substantial evidence of ideological and issue clarity if the southern party system
is undergoing the strains of partisan realignment. In the section that follows,
ideology, issues, ideological perceptions of the two parties, and selected dimensions of candidate orientation and party loyalty all are examined in an investigation of partisan issue and ideological clarity. The analysis focuses broadly
on the two state parties.

FINDINGS

Political Philosophy

Table 6.1 reports data by party on the delegates' political philosophy on a
question utilizing a standard seven-point ideological scale ranging from "ex-

tremely conservative to extremely liberal.'' Activists in the two parties differentiate quite clearly in terms of political philosophy: in general, the Republican delegates perceived themselves as a party of the right, and Democrats saw themselves (somewhat less strongly) as a party of the left. Over 80 percent of the Republicans described themselves as "conservative" or "extremely conservative." When those describing themselves as "slightly conservative" (11 percent) are added, the Republicans approached a substantial degree of ideological unanimity. Conversely, only a small portion (18 percent) of the Democrats described themselves as any kind of conservative, and just 7 percent fell in the two most conservative categories. Almost two-thirds of the Democrats (and only 2 percent of the Republicans) described themselves as some kind of liberal. The ideological pattern revealed in Table 6.1 strongly supports the hypothesis that the Republican and Democratic state parties in the South have each developed a distinctive ideological center of gravity.

A secondary point regarding the data in Table 6.1 is that, for the Democrats, blacks tended to anchor the liberal wing of the party. Even so, nearly 60 percent of the whites described themselves as some type of liberal (as compared with nearly 80 percent of black Democrats). Thus the distinctive ideological cast of the Democratic party is a product of both racial groups, albeit with a somewhat greater concentration of blacks in the dominant liberal wing.

Table 6.1 suggests the final point that southern Republicans were more uniformly conservative than southern Democrats were uniformly liberal. While the Democratic state party activists were not at all cvenly distributed across the liberal-conservative spectrum, they were more widely scattered than their Republican counterparts. This pattern suggests that the Democratic party elite has retained some measure of a broadly based party even as its strength in the electorate eroded.

Issue Positions

The delegates' general ideological placement is more clearly understood through an analysis of their responses to three sets of issues: twelve "new politics" or social issues, four economic issues, and five foreign policy/defense issues. (See Table 6.2) Their responses on these issues give further evidence of the distinctive outlooks of Republican and Democratic state party activists. A majority of Democrats were opposed by a majority of Republicans on fifteen of the twenty-one issues examined.[17]

Of the twelve social issues, a majority of Democrats opposed a majority of Republicans on nine of them. On two social issues—the immorality of homosexual behavior and marijuana use—there was some agreement, although the Democrats exhibited large clusters of differing opinion. While Republicans were nearly unanimous on both (92 percent on homosexuality and 85 percent on marijuana), the Democrats were not as unified: smaller majorities (65 percent on homosexuality and 58 percent on marijuana) of Democrats agreed on the

Table 6.2
Issue Positions of Delegates* (in percent approving)

Issue	Demo- crats	Repub- licans	Differ- ence
Social Issues			
ERA	85	16	69
Affirmative action	78	15	63
Conservative Christian organizations	14	76	62
Nuclear power	20	82	62
Taxes for public education	85	26	59
Environmental regulation excess	28	74	46
Handgun control	69	24	45
Reduction in food stamps	50	94	44
Prayer, Bible-reading Amendment	44	82	38
Homosexual behavior morally wrong	65	92	27
Marijuana morally wrong	58	85	26
Anti-abortion Amendment	32	57	25
Average difference			47
Economic Issues			
National health insurance	75	10	65
Public works to reduce unemployment	61	7	42
Spending cuts to balance budget	59	92	33
Tax increase to reduce deficit	50	17	33
Average difference			43
Military/Defense Issues			
Increase defense spending	15	91	76
Increase mil. presence in Lat. America	13	78	65
Nuclear freeze	92	47	45
Increase mil. presence in Mid. East	10	52	42
More arms control negotiation	94	74	20
Average difference			50

*Responses of "strongly favor" and "favor" (or "strongly agree" and "agree") were collapsed into a single favorable category; "undecided" responses were dropped. Thus the table reports the distribution of opinion among those expressing an opinion. For the complete wording of each questionnaire item, see the Appendix.

immorality of these two types of behavior. On one social issue—reducing the number of people on food stamps—Democrats were evenly divided while Republican state party elites overwhelmingly favored such steps (by 94 percent).

On two of the four economic issues (national health insurance and public works programs), a majority of Democrats opposed a majority of Republicans. Both groups of activists agreed that spending should be cut in order to balance the federal budget, though with quite distinctive levels of support. As with the two social issues where majorities of each party agreed, Republican activists (at 92 percent) were much more unified than their Democratic counterparts (at 59 percent). On the final economic issue—a tax increase to reduce the federal

Table 6.3
Delegates' Ideological Perceptions of the Democratic Party and the Republican Party in Their Own States (in percent)

Item	Democrats		Republicans	
	Own Party	Republican Party	Democratic Party	Own Party
Very liberal	4	3	28	1
Liberal	13	2	39	*
Slightly liberal	26	2	20	1
Middle-of-the-road	27	4	7	4
Slightly conservative	20	7	4	13
Conservative	8	28	2	66
Very conservative	2	56	*	15
Totals	100	102	100	100
(N=)	(2625)	(2613)	(1837)	(1874)

*less than 0.5 percent

deficit—the Democrats split evenly in contrast to the Republican disapproval margin of 83 percent.

On four of the five military/defense related issues, majorities of activists in the two parties opposed each other. On one issue—more intensive negotiation on nuclear arms control—majorities of activists in both parties agreed, support being 94 percent among Democrats and 74 percent among Republicans.

The *average* percentage difference between party activists on the three types of issues were fairly consistent. (See Table 6.2) On social issues, the average percentage point difference between Democrats and Republicans was 47 percent; on economic issues, 43 percent; and, on military/defense related issues, 50 percent. These average percentage point differences are large and occur consistently across several issue dimensions. They support the ideological clarity, even polarization, suggested by the delegate responses to the ideological self-placement item discussed above.

Ideological Perceptions of the Opposing Party

Another measure of ideological polarity relates to the perceptions held by party delegates regarding the opposing party. (See Table 6.3.) Democratic delegates, for example, viewed the Republican parties at the state level in the six southern states as overwhelmingly conservative (91 percent; 56 percent, moreover, place Republicans in the "very conservative" category). In contrast, they saw themselves comprising a moderate to liberal party (70 percent). In near mirror image, the Republicans perceived their state Democratic parties as liberal (87 percent) and themselves as conservative (94 percent).

These extreme perceptions are striking, and particularly so in the case of the

Table 6.4
Candidate and Party Orientation (in percent)

Item	Democrats	Republicans
What is the most important factor in candidate selection?		
Candidate position on issues	73	85
Prior party loyalty and service	18	5
Chance for election victory	5	7
Can't decide	4	2
Totals	100	99
(N=)	(2831)	(1868)
Which is more important--issue acceptability or electoral success?*		
Electoral success	70	62
Issue acceptability	13	24
Can't decide	17	14
Totals	100	100
(N=)	(2786)	(1803)

*"Issue acceptability" percentage indicates those who agreed with this statement: "If I disagreed with a major stand of my party which was important to me, I would stop working for the party." "Electoral success" percentage indicates those who agreed with this statement: "It is more important to me that my party make a broad electoral appeal than for my party to take stands on issues which I personally agree with."

Republicans. Democratic party activists were somewhat more reticent to view the parties as ideological opposites inasmuch as they were not as likely to perceive their own party to be as liberal as the Republicans did. Republican state party activists, however, saw themselves to be almost as conservative as did Democrats.

Candidate Orientation and Party Loyalty

The orientations of the delegates toward candidates and party offer additional evidence regarding the party sorting hypothesis by testing their strength of commitment to issues and ideology. (See Table 6.4.) On the one hand, the state convention delegates in both parties perceived a potential party nominee's issue positions as far more important than party loyalty and service or even his or her chances for electoral victory. On the other hand, if the party took a personally unacceptable position on an issue perceived as important, most reported they would not quit the party. Even so, nearly a quarter of the Republican state party activists indicated they would indeed leave the party, while about half as many Democrats so responded. The rather impressive percentage for the Republicans is consistent with other data reviewed above on the importance of issues to the Republican party activists.

Table 6.5
Reasons for Political Involvement in 1984 (in percent)

Single Most Important Reason	Democrats	Republicans
To support my party	42	36
To work for issues	19	27
To support a particular candidate	21	23
To fulfill my civic responsibilities	9	9
To make business/professional contacts	3	2
To help my political career	3	2
To enjoy campaign excitement	2	1
To meet other people	2	1
To enjoy visibility as a delegate	*	*
Totals	101	101
(N=)	(3011)	(1938)

*less than 0.5 percent

A final measure of the issue basis for southern parties tests personal motivations for 1984 political activity. (See Table 6.5.) The data indicate that support for one's party was the most important motivational reason (42 percent for Democrats and 36 percent for Republicans) followed by support for particular issues and support for particular candidates. However, these data may underreport the importance of issues as a motivating factor because candidate support may well mask an issue orientation, particularly for Republicans who were working for President Ronald Reagan's reelection and for black Democrats who were supporting Jesse Jackson. Even so, issue support was particularly large for Republican activists with over a quarter of them indicating that "to work for issues" was the most important factor in their 1984 political activity.

Finally, other evidence also supports the party sorting hypothesis. See Chapter 9 for the ideological impact of migration and Chapter 10 for the impact of party switching. Perhaps it is worth noting, in anticipation of Chapter 10, that party switchers have strongly confirmed the ideological trends noted above: Democrats who became Republicans were as conservative as the Republicans they joined and thus were far more conservative than the particular state Democratic party they left; and Republicans who became Democrats, while not so liberal as the party they joined, were clearly much more liberal than the Republicans they left.

CONCLUSION

The evidence reviewed in this chapter lends substantial support to the party sorting hypothesis as it relates to southern state party systems, at least at the level of state party activists. Each party, through its state level partisans, has developed an implicit but clear ideological center of gravity. This was especially so for the Republicans. Republican activists, clustered quite closely, were remarkably conservative in almost every measurable way: they saw themselves as conservative; they took conservative stances on a variety of types of issues; they characterized their party as conservative; and they saw issues and ideology as important dimensions in candidate selection and party support.

In remarkable contrast to the 1940s, when the Democratic party had been a large and inclusive umbrella party, the evidence supports observations quite similar to those cited above for the Republicans. While the Democratic state party activists were somewhat less closely clustered, they nevertheless were quite unevenly distributed across the issue and ideological spectrums. Even though they did not perceive their state party as being as liberal as the Republicans perceived it, their attitudinal patterns reveal a liberal general orientation. Although black Democrats, at least in the abstract, concentrate in the liberal wing of the party more so than whites, both racial groups contribute to the ideological structuring that has increasingly given the southern party system greater philosophical clarity.

The party realignment literature has suggested a number of sign posts that point to a party system undergoing fundamental changes, whether such changes are dealignment or realignment. One such sign post at the elite level is whether or not ideological structuring is occurring between the two parties, that is, whether greater philosophical clarity illuminates the party system. The data reviewed above demonstrates that, at least among party activists in the six southern states of this study, party sorting has occurred in the South. Whether this development is called "convergence,"[18] "nationalization,"[19] or even "the southernization of the national party system,"[20] is not as important as the conclusion that the southern state party systems now operate in ways that are philosophically competitive and that are more congruent with non-Southern party systems. In short, the data reviewed here support and confirm the realignment thesis for southern state party systems.[21]

Similar changes have occurred among the mass of southern voters as well. The southern electorate has more and more come to reflect the kinds of divisions that are characteristic of non-Southern voters. Analyses of presidential voting, poll data, and other data sources have repeatedly confirmed the increasing competitiveness, even polarization, of the two parties in the South.[22]

The old one-party Democratic South is clearly gone, although there is no evidence to suggest that a new one-party Republican South looms in the future. But certainly the Democratic party has changed as the political environment, reflecting social and economic changes, has undergone striking transformations. No longer a party of fluid factions both diverse and flexible in their issue and ideological orientations, the Democratic party, like the Republican party, has become a remarkable cluster of opinion-holding. The southern party system, in short, has become newly restructured not only competitively but philosophically as well.

NOTES

1. A somewhat different treatment of the part of this chapter that deals with ideology and specific political issues appears as "Ideology, Issues, and Realignment among South-

ern Party Activists," in *Party Realignment and Dealignment in the South*, David Brodsky and Robert Swansbrough, eds. (Columbia: University of South Carolina Press, 1988), 268–281.

2. For a discussion of issues, ideology, and party differences in relation to the mass electorate and for a citation of sources, see William Goodman, *The Party System in America* (Englewood Cliffs, N.J.: Prentice-Hall, 1980), 183–205. The classic studies are, of course, Angus Campbell, Philip E. Converse, Warren E. Miller, and Donald F. Stokes, *The American Voter* (New York: John Wiley and Sons, 1960), chaps. 8–10; and Philip E. Converse, "The Nature of Belief Systems in Mass Publics," in *Ideology and Discontent*, ed. David Apter (New York: The Free Press, 1964), 206–261.

3. See Herbert McClosky, Paul J. Hoffman, and Rosemary O'Hara, "Issue Conflict and Consensus among Party Leaders and Followers," *American Political Science Review* 54 (June 1960): 406–427.

4. See Norman H. Nie, Sidney Verba, and John R. Petrocik, *The Changing American Voter* (Cambridge, Mass.: Harvard University Press, 1976); Warren E. Miller and Teresa E. Levitin, *Leadership and Change: Presidential Elections from 1952 to 1976* (Cambridge, Mass.: Winthrop Publishers, 1976); Benjamin I. Page and Richard A. Brody, "Policy Voting and the Electoral Process: The Vietnam War Issue," *American Political Science Review* 66 (September 1972): 979–995; William R. Shaffer, "Partisan Loyalty and the Perceptions of Party, Candidates and Issues," *Western Political Quarterly* 25 (September 1972): 424–433; Arthur H. Miller, Warren E. Miller, Alden S. Raine, and Thad A. Brown, "A Majority Party in Disarray: Policy Polarization in the 1972 Election," paper presented at the 1973 annual meeting of the American Political Science Association; Norman H. Nie and Kristi Andersen, "Mass Belief Systems Revisited: Political Change and Attitude Structure," *Journal of Politics* 36 (August 1974): 540–591; and Stephen Earl Bennett, "Consistency among the Public's Social Welfare Policy Attitudes in the 1960s," *American Journal of Political Science* 17 (August 1973): 544–570.

5. See James W. Soule and James W. Clarke, "Issue Conflict and Consensus: A Comparative Study of Democratic and Republican Delegates to the 1968 National Conventions," *Journal of Politics* 33 (August 1971): 72–91; Jeane Kirkpatrick, *The New Presidential Elite: Men and Women in National Politics* (New York: Russell Sage Foundation and Twentieth Century Fund, 1976); Dennis S. Ippolito, "Political Perspectives of Suburban Party Leaders," *Social Science Quarterly* 49 (March 1969): 800–815; Robert S. Hirschfield, Bert E. Swanson, and Blanche D. Blank, "A Profile of Political Activists in Manhattan," *Western Political Quarterly* 15 (September 1962): 489–506; M. Margaret Conway and Frank B. Feigert, "Motivation, Incentive Systems, and the Political Party Organization," *American Political Science Review* 62 (December 1968): 1169–1183; and Everett Carll Ladd, Jr. and Charles D. Hadley, *Political Parties and Political Issues* (Beverly Hills: SAGE Professional Paper in American Politics, 1973), 20–60.

6. See generally V. O. Key, Jr., *Southern Politics in State and Nation* (New York: Alfred A. Knopf, 1949).

7. Key, *Southern Politics*, 146; see generally 142–147. In South Carolina, for example, Key noted that the careers of "Pitchfork" Ben Tillman and Olin Johnston, both U.S. Senators, well illustrated the fluidity of southern politics.

8. See Allan P. Sindler, *Huey Long's Louisiana* (Baltimore: Johns Hopkins University Press, 1956), 282–286.

9. Everett Carll Ladd, Jr. and Charles D. Hadley, *Transformations of the American Party System* (New York: W. W. Norton, 1975), 129–177.

10. See generally Robert P. Steed, Laurence W. Moreland, and Tod A. Baker, eds., *The 1984 Presidential Election in the South* (New York: Praeger, 1986).

11. See note 8 in Chapter 1 of this volume.

12. See the discussion in David Castle and Harold W. Stanley, "Partisan Realignment in the South: Making Sense of Scholarly Dissonance," paper presented at the 1982 annual meeting of the Southern Political Science Association. See also, for example, Gerald M. Pomper, *Elections in America* (New York: Dodd, Mead and Co., 1972); Gerald M. Pomper, "Classification of Presidential Elections," *Journal of Politics* 29 (August, 1967): 535–566; James L. Sundquist, *Dynamics of the Party System: Alignment and Dealignment of Political Parties in the United States* (Washington, D.C.: Brookings Institution, rev. ed., 1983); Walter Dean Burnham, *Critical Elections and the Mainstreams of American Politics* (New York: W. W. Norton, 1970); and Paul Allen Beck, "Partisan Dealignment in the Postwar South," *American Political Science Review* 71 (June 1977): 477–496.

13. See, for example, V. O. Key, Jr., "A Theory of Critical Elections," *Journal of Politics* 17 (February 1955): 3–18; James F. Ward, "Toward a Sixth Party System? Partisanship and Political Development," *Western Political Quarterly* 26 (September 1973): 406–407; Sundquist, *Dynamics of the Party System*, 294–295; Harold W. Stanley, "Southern Partisan Changes: Dealignment, Realignment or Both?" *Journal of Politics* 50 (February 1988): 64–88; and Burnham, *Critical Elections*, 6.

14. See, for example, Sundquist, *Dynamics of the Party System*, chaps. 1 and 16.

15. See Sundquist, *Dynamics of the Party System*, 297. Congressional voting, for example, has been more polarized during periods of realignment. See W. Wayne Shannon, *Party, Constituency and Congressional Voting: A Study of Legislative Behavior in the United States House of Representatives* (Baton Rouge: Louisiana State University Press, 1968), 175–176, 180–181; and Barbara D. Sinclair, "Party Realignment and the Transformation of the Political Agenda: The House of Representatives, 1925–1938," *American Political Science Review* 71 (September 1977): 940–953. For such polarization at the state level, see, for example, Alan I. Abramowitz, "Ideological Realignment and the Nationalization of Southern Politics," paper presented at the 1979 annual meeting of the Southern Political Science Association.

16. Burnham, *Critical Elections*, 10.

17. For the purposes of Table 6.2 the questionnaire responses were collapsed from five categories ("strong favor," "favor," "undecided," "oppose," and "strongly oppose") into two ("favor" and "oppose") with "undecided" responses dropped. A more detailed examination of the data based on the original five categories indicates that the two parties may be even more divergent on issues than a simple conservative-liberal comparison of modal responses might suggest. even though that dimension alone indicates significant differences. The Democrats, although as a group notably much more liberal than the Republicans, were much less likely to be concentrated in a single response category. In other words, the Democrats were considerably more heterogeneous in their attitudes. The Republicans, on the other hand, were much more likely to load up in one of the polar categories ("strongly favor" or "strongly oppose") which, in addition, is suggestive of a higher level of intensity of feeling among Republican delegates.

Moreover, grouping together the respondents in the six states does not necessarily hide significant differences from state to state. For example, the ideology-issues pattern of South Carolina delegates closely resembles that of the delegates in the other five southern states; see Laurence W. Moreland, "Ideological and Issue Orientations among South

Carolina Party Activists at the 1984 State Party Conventions,'' paper presented at the 1985 annual meeting of the South Carolina Political Science Association.

18. See, for example, Phillip Converse, "On the Possibility of Major Political Re-alignment in the South," in Allen P. Sindler, ed., *Change in the Contemporary South* (Durham: Duke University Press, 1963), 195–222.

19. See, for example, Paul Allen Beck and Paul Lopatto, "The End of Southern Distinctiveness," in Moreland et al., *Contemporary Southern Political Attitudes*, chap. 8; and John C. McKinney and Linda B. Bourque, "The Changing South: National Incorporation of a Region," *American Sociological Review* 36 (June 1971): 399–412.

20. See, for example, John Shelton Reed, *The Enduring South: Subcultural Persistence in Mass Society* (Chapel Hill: University of North Carolina Press, 1972), chap. 5, for the contention that, at least on certain issues, the nonsouth has moved toward positions taken in the South. See also Earl W. Hawkey, "Southern Conservatism 1956–1976," in Moreland et al., *Contemporary Southern Political Attitudes*, chap. 3.

21. See Stanley, "Southern Partisan Changes." Cf. Charles D. Hadley and Susan E. Howell, "The Southern Split Ticket Voter, 1952–1976: Republican Conversion or Dem-ocratic Decline?" in Robert P. Steed, Laurence W. Moreland, and Tod A. Baker, eds., *Party Politics in the South* (New York: Praeger, 1980), 127–151.

22. See, for example, Steed et al., *The 1984 Presidential Election in the South*; and Stephen D. Shaffer, "The Nationalization of Mississippi Politics," paper presented at the 1986 Citadel Symposium on Southern Politics, March 6–7, 1986.

7

The Emergence of the Religious
Right and the Development of the
Two-Party System in the South

Tod A. Baker

During the past few decades the South has undergone a rather profound transformation. Industrialization, urbanization, a pattern of in-migration, the development of the Republican party, and the emergence of blacks as politically relevant actors have all caught the attention of students of the region.[1] Whereas some analysts have argued that this transformation has tended to break down a distinctively southern subculture, others have asserted that in spite of these changes white southerners have continued to persist as an ethnocultural or ethnic group.[2]

In terms of the above debate, the emergence of the religious right during the 1980s is of considerable interest. To begin with, this fundamentalist and evangelical movement should find considerable support in the South since fundamentalism and evangelicalism have long been considered important components of the southern subculture. Second, the conservative and Republican orientations of the religious right should induce fundamentalist and evangelical southerners to shift to the Republican party, particularly at the level of the political elite. Thus the religious right can be thought of as appealing to very traditional elements of the southern mindset while simultaneously contributing to the breakdown of a southern institution, the one-party system.[3]

This chapter seeks to determine the impact of the religious right on party coalitions in the six states included in this study. The chapter begins with a discussion of the bases of support for the religious right. Next, the effects of a favorable attitude toward the religious right or delegates' attachment to their respective parties is examined. Third, the ideological and issue positions of

A different version of this chapter appears in Charles W. Dunn, ed., *Religion in American Politics*, (Washington, D.C.: Congressional Quarterly Press, 1989). Used by permission.

Table 7.1
Religious Preference and Orientation Toward the Religious Right (in percent)

| Orientation Toward the Religious Right | Religious Preference | | | |
	Evangelical Protestant	Nonevangel. Protestant	Catholic	Jewish
Member	7	3	2	
Sympathizer	32	27	20	3
Undecided	24	18	27	8
Opponent	37	52	51	89
	100	100	100	100
(N=)	(1643)	(1959)	(420)	(37)

delegates are examined. And finally, the religious right as a contributor to partisan realignment in the South is examined.

BASES OF SUPPORT FOR THE RELIGIOUS RIGHT

Four religious variables (the evangelical-nonevangelical distinction, the presence or absence of a born-again experience, a literal or nonliteral belief in the Bible, and the frequency of church attendance) are analyzed as bases of support. In addition, two nonreligious variables, party identification and race, are examined.

As indicated by Tables 7.1 through 7.4, religious variables appear to be quite important. To begin with, evangelical Protestants are most likely to be members or sympathizers of religious right organizations followed by nonevangelical Protestants, Catholics, and Jews (see Table 7.1). Thus 39 percent are drawn from evangelical denominations, 30 percent from nonevangelical Protestants, 22 percent from the Catholic church and 3 percent from the Jewish faith; conversely, 37 percent of the opponents are evangelicals as compared with 52 percent of the nonevangelicals, 51 percent of the Catholics, and 89 percent of the Jews.

Second, 48 percent of the born agains are members or sympathizers as compared with 20 percent of those who have not been reborn (see Table 7.2) and 32 percent of the born agains are opponents as compared with 61 percent of those who have not undergone this experience.

The effect of literal belief in the Bible is similar to that of a born-again experience (see Table 7.3). Forty-seven percent of those who have a literal belief in the Bible are members or sympathizers as compared with 20 percent of those who do not. At the opposite pole, 27 percent of those with a literal belief in the Bible are opponents as compared with 63 percent of those whose belief is not literal.

Finally, those who attend church regularly are most likely to be members or sympathizers of religious right organizations (see Table 7.4). Forty-three percent

Table 7.2
Born Again Experience and Orientation Toward the Religious Right (in percent)

Orientation Toward the Religious Right	Born-Again Experience	
	Yes	No
Member	9	1
Sympathizer	38	19
Undecided	20	20
Opponent	32	61
	99	101
(N=)	(1721)	(2339)

Table 7.3
Literal Belief in the Bible and Orientation Toward the Religious Right (in percent)

Orientation Toward the Religious Right	Belief in the Bible	
	Literal	Not Literal
Member	9	1
Sympathizer	38	19
Undecided	26	17
Opponent	27	63
	100	100
(N=)	(1877)	(2559)

Table 7.4
Frequency of Church Attendance and Orientation Toward the Religious Right (in percent)

Orientation Toward the Religious Right	Frequency of Church Attendance				
	Every Week	Almost Every Week	Once or Twice a Month	Few Times a Year	Never
Member	8	3	1	1	0
Sympathizer	35	24	22	19	9
Undecided	22	23	22	20	8
Opponent	36	50	55	60	83
	101	100	100	100	100
(N=)	(1945)	(897)	(531)	(833)	(279)

Table 7.5
Religiosity and Orientation Toward the Religious Right (in percent)

Orientation Toward the Religious Right	Religiosity Index		
	Low	Medium	High
Member	1	2	10
Sympathizer	19	27	41
Undecided	19	27	22
Opponent	62	45	27
	101	101	100
(N=)	(1687)	(773)	(1408)

of those who attend church every week are members or sympathizers compared with only 9 percent of those who never attend church. Opponents constitute 36 percent of those who attend church every week but 83 percent of those who never attend church.

Whereas the above four tables reveal that members and sympathizers of religious right organizations are not drawn exclusively from the more religious respondents and many opponents are evangelical, and/or have had a born-again experience, and/or have a literal belief in the Bible, and/or attend church regularly, there is a fairly pronounced tendency for those who are classified as religious to be more favorably inclined toward the religious right. This tendency can perhaps be seen with greater clarity in terms of a three-point religiosity index constructed for the four religious items (see Table 7.5).[4] Members and sympathizers make up only 20 percent of those who rank low on religiosity but 5 percent of those who rank high; on the other hand, 62 percent of those who rank low on religiosity are opponents as compared with 27 percent who rank high.

Party identification was selected as a basis for support on the assumption that Republicans should find the religious right much more compatible than is the case for Democrats. This appears to be the case (see Table 7.6). Whereas only 11 percent of the Democrats are members or sympathizers of religious right organizations, 63 percent of the Republicans fit in this category. Likewise, whereas 67 percent of the Democrats are opponents of the religious right, only 20 percent of the Republicans have an unfavorable orientation.

This difference could occur simply because Republicans rank higher on religiosity. This, however, does not turn out to be the case (see Table 7.7). Although for both Democrats and Republicans, there is a positive relationship between religiosity and favorable orientation toward the religious right, at each level of religiosity Republicans are more supportive of the religious right than are Democrats. Party identification, thus, tends to have an independent effect.

Race was selected as a basis of support on the assumption that within the Democratic party blacks constitute a progressive or liberalizing influence, re-

Table 7.6
Party Identification and Orientation Toward the Religious Right (in percent)

Orientation Toward the Religious Right	Party Identification	
	Democratic	Republican
Member	2	9
Sympathizer	9	54
Undecided	23	18
Opponent	67	20
	101	101
(N=)	(2799)	(1800)

Table 7.7
Party Identification and Orientation Toward the Religious Right, Controlling for Religiosity (in percent)

Orientation Toward the Religious Right	Religiosity					
	Low		Medium		High	
	Dem.	Rep.	Dem.	Rep.	Dem.	Rep.
Member	1	2	1	4	4	18
Sympathizer	5	41	8	57	19	67
Undecided	15	24	28	24	34	8
Opponent	80	33	63	14	44	6
	100	100	100	99	101	99
(N=)	(1041)	(644)	(487)	(286)	(765)	(642)

sulting in a situation in which the religious right appeals mainly to whites. The findings tend not to bear this out (see Table 7.8). With regard to favorable attitude toward the religious right, there is little difference between black Democrats and white Democrats. With regard to unfavorable attitudes, a considerably higher percentage of whites classify themselves as opponents. This, however, is counter-balanced by the higher percentage of blacks who are undecided. This latter point is, perhaps, the most salient finding with regard to blacks. In a sense, they can be thought of as poised between shifting to a relatively strong favorable orientation or to an unfavorable position similar to that of their white counterparts.

ATTACHMENT TO POLITICAL PARTY

The assumption here is that delegates' orientation toward the religious right affects the strength of attachment to their political party. Since the religious right is a conservative movement and the Democratic party is the more liberal of the

Table 7.8
Race and Orientation Toward the Religious Right for Democratic Delegates (in percent)

Orientation Toward the Religious Right	Race	
	White	Black
Member	1	3
Sympathizer	9	9
Undecided	17	36
Opponent	73	51
	100	99
(N=)	(1950)	(755)

Table 7.9
Orientation Toward the Religious Right and the National Party Identification of Delegates (in percent)

Party Identi-fication	Democrats						Republicans			
	White			Black						
	M/S*	U	O	M/S*	U	O	M	S	U	O
Strong Dem.	46	65	77	80	77	78	0	0	0	0
Weak Dem.	26	22	12	16	20	14	0	0	0	0
Ind. Dem.	12	7	8	4	2	7	0	0	0	0
Independent	10	5	1	0	1	1	1	1	0	1
Ind. Repub.	5	1	1	0	0	0	9	5	4	5
Weak Repub.	1	0	0	0	0	0	7	4	7	8
Strong Repub.	1	0	0	0	0	0	84	90	89	86
	101	100	99	100	100	100	101	100	100	100
(N=)	(189)	(322)	(1390)	(90)	(272)	(375)	(153)	(928)	(301)	(341)

*Due to the small number of Democrats who are members of religious right groups, members and sympathizers were collapsed into a member/sympathizer category.

two parties, a supportive attitude toward the religious right should weaken the attachment of Democratic delegates to the Democratic party but not the attachment of Republican delegates to the Republican party. This hypothesis is tested by examining the strength of delegates' party identification, by measuring their ideological proximity to parties and presidential candidates, by ascertaining their attitudes toward party supporters voting a split ticket, and by determining their defection rates in the 1980 presidential election contest.

As indicated by Tables 7.9 and 7.10, orientation toward the religious right has a considerable effect on the strength of party attachment of white Democrats

Table 7.10
Orientation Toward the Religious Right and the State Party Identification of Delegates (in percent)

Party Identi-fication	Democrats						Republicans			
	White			Black						
	M/S	U	O	M/S	U	O	M	S	U	O
Strong Dem.	63	79	84	81	81	81	0	0	0	0
Weak Dem.	22	12	9	12	16	10	1	0	0	0
Ind. Dem.	7	5	7	7	2	8	0	0	0	0
Independent	4	3	1	0	1	0	1	0	1	0
Ind. Rep.	3	1	0	1	0	0	10	7	5	6
Weak Rep.	0	0	0	0	0	0	7	8	11	13
Strong Rep.	0	0	0	0	0	0	82	84	83	80
	99	100	101	101	100	99	101	99	100	99
(N=)	(188)	(320)	(1392)	(90)	(272)	(377)	(152)	(927)	(302)	(304)

but little or no effect on the strength of attachment of black Democrats or Republicans. Thus, in terms of national party identification, 46 percent of white Democrats who are members or sympathizers are strong Democrats as compared with 65 percent of the undecided and 77 percent of the opponents; the percentages for black Democrats are 80, 77, and 78 respectively whereas the percentage of Republicans who classify themselves as strong party identifiers are 84 for members, 90 for sympathizers, 89 for undecided, and 86 for opponents. The findings for the state party identification are similar. Among white Democrats, 63 percent of those who are members or sympathizers classify themselves as strong Democrats as compared with 79 percent of the undecided and 84 percent of the opponents. For black Democrats the percentages are 81, 81, and 81 and for Republicans 82, 84, 83, and 80.

In terms of ideological proximity to candidates and parties, white Democratic members and sympathizers again emerge as relatively disaffected (see Table 7.11). Members and sympathizers are at a considerably greater distance from Mondale and the national Democratic party and are slightly more distant from the state Democratic party than is the case for those in the undecided and opponent categories. Indeed, members and sympathizers are closer to Reagan than to Mondale, closer to the national Republican party than to the national Democratic party, and almost as close to the state Republican party as to the state Democratic one.

Orientation toward the religious right also affects the mean proximity scores of black Democrats, although the effect is not as strong as for whites. However, race may be a more important predictor of party attachment than attitude toward the religious right; for example, differences in mean proximity scores between

Table 7.11
Orientation Toward the Religious Right and the Mean Ideological Proximity of Delegates to Candidates and Parties

Mean Ideological Proximity*	Democrats						Republicans			
	White			Black						
	M/S	U	O	M/S	U	O	M	S	U	O
Mondale	2.5	1.8	1.1	1.3	1.1	1.0	5.1	4.8	4.3	4.1
Reagan	1.8	2.2	3.7	3.5	3.7	4.3	.5	.5	.5	.7
National Democratic Party	2.2	1.5	1.2	1.1	1.2	1.3	4.9	4.6	4.1	3.9
State Democratic Party	1.7	1.4	1.5	1.2	1.5	1.9	4.2	3.9	3.4	3.2
National Republican Party	1.7	2.3	3.3	3.4	3.7	4.0	1.0	.8	.7	.6
State Republican Party	1.9	2.4	3.7	3.4	3.7	4.2	.8	.6	.6	.7

*The mean ideological proximity of each group was calculated by taking the mean of the absolute value of the respondents' ideology minus the ideology of the candidate or party.

Table 7.12
Orientation Toward the Religious Right and the Attitude of Delegates Toward Party Supporters Voting a Split Ticket (in percent)

Attitude Toward Split Ticket	Democrats						Republicans			
	White			Black						
	M/S	U	O	M/S	U	O	M	S	U	O
Permissible	63	38	40	38	27	25	56	59	56	62
Not Permissible	32	51	53	51	59	68	33	33	32	30
Don't Know	5	11	7	11	14	7	11	8	12	8
	100	100	100	100	100	100	100	100	100	100
(N=)	(192)	(317)	(1383)	(88)	(266)	(371)	(151)	(919)	(295)	(339)

black members and sympathizers on the one hand and white opponents on the other tend to be small, suggesting that black members and sympathizers tend not to be disaffected Democrats.

For Republicans, support or nonsupport for the religious right has little or no effect on mean proximity scores for Reagan, the national Republican party, or the state Republican party. Republicans in each of the four categories feel quite close to their president and their party.

Third, with regard to attitude toward party supporters voting a split ticket, the findings support those for strength of party identification and ideological proximity (see Table 7.12). Among white Democrats about two out of three members and sympathizers state that it is or was permissible for party supporters to vote

Table 7.13

Orientation Toward the Religious Right and the Defection Rate in the 1980 Presidential Election Contest (in percent)

Presidential Vote in 1980	Democrats						Republicans			
	White			Black						
	M/S	U	O	M/S	U	O	M	S	U	O
Carter	63	73	84	98	94	96	1	1	0	1
Reagan	33	18	6	0	2	1	97	98	97	96
Anderson	2	2	7	0	1	2	0	0	1	2
Other	2	2	1	1	0	0	2	1	3	1
Didn't Vote	1	4	2	1	4	1	0	0	0	0
	101	99	100	100	101	100	100	100	101	100
(N=)	(185)	(314)	(1402)	(92)	(274)	(381)	(141)	(874)	(293)	(330)

a split ticket as compared to two of every five opponents. This relationship is also found among black Democrats although it is not nearly so pronounced—two of every five members and sympathizers compared to one of every four opponents. For Republicans, orientation toward the religious right has little or no effect on attitudes toward a split-ticket vote. This is not surprising inasmuch as the Republican party often does not offer candidates for all offices.

Finally, whereas in the 1980 presidential election contest white Democrats tended to exhibit a higher defection rate than black Democrats or Republicans, this tendency was most pronounced for members and sympathizers (see Table 7.13). Sixty-three percent of the white Democratic members and sympathizers voted for Carter as compared with 84 percent of the opponents; the black Democratic vote for Carter was 98, 94, and 96 percent respectively and the Republican percentages for Reagan were 97, 98, 97, and 96.

White Democratic members and sympathizers who defected also exhibited a pronounced tendency to vote for Reagan whereas opponents divided about equally between Reagan and Anderson.

IDEOLOGY AND ISSUE POSITIONS

Since the religious right is a conservative movement, orientation toward the religious right should be related to both political ideology and issue positions (see Table 7.14). With regard to political ideology, this tends to be the case for white Democrats; whereas only 23 percent of the members and sympathizers consider themselves liberal, 68 percent of the opponents do so. Conversely, 50 percent of the opponents consider themselves conservative but only 14 percent of the opponents place themselves in this category. Orientation toward the religious right has little or no effect on the political ideology of black Democrats (71 percent of the members and sympathizers, 71 percent of the undecided, and

Table 7.14
Orientation Toward the Religious Right and the Political Ideology of Delegates (in percent)

Political Ideology	Democrats						Republicans			
	White			Black						
	M/S	U	O	M/S	U	O	M	S	U	O
Liberal	23	38	68	71	71	74	2	1	4	3
Mid.-of-road	27	27	18	12	18	11	0	2	5	9
Conservative	50	35	14	17	11	14	98	97	91	88
	100	100	100	100	100	99	100	100	100	100
(N=)	(188)	(307)	(1383)	(85)	(267)	(370)	(142)	(875)	(295)	(332)

74 percent of the opponents classify themselves as liberal) and very little effect on Republicans—although there is a 10 percentage point difference between members and opponents, the fact that 88 percent of the opponents consider themselves conservative indicates that for Republicans partisanship is probably more important than orientation toward the religious right.

Delegates also expressed their viewpoints on twenty-one issues—six economic, five defense, two minority rights, three energy-environment, four moral, and one gun control.[5] An effort is made to ascertain the manner in which these twenty-one issues discriminate among the ten groups of delegates through the use of discriminant analysis. This analysis reveals two substantively significant functions; the first has a canonical correlation of .858 and accounts for 75 percent of the variance whereas the second has a canonical correlation of .631 and explains 18 percent of the variance. Forty-nine percent of the grouped cases are classified correctly, a considerable improvement over 10 percent random choice.

The first function can be thought of as lying on a general liberalism-conservatism dimension since issues from the defense, minority rights, economic, and energy–environmental issue areas are dominant on it (see Table 7.15). In terms of group means, party identification tends to be the basic cleavage; the six most liberal groups are Democratic and/or the four most conservative are Republican (see Table 7.16). Orientation toward the religious right does, however, have some salience. Among Republicans, those in the undecided category are more conservative than opponents, sympathizers are more conservative than the undecided, and members are more conservative than sympathizers. A similar pattern exists for the Democrats. For both blacks and whites opponents are more liberal than the undecided and the undecided are more liberal than members and sympathizers. Finally, within the Democratic party race tends to be important since three of the four most liberal groups are blacks.

The second function is much more specialized since moral issues tend to be dominant on it. Among the seven white groups, orientation toward the religious

Table 7.15
Pooled Within-Groups Correlations Between Discriminating Variables and Canonical Discriminant Functions

Discriminating Variables*	Function 1	Function 2
Increase Defense Spending	.70324	-.00801
Equal Rights Amendment	.67260	-.00624
Affirmative Action	.54077	-.45458
National Health Insurance	.50561	-.23453
Increase Mil. Presence in Latin America	.50176	-.11100
More Rapid Develop. of Nuclear Power	.45136	-.00369
Public Works Program	.42938	-.11199
Tax for Public Education	.41807	-.10964
Reduce No. of People on Food Stamps	.39662	-.03937
Reg. of Bus. to Protect Environ. is Excess.	.34921	-.22897
Legislation to Control Handguns	.34799	-.01968
School Prayer Amendment	.40628	.58832
Amendment to Prohibit Abortion	.29013	.57355
Use of Marijuana is Morally Wrong	.26695	.31894
Increase Energy Resources	.18985	.13826
Nuclear Freeze	.40106	.04744
Homosexual Behavior is Morally Wrong	.32227	.36040
Increase Mil. Presence in Middle East	.34380	.09024
Cut Spending to Balance Budget	.31234	-.02094
Negotiate on Arms Control	.28701	.15024
Tax Increase to Reduce Deficit	.24415	.14639

*See Appendix for wording of the issues questions

Table 7.16
Group Means on the Discriminant Functions

Groups	Group Means	
	Function 1	Function 2
Wht. Dem. Member/Sympathizers	.48505	.44169
Wht. Dem. Undecided	-.23225	.37182
Wht. Dem. Opponents	-1.51471	-.67922
Blk. Dem. Member/Sympathizers	-1.40655	2.18820
Blk. Dem. Undecided	-1.52633	2.19450
Blk. Dem. Opponents	-2.05080	.94453
Wht. Rep. Members	2.61828	.57478
Wht. Rep. Sympathizers	2.16125	.16023
Wht. Rep. Undecided	1.40535	-.21703
Wht. Rep. Opponents	1.07444	-.94375

right tends to be a much more important cleavage than party identification—of the three groups that take a liberal position on the second function two are Republican and one is Democratic. The two most liberal groups are Republican opponents and Democratic opponents and the two most conservative are Democratic members and sympathizers and Republican members.

Although orientation toward the religious right does affect the rank ordering

Table 7.17
The Effect of Orientation Toward the Religious Right on the Decision of
Democrats to Switch to the Republican Party (in percent)

Switched Parties	Orientation Toward the Religious Right			
	Member	Sympathizer	Undecided	Opponent
Yes	36	32	31	28
No	64	68	69	72
	100	100	100	100
(N=)	(152)	(944)	(318)	(354)

of black groups, the fact that the three most conservative groups are black suggests that race is more important in determining their placement.

THE RELIGIOUS RIGHT AND REALIGNMENT

Inasmuch as white Democrats who are members and sympathizers of religious right organizations tend to have a rather tenuous attachment to the Democratic party, tend to express a conservative political ideology, and are the most conservative Democratic group on each of the two functions, it seems plausible to assume that at least at the level of the party of the activists the religious right can be thought of as a bridge across which people are moving from the ranks of the Democratic party to the Republican faith. The evidence suggests that there may be some validity to the hypothesis, although the religious right is by no means the only conduit to the Republican party (see Table 7.17). Thus 36 percent of Republicans who are members of religious right organizations indicated that they have switched parties as compared with 32 percent of the sympathizers, 31 percent of the undecided, and 28 percent of the opponents.

SUMMARY AND CONCLUSIONS

Quite obviously orientation toward the religious right has had the greatest impact on the traditional party of the South, i.e., white Democrats. To a considerable degree the sense of party attachment among white Democrats who are members or sympathizers with religious right groups is so slight that, at least at the national level, they can be thought of as Democrats in name only. Furthermore, their rather conservative political stance tends to inhibit the leftward shift of the southern Democratic party. It may well be that over the long run these disaffected Democrats will tend to disappear. Since Republicans tend to be more favorably inclined toward the religious right, it seems not unreasonable to assume that politically active members and sympathizers should gravitate to the Republican party. To some degree the evidence does suggest that the religious right is performing this bridging function. When death and retirement from politics are taken into consideration it may not be unreasonable to suggest that among white Democrats the religious right is making its last stand.

The situation with regard to black Democrats appears to be quite different. Orientation toward the religious right has little effect on blacks' attachment to the Democratic party and relative to whites their attachment tends to be strong. Likewise, orientation toward the religious right tends to have a relatively slight effect on the positions of blacks on the issues. While the group means on the functions are ordered by orientation toward the religious right, race appears to be considerably more important in determining the relative liberalism or conservatism of blacks. Thus on the first function three of the four most liberal groups are blacks whereas on the second blacks constitute the three most conservative groups.

For Republicans, a favorable attitude toward the religious right tends to pull the party toward the right, not only on political ideology but on each of the two functions. This suggests that if those who are responsive to the appeal of the religious right tend to move into the Republican party, interparty differences should become greater.

Finally, in terms of moral issues intraparty differences are greater than interparty ones. This suggests that if moral issues became salient, partisan alignments could take a rather strange turn.

NOTES

1. See Chapter 1, note 8.

2. For the former position, see V. O. Key, Jr., *Southern Politics in State and Nation* (New York: Alfred A. Knopf, 1949); and I. A. Newby, *The South: A History* (New York: Holt, Rinehart, and Winston, 1978), 505–506. For the latter position, see Numan V. Bartley, "The South and Sectionalism in Southern Politics," *Journal of Politics* 38 (August 1976): 257; and John Shelton Reed, *The Enduring South: Subcultural Persistence in a Mass Society* (Lexington, Mass.: Lexington Books, 1972).

3. Lyman A. Kellstedt, "Evangelical Religion and Support for Falwell Policy Positions: An Examination of Regional Variation," paper presented at The Citadel Symposium on Southern Politics, Charleston South Carolina, March 6–7, 1986; and Robert P. Steed, Laurence W. Moreland, and Tod A. Baker, "Religion and Party Activists: Fundamentalism and Politics in Regional Perspective" in Tod A. Baker, Robert P. Steed, and Laurence W. Moreland, *Religion and Politics in the South* (New York: Praeger, 1983), 105–132.

4. Each item was coded zero or one, yielding a five-point index ranging from zero, religious on none of the items, to four, religious on each of them. This was collapsed into a three-point index by recoding zero and one as low, two as medium, and three or four as high.

5. For the wording of the questions see the Appendix.

8

The Impact of Urbanization on Party Coalitions

Tod A. Baker

Forty years ago the South was a one-party region characterized by a relatively low literacy rate, poverty, Jim Crow laws, and a small town, rural life style. Since then considerable changes have occurred: the Republican party is no longer merely a conspiracy for plunder; the literacy rate has gone up and southerners are more affluent; blacks have made substantial political and social advancements; and the region has experienced considerable urbanization and suburbanization.

This chapter focuses on the last of these transformations. Certainly, urbanization has had an impact. In rather broad cultural terms the urbanization of the South has been a major contributor to the breakdown of the traditionalistic subculture that has long characterized the region.[1] In the words of Earl Black and Merle Black, southern cities "are gradually becoming zones of heterogeneity and political diversity in a region . . . long known to be homogeneous."[2] More narrowly, scholars have pointed to the impact of urbanization on the development of a Republican electoral base: in the late 1960s Kevin B. Phillips discussed the growth of urban Republicanism in Florida and Texas; in the mid–1970s Louis Seagull indicated the importance of urbanization and suburbanization on political change in the South; and in the late 1980s Black and Black noted that urban Republicanism is one of the three leading sources of presidential Republicanism.[3]

Given the importance of urbanization on political change, it seems plausible to assume that an analysis of delegates by type of community might reveal relatively systematic intraparty differences. Four topics are covered—personal characteristics of the delegates, strength of party attachment, the group bases of the parties, and ideological and issue differences.

Table 8.1
Race, Gender, and Migration Status of Delegates

Type of Community	Race of Delegates*	
	White Democrats	Black Democrats
Urban	29	31
Suburban	21	16
Small Town	32	37
Rural	18	17
	100	101
(N=)	(2011)	(775)

	Gender of Delegates			
	Democratic Women	Democratic Men	Republican Women	Republican Men
Urban	30	29	28	26
Suburban	19	21	28	30
Small Town	34	33	28	30
Rural	17	17	17	14
	100	100	101	100
(N=)	(1458)	(1413)	(809)	(1059)

	Migration Status of Delegates					
	Native Dem.	Southern Dem.	Non-Southern Dem.	Native Rep.	Southern Rep.	Non-Southern Rep.
Urban	26	38	42	25	29	28
Suburban	19	22	26	27	34	32
Small Town	37	27	19	31	22	28
Rural	19	13	14	17	14	12
	101	100	101	100	99	100
(N=)	(2141)	(299)	(367)	(983)	(253)	(545)

*Since there are just 29 black Republicans, only the Democrats are included.

PERSONAL CHARACTERISTICS OF THE DELEGATES

Race, gender, migration status, and religious beliefs and practices are covered here. The first three are included because blacks, women, and immigrants are relatively new actors on the southern political scene. Hence it could be useful to ascertain whether blacks, women, or immigrants tend to be concentrated in a particular type of community. On the other hand, evangelical beliefs and practices and frequent church attendance have long been characteristic of southerners. It would, thus, seem that the more religious activists would be found in small town and rural areas.

With regard to race and gender, differences among delegates are slight to nonexistent. (See Table 8.1.) Within the Democratic party, whites and blacks tend to be relatively equally distributed among the four types of communities, with a slightly higher percentage of whites in suburbs and a slightly higher percentage of blacks in small towns. Within both parties community differences between men and women tend to be nonexistent. On the other hand, in terms of migration status, both Democratic and Republican in-migrants are more likely to be found in urban and suburban areas whereas the native born are more likely to be found in small town and rural communities. This tendency is somewhat more pronounced for the Democrats, particularly in urban areas.

Religious beliefs and practices are included because a rather substantial body of literature attests to the importance of religion in the South, particularly evangelical religion.[4] It thus seems plausible to assume that the urbanization of the South should dilute traditional religious practices, thereby contributing to secularization. If this is the case small town and rural delegates should be more apt to express religious beliefs and practices than suburban and urban ones.

Three religious variables are examined—the presence or absence of a born-again experience, viewpoint on the inerrancy of the Bible, and the frequency of church attendance. With regard to the first two variables, the findings do tend to support the hypothesis. For both Democrats and Republicans urban and suburban delegates are less likely to have been born again or to have a literal belief in the Bible (See Table 8.2.) While these differences are not great they are in the expected direction and do suggest that party activists in urban and suburban areas tend not to be as committed to evangelicalism as those in small town and rural communities.

With regard to frequency of church attendance, the hypothesis tends to be borne out only for the Democrats. Thus, whereas 75 percent of those who never attend church live in urban or suburban areas compared to 42 percent of those who attend church frequently, the percentages for small towns and rural areas are 25 and 58 respectively. Of those never attending church, 52 percent live in urban and suburban communities whereas of those who attend church frequently 54 percent live in these types of communities. The percentages for small towns and rural areas are 49 and 47 respectively. Thus, whereby relatively few urban and suburban Democrats are exposed to religious messages through church attendance and hence are not as likely to be tied into religious networks as small town and rural ones are, among Republicans exposure to religious information is about the same regardless of type of community.

STRENGTH OF PARTY IDENTIFICATION

This section seeks to ascertain the impact of urbanization and suburbanization on the party attachment of delegates. Three variables are analyzed—national party identification, state party identification, and delegates' ideological proximity to presidential candidates and the parties.

With respect to national and state party identification, type of community makes little or no difference. (See Table 8.3.) Among Democrats 77 percent of those living in urban areas consider themselves strong national Democrats compared to 72 percent of the suburbanites, 72 percent of those living in small towns,

Table 8.2
Religious Beliefs, Experiences, and Practices of Delegates

Type of Community	Born Again Experience of Delegates			
	Born Again Dem.	Not Born Again Dem.	Born Again Rep.	Not Born Again Rep.
Urban	25	32	24	29
Suburban	14	23	27	30
Small Town	37	32	32	27
Rural	24	13	17	14
	100	100	100	100
(N=)	(1034)	(1521)	(778)	(922)

	Delegates' Belief on the Inerrancy of the Bible			
	Literal Belief Dem.	Nonliteral Belief Dem.	Literal Belief Rep.	Nonliteral Belief Rep.
Urban	22	34	24	29
Suburban	16	23	27	30
Small Town	39	30	32	27
Rural	23	13	17	14
	100	100	100	100
(N=)	(1015)	(1759)	(935)	(913)

	Frequency of Delegates' Church Attendance					
	Never (Dem.)	Occasionally* (Dem.)	Freq.** (Dem.)	Never (Rep.)	Occasionally* (Rep.)	Freq.** (Rep.)
Urban	42	32	26	22	28	25
Suburban	33	25	16	30	32	28
Small Town	14	27	39	26	27	31
Rural	11	15	19	23	13	16
	100	99	100	101	100	100
(N=)	(204)	(885)	(1757)	(78)	(540)	(1253)

*Occasionally ranges from a few times a year to once or twice a month.

**Frequently ranges from almost every week to every week.

and 73 percent of those living in rural areas; the Republican figures are 87, 90, 88, and 87 respectively. At the state level the Democratic percentages are 83, 77, 81, and 80 and the Republican ones are 82, 84, 82, and 82.

In terms of ideological proximity to presidential candidates and parties, the urbanization process seems to have little effect on delegates' proximity to their candidate and party but does appear to affect delegates' proximity to the opposite candidate and party. (See Table 8.4.) Democrats tend to be uniformly close to Mondale, the national Democratic party, and the state Democratic party and Republicans tend to be uniformly close to Reagan, the national Republican party, and the state Republican party. On the other hand, urban and suburban Democrats are further from Reagan and the Republican party than is the case for their small town and rural counterparts, whereas urban and suburban Republicans are closer to Mondale and the Democratic party than are small town and rural ones.

Table 8.3
Strength of Party Identification among the Delegates

Party Identification	National Party Identification of Delegates							
	Urban Dem.	Sub-urban Dem.	Small Town Dem.	Rural Dem.	Urban Rep.	Sub-urban Rep.	Small Town Rep.	Rural Rep.
Strong Democrat	77	72	72	73	0	0	0	0
Weak Democrat	13	18	16	17	0	0	0	0
Ind. Closer to Dem.	8	7	8	6	0	0	0	0
Independent	2	2	3	3	1	1	1	0
Ind. Closer to Rep.	1	1	1	1	6	5	5	6
Weak Republican	0	0	0	0	6	4	7	6
Strong Republican	0	0	0	1	87	90	88	87
	101	100	100	101	100	100	101	99
(N=)	(867)	(579)	(975)	(504)	(502)	(552)	(559)	(291)

	State Party Identification of Delegates							
	Urban Dem.	Sub-urban Dem.	Small Town Dem.	Rural Dem.	Urban Rep.	Sub-urban Rep.	Small Town Rep.	Rural Rep.
Strong Democrat	83	77	81	80	0	0	0	0
Weak Democrat	9	15	10	12	0	0	0	0
Ind. Closer to Dem.	7	7	6	5	0	0	0	0
Independent	1	1	1	1	1	0	1	1
Ind. Closer to Rep.	0	0	1	1	6	8	5	8
Weak Republican	0	0	0	0	10	7	12	8
Strong Republican	0	0	0	0	82	84	82	82
	100	100	99	99	99	99	100	99
(N=)	(869)	(582)	(974)	(504)	(502)	(551)	(556)	(291)

Table 8.4
Ideological Proximity of Delegates to Candidates and Parties

	Democrats				Republicans			
	Urban	Sub-urban	Small Town	Rural	Urban	Sub-urban	Small Town	Rural
Reagan	3.9	3.7	3.1	3.0	.5	.5	.6	.6
Mondale	1.2	1.2	1.4	1.4	4.5	4.6	4.6	4.8
Nat. Dem. Party	1.3	1.4	1.4	4.2	4.4	4.4	4.7	4.7
State Dem. Party	1.7	1.4	1.5	3.6	3.7	3.7	4.0	4.0
Nat. Rep. Party	3.6	3.4	2.9	2.9	.7	.7	.7	.8
State Rep. Party	3.9	2.7	3.1	3.0	.6	.6	.7	.7

GROUP BASES OF POLITICS

Respondents were asked to indicate their activity in ten types of groups as well as their orientation toward religious right organizations. For both Democrats and Republicans the evidence tends to suggest that urbanization has tended to alter the group bases of the parties.

Among the Democrats farm groups tend to be much more strongly represented

Table 8.5
Group Activities of Delegates (in percent)

Group in Which Delegates Are Active	Democrats				Republicans			
	Urban	Sub-urban	Small Town	Rural	Urban	Sub-urban	Small Town	Rural
Labor Unions	18	23	11	14	4	2	5	6
Business	30	29	33	25	47	44	42	33
Religious-Related	37	37	40	41	52	54	52	53
Civil Rights	38	27	26	24	4	2	3	3
Education	23	25	28	28	14	12	17	14
Environmental	19	16	12	13	9	8	10	11
Antiabortion	4	3	2	3	13	15	14	13
Farm	5	5	14	25	4	3	13	30
Women's Rights	33	28	18	15	5	3	3	3
Public Interest	46	36	39	32	31	31	30	23

among small town and rural delegates and labor unions among urban and suburban ones. (See Table 8.5.) While it is not surprising that urbanization has reduced the proportion of delegates who are members of farm groups, the greater proportion of labor union members among urban and suburban delegates suggests that urbanization is tending to have a nationalizing effect on the Democratic party; i.e., in a region long characterized by an antipathy to the union movement, the increase in union membership suggests that the Democratic party in the South is moving toward convergence with the national party.

Other principal differences among the Democrats fall in the social issue area—civil rights, women's rights, and the environment. These differences also suggest that urbanization is having a nationalizing effect. Hence, as urbanization progresses, the group basis of the southern Democratic party should more and more resemble the group basis at the national level.

Among Republicans principal differences exist for business groups and farm groups. Thus, as urbanization continues, some change should occur in the group basis of the Republican party. Since the Republican party is already the party of business, this shift in group basis should not affect the nature of the policies espoused by Republicans.

Respondents were also asked to indicate their position toward the religious right with orientation ranging from member to opponent. Here too urbanization has an effect, with the greater effect being felt by the Democrats. (See Table 8.6.) Beginning with the Democrats, differences for members and sympathizers are not great—9 percent for urban delegates, 8 percent for suburban ones, 12 percent for small town residents, and 13 percent for those living in rural areas. However, relatively sharp differences exist in the undecided and opponent categories. Of the urban delegates 15 percent are undecided compared to 19 percent of the suburban ones, 28 percent of those in small towns, and 31 percent of delegates living in rural areas. The percentages for opponents are 77, 73, 59, and 56 respectively. Small town and rural delegates are, thus, considerably more

Table 8.6
Delegates' Orientation Toward Religious Right Organizations

Orientation Toward the Religious Right	Democrats				Republicans			
	Urban	Sub-urban	Small Town	Rural	Urban	Sub-urban	Small Town	Rural
Member	2	1	1	2	7	9	8	11
Sympathizer	7	7	11	11	51	54	54	55
Undecided	15	19	28	31	19	17	17	20
Opponent	77	73	59	56	23	19	21	14
	101	100	99	100	100	99	100	100
(N=)	(852)	(572)	(952)	(491)	(473)	(522)	(531)	(285)

likely to take a fence-sitting position whereas urban and suburban ones have a greater tendency to take an opposition stance.

The differences among the Republicans are in the same direction as those for the Democrats but are considerably more moderate. Among members there is only a 4 percentage point difference between urban and rural delegates, with the difference for sympathizers, undecided, and opponents being 4, 1, and 9 respectively.

At least for the Democrats the differences in orientation toward religious right groups tend to support other differences. As pointed out in the previous chapter the religious right tends to draw its members and sympathizers from evangelical Christians who attend church regularly. These beliefs and behaviors tend to be more characteristic of Democrats living in small towns and rural areas. It is, thus, not surprising that the religious right has a greater appeal among small town and rural Democrats. As a result as urbanization continues Democratic opposition to the religious right should increase.

For the Republicans there are probably several reasons for the moderate effect of urbanization on orientation toward the religious right. To begin with, through relatively frequent church attendance urban Republicans have a relatively high probability of being exposed to messages supportive of the religious right. Second, since the Republican party is the conservative party, Republicans and the religious right may have a community of interest.

IDEOLOGY AND ISSUES

Respondents were asked to indicate their political ideology as well as their positions on twenty-one issues—six economic, two minority rights, three energy-environmental, five defense, four moral, and one handgun control.

In terms of political ideology, differences within the Democratic party tend to be relatively sharp, with urbanization having a rather pronounced liberalizing effect. (See Table 8.7.) Thus, 58 percent of the urban Democrats consider themselves liberal or very liberal compared with 47 percent of the suburban

Table 8.7
The Political Ideology of Delegates (in percent)

Political Ideology	Democrats				Republicans			
	Urban	Sub-urban	Small Town	Rural	Urban	Sub-urban	Small Town	Rural
Very Liberal	14	10	9	7	0	0	1	0
Liberal	44	37	27	29	1	1	2	1
Mod. Liberal	16	23	18	16	1	1	1	1
Neutral	13	15	23	21	4	3	4	4
Mod. Conser.	9	11	12	14	16	9	12	7
Conservative	4	4	8	11	66	69	62	61
Very Conser.	0	1	2	2	12	17	19	26
	100	100	99	100	100	100	101	100
(N=)	(852)	(572)	(952)	(493)	(473)	(520)	(536)	(286)

Democrats, and 36 percent of both the small town and rural ones. Republican differences are more moderate. Although small town and rural Republicans are more likely to consider themselves very conservative, combining the conservative and very conservative categories reveals little or no differences among the four types of communities.

Intraparty differences on the issues tend to mirror those on political ideology, with Democratic differences ranging from relatively slight to fairly substantial and Republican differences slight to nonexistent. (See Table 8.8.) Indeed, food stamps, abortion, the morality of marijuana, the morality of homosexuality, school prayer, and handgun control are the only issues on which Democratic intraparty differences are fairly substantial. It thus appears that social issues, particularly moral ones, have the greatest potential for creating cleavages between urban-suburban Democrats on the one hand and small town-rural ones on the other.

SUMMARY AND CONCLUSIONS

Although the impact of urbanization on party coalitions appears to be at most moderate, for at least the Democrats differences between urban and suburban Democrats on the one hand and small town and rural ones on the other do seem to be worthy of comment. Urban and suburban Democrats, for example, are somewhat less likely to consider themselves born again or to have a literal belief in the Bible and are considerably less likely to attend church frequently. For these Democrats the South as the Bible Belt has begun to recede into the past. Urban and suburban party activists are also more likely to be members of groups (labor unions, environmental, women's rights, and civil rights) whose wants and demands have traditionally not been expressed by the Democratic party in the South. Therefore, it appears that here too Democratic party activists are moving away from what could be called distinctively southern viewpoints and moving

Table 8.8
Mean Position of Delegates on the Issues*

Issue	Democrats				Republicans			
	Urban	Sub-urban	Small Town	Rural	Urban	Sub-urban	Small Town	Rural
Nat. Health Ins.	2.3	2.4	2.6	2.5	4.2	4.3	4.2	4.1
Cut Spend/Bal. Bud.	3.0	3.2	3.4	3.3	4.2	4.2	4.2	4.3
Tax Inc./Red. Def.	3.0	3.0	3.1	3.1	4.0	4.0	3.8	4.0
Public Works Proj.	2.7	2.7	2.8	2.9	4.2	4.2	4.2	4.2
Tax for Education	2.0	2.0	2.1	2.2	3.6	3.7	3.5	3.6
Red. No. People on Food Stamps	2.7	2.9	3.2	3.3	4.2	4.3	4.3	4.3
Equal Rights Amend.	1.6	1.8	2.0	2.1	3.9	4.1	4.0	4.0
Affirmative Action	2.0	2.2	2.3	2.5	3.9	4.0	3.9	3.9
Develop Nuc. Power	2.0	2.2	2.4	2.3	3.7	3.8	3.7	3.6
Inc. Energy Res.	2.3	2.3	2.5	2.5	3.0	3.1	3.0	2.9
Govt. Reg. Bus. to Protect Env. in Exc.	2.2	2.3	2.7	2.6	3.6	3.6	3.6	3.5
Inc. Defense spend.	1.7	1.9	2.2	2.2	4.0	4.2	4.1	4.2
Inc. Mil. in ME	1.9	2.0	2.2	2.2	3.0	3.0	3.1	3.1
Inc. Mil. in LA	1.9	2.0	2.6	2.3	3.5	3.6	3.7	3.6
Arms Control Neg.	1.6	1.7	1.8	1.9	2.5	2.5	2.5	2.6
Bilat. Nuc. Freeze	1.7	1.7	1.8	1.9	3.2	3.2	3.2	3.1
Amend. to Prohibit Abortions	2.1	2.3	2.7	2.9	3.1	3.3	3.4	3.5
Use of Marijuana Is Morally Wrong	3.0	3.0	3.6	3.8	4.1	4.2	4.2	4.2
Homosexual Behav. Is Morally Wrong	3.0	3.2	3.7	4.0	4.4	4.5	4.5	4.5
School Prayer Amend.	2.4	2.6	3.1	3.3	3.9	4.0	4.1	4.1
Handgun Control	2.1	2.4	2.6	2.9	3.7	3.8	3.8	3.9

*Variables are coded from liberal to conservative on a five point scale.
See the Appendix for the wording of the questions.

toward convergence with the National Democratic party. Finally, differences on issues between the Democrats tend to be moderately substantial on social issues and particularly on those that could be classified as moral. Thus the principal issue cleavages among Democrats appear to be noneconomic in nature.

In summary it appears that urban and suburban Democratic parties are leading the way in shedding the mantle of southern distinctiveness and bringing greater heterogeneity and diversity to the politics of the region. This, however, appears not to be the case for the Republicans. Although there are some differences among the four sets of Republican activists, these differences tend to be so slight that in terms of the urban-rural cleavage the Republican party emerges as very close to monolithic.

NOTES

1. Earl Black and Merle Black, *Politics and Society in the South* (Cambridge, Mass.: Harvard University Press, 1987), 43–47.

2. Black and Black, *Politics and Society in the South*, 47.

3. Kevin B. Phillips, *The Emerging Republican Majority* (New Rochelle, N.Y.: Arlington House, 1969), 270–280; Louis M. Seagull, *Southern Republicanism* (New York: John Wiley and Sons, 1975), 6–7; and Black and Black, *Politics and Society in the South*, 268–269.

4. See John Shelton Reed, *The Enduring South: Subcultural Persistence in a Mass Society* (Lexington, Mass.: Lexington Books, 1972), chap. 6; Lyman A. Kellstedt, "Evangelical Religion and Support for Falwell Policy Positions: An Examination of Regional Variation," paper presented at The Citadel Symposium on Southern Politics, Charleston, South Carolina, March 6–7, 1986; and Robert P. Steed, Laurence W. Moreland, and Tod A. Baker, "Religion and Party Activists: Fundamentalism and Politics in Regional Perspective" in Tod A. Baker, Robert P. Steed, and Laurence W. Moreland, *Religions and Politics in the South* (New York: Praeger Publishers, 1983), 105–132.

9

The Impact of Immigration on the Composition of Party Coalitions

Laurence W. Moreland

The dramatic social, economic, and cultural changes that characterized the post–World War II South have contributed to significant alterations in the region's politics. Industrialization, urbanization, migration, and changing patterns in race relations have all been factors in a series of political changes that helped move the South toward the nation's political mainstream.[1]

One of the clearest and most important of these political changes was the dissolution of the traditional one-party politics of much of the South and the attendant increase in both Republican party strength and interparty competition.[2] Many factors contributed to this key development, but one less studied than others is the influence of migrants moving into the South from other parts of the nation. The South was attractive to a variety of in-migrants, including retirees, business entrepreneurs and others seeking new employment, managerial representatives of national corporations moving into the region, and those generally wanting to take advantage of the South's business and meteorological climates.[3] Politically, in-migrants helped to crack the traditional Democratic control of southern politics and contributed to changes within the state Democratic parties themselves by bringing them, variously, partisan identifications, programmatic and political orientations, and voting patterns different from the traditional one-party Democratic politics of the region.[4]

On a general level, demographers and economists have analyzed the effects of population movements to assess changes in industrialization, income, and race relations.[5] At the political level, research has identified population movement (both from the South and into the South) as an important contributing factor in the changing politics of the region, its strongest impact being on partisan voting patterns.[6] This influx of non-Southern and often strongly Republican voters into the southern electorate significantly altered the character and importance of the general election that pits Democratic candidates against Republicans. While native white southerners (especially those of the professional and business classes in the rapidly growing urban and suburban centers of the region) fuel the growth in Republican voting even more than in-migrants, the contribution of in-migrants to the dynamism of southern politics remains an important factor.

In their landmark study, *The American Voter*, Angus Campbell et al. identified three kinds of political effects as potential consequences of population movement.[7] First, there was the impact on the political composition of the areas from which migrants leave and into which they come. Second, there was the impact on the migrant of the move itself, an impact that may in turn reflect other factors promoting political change (such as a dramatically improved financial status). And, third, there is the impact of the new environment on the migrant. Most research on in-migration and southern politics focused on the first effect of population movement, the impact on the political environment (particularly partisan voting patterns); this electoral impact emphasis on population movement is a useful initial step in the analysis of the implications of population movement. It is understandable as well in light of the political significance of evolving southern voting patterns.

However, much of the importance of in-migration for southern politics may lie in areas other than partisan voting patterns. For example, in-migrants within the ranks of political party activists in the region may play an important role in the development and direction of state party organizers. Samuel Patterson suggested such a possibility in early research identifying in-migrants as relatively important to the development of a viable Republican party organization in Oklahoma during the early 1960s.[8]

Although state party activists have received some attention by scholars, only relatively recently were data collected on a wide enough scale to examine systematically in-migrants as a party subgroup,[9] and the CSPAS data offers a particularly good opportunity for such analysis. This chapter seeks to contribute to our understanding of the political effects of population movement by describing and analyzing the impact of in-migrants on the traditional southern party system through examination of variations between in-migrants and native southerners; three areas are examined: background characteristics, ideology and issues, and party orientation and penetration. Three dimensions—region of childhood, race, and partisan identification—are examined.

A comparison of white in-migrants with white natives may be especially useful in assessing the impact of population movement; in other words, to what extent has the traditional southern party system (almost exclusively native whites) been altered by the in-migrants and their participation in state party organizations? Although the party system was influenced greatly by the reenfranchisement of native blacks[10] (and more mildly so by other factors), this analysis is limited to addressing the impact of *nonnative whites* moving into the system.

While blacks are not the central focus of the analysis, data on black Democrats are provided for the purpose of comparisons with the white groups. Blacks make up over 28 percent of the Democratic respondents, but almost all (90 percent) are native to the South, providing only a small number (approximately 75 respondents) of black in-migrants for purposes of analysis. Although data on in-migrant blacks are included, these data are more suggestive than conclusive. On the other hand, black Republicans are excluded altogether as only a little more than one percent of the Republican delegates participating in the survey are black (about 30 respondents, only five of whom are in-migrants), a number too small for reliable analysis.

For the purposes of the analysis that follows, all white respondents were divided into four groups based on their state or region of childhood and on their partisan identification. The two groups designated here as white migrants consist of those delegates whose childhoods were spent outside the South (the eleven states of the Confederacy). These two groups comprise 25 percent of the total number of white delegates. By party, about 18 percent of the white Democrats and about 34 percent of the white Republicans are nonnative to the region. Two additional groups, comprising the remaining 75 percent of the white respondents, are designated as white natives and also are divided by party. These delegates consist of those delegates who spent their childhoods in the South and now live in one of the six states under study. While these white southerners are not necessarily natives of the states where they now reside, they share a common regional heritage and a range of cultural experiences. In addition, they have in common the backgrounds, attitudes, and orientations developed from the traditional one-party politics dominant in the region. Finally, as noted above, two black Democratic groups (migrant blacks and native blacks) are included and are defined in the same way as the white groups.

BACKGROUND CHARACTERISTICS

State convention delegates were surveyed on seven background characteristics—age, sex, education, income, occupation, church attendance, and born-again status. (See Table 9.1.)

On these seven characteristics the Republican delegates were relatively consistent; migrants showed few differences with native whites. The largest and most striking variation occurred on age where the migrants were considerably older than native Republicans; only about an eighth were age 18–34 as compared with a quarter of the natives. Nearly half of the migrants were over age 55 as compared with fewer than a third of the natives. Migrants were somewhat better educated and more likely to hold professional occupations but earned lower family incomes than natives. This apparent anomaly likely is explained in part by the higher proportion of migrants listing education or teaching as their occupation (13 percent for migrants as compared with 8 percent for natives). Delegates who were migrants also were slightly more likely to be female than the native delegates.

Both Republican groups reported high levels of religiosity on the two religious

Table 9.1
Selected Background Characteristics (in percent)

| | Democrats | | | | Republicans | |
	White Migrant	White Native	Black Migrant	Black Native	White Migrant	White Native
Age						
18-34	23	24	16	23	12	24
35-54	51	48	50	49	42	46
55+	27	28	34	27	45	30
Totals	101	100	100	99*	99	100
(N=)	(356)	(1678)	(76)	(715)	(621)	(1218)
Gender						
Female	53	49	56	55	47	42
Male	48	52	44	45	53	58
Totals	101	101	101	100	100	100
(N=)	(356)	(1679)	(75)	(716)	(623)	(1219)
Education						
High school or less	8	19	22	18	11	16
Some college	19	27	14	23	29	29
College	19	17	21	20	26	26
Graduate training	55	37	43	39	34	29
Totals	101	100	100	100	100	100
(N=)	(352)	(1663)	(77)	(716)	(615)	(1210)
Income						
0-$14,999	7	8	19	22	8	8
$15,000-24,999	19	19	26	26	18	15
$25,000-34,999	26	23	17	22	21	18
$35,000-44,999	21	20	22	15	18	19
$45,000-59,999	12	15	7	10	16	17
$60,000+	14	15	8	5	19	23
Totals	99	100	99	100	100	100
(N=)	(337)	(1587)	(72)	(664)	(585)	(1148)
Occupation						
Professional (education)	51 (19)	40 (17)	53 (27)	51 (33)	37 (13)	32 (8)
Self-employed or business manage.	18	21	16	15	30	32
Housewife	7	7	7	3	16	14
Real estate, ins., retail sales	8	9	8	7	10	11
Skilled, semi-skilled	3	7	10	12	3	4
Public employee or official or non-profit	10	11	3	8	3	4
Student or unemployed	2	5	3	4	1	4
Totals	99	100	100	100	100	101
(N=)	(311)	(1531)	(62)	(651)	(561)	(1110)

Table 9.1 (continued)

| | Democrats | | | | Republicans | |
	White Migrant	White Native	Black Migrant	Black Native	White Migrant	White Native
Church Attendance						
Every week	29	36	57	56	51	47
Almost every week	18	21	24	23	14	20
Once or twice a month	14	12	11	12	9	12
A few times a year	22	23	7	8	20	17
Never	17	8	1	1	6	4
Totals	100	100	100	100	100	100
(N=)	(339)	(1639)	(74)	(696)	(613)	(1195)
Born-Again Experience?						
Yes	20	35	54	48	37	46
No	75	58	36	40	57	47
Don't know	5	7	10	12	6	7
Totals	100	100	100	100	100	100
(N=)	(339)	(1591)	(70)	(685)	(597)	(1162)

*Percentages may not total 100 because of rounding

dimensions. Overall, native whites were only slightly more regular in their church attendance than migrants (with over two-thirds of each group attending church every week or almost every week). Natives were more likely, however, to report a born-again religious experience than were the migrants (46 percent to 37 percent).

The Democratic groups showed a rather different pattern of variations. The white migrants generally fell in the same age groups as both native whites and native blacks. They were somewhat more likely to be female and substantially more likely to have postundergraduate educations and to hold noneducation professional occupations. Their incomes were similar to those of white natives. In these characteristics, migrant Democrats tend to look like prototypical young urban professionals (Yuppies).[11] The characterization is supported further by the two religious dimensions. White migrants were both much less regular in their church attendance and substantially less likely to have had a born-again experience. Both migrant and native black Democrats, however, exceed Republican percentages on both church attendance and born-again status.

The picture of white in-migrants that emerges is that, for both parties, they tended to be better educated and more likely to hold a professional occupation than native white southerners although their income levels tended to be somewhat lower. In addition, migrants for both parties, especially the Democratic party, tended to attend church less often and to be less likely to be born-again than native white Democrats.

Table 9.2
Ideological Position (in percent)*

Ideological Position	Democrats				Republicans	
	White Migrant	White Native	Black Migrant	Black Native	White Migrant	White Native
Extremely liberal	16	6	17	16	*	*
Liberal	37	28	49	49	2	1
Slightly liberal	21	20	16	14	1	1
Middle-of-the-road	14	22	4	12	4	3
Slightly conserv.	6	15	6	5	10	12
Conservative	4	9	6	3	66	65
Extremely conserv.	1	1	1	1	17	19
Totals	99	101	99	100	100	101
(N=)	(348)	(1608)	(69)	(687)	(597)	(1144)

*Less than 0.5 percent

IDEOLOGY AND ISSUE POSITIONS

As might be expected from recent research indicating an evolving ideological nationalization of southern party elites,[12] there were dramatic ideological and issue differences between activists in the two parties. Respondents were asked to place themselves on a standard seven-point ideological scale as well as to respond to a series of 21 contemporary political issues.

Ideology

The Republicans were concentrated in just two categories regardless of migrant or native status: nearly 85 percent of both groups responded that they were either "conservative" or "extremely conservative" (Table 9.2). Democrats, on the other hand, while not at all evenly distributed across the ideological spectrum, showed substantially more ideological heterogeneity. The Democratic party in the six states thus provides a larger ideological umbrella than does the Republican party. Within this context Democratic migrants identified themselves as more liberal than natives. About three-fourths of the migrants identified themselves as one of the three variations of "liberal" on the seven-point scale (compared with a little over half—54 percent—of the natives). Indeed, white migrant Democrats were nearly as liberal as black Democrats, whether migrant or native.

Clearly, the involvement of in-migrants and blacks in the state Democratic party conventions had the potential for liberalization of the state Democratic parties. The in-migrant impact within the Republican party was more limited, although the involvement of in-migrants reinforced the already strong conservatism of the Republican state convention delegates.

Issues

The delegates were asked to respond to a series of twenty-one issues falling into three categories: social issues (12 items), economic issues (4 items), and military/defense issues (5 items) (Table 9.3).

Essentially the same pattern emerges on issues as on ideological self-placement. On those issues readily amenable to a liberal-conservative continuum, the Democratic groups were consistently more liberal than the Republican groups, and the Republicans were far more homogeneous. Within the Republican party, differences between the two groups were small, often very small. The variation never exceeded more than 8 percentage points on any one issue. On 15 of the 21 issues it did not exceed 3 percentage points. The pattern reflects a striking consistency, regardless of the kind of issue addressed.

As with ideological self-placement, the differences among the Democratic groups were much more pronounced than among the Republicans. The percentage point differences between the white migrants and white natives equaled or exceeded 10 on just over half (11) of the 21 issues. These differences were particularly pronounced on the social issues. The percentage point distance between the two groups equaled or exceeded 20 on marijuana, prayers/Bible-reading in the public schools, affirmative action, handgun regulation, and food stamps. On only three social issues—nuclear power, increasing taxes for public education, and attitude toward conservative Christian organizations—was the percentage difference less than 10. On all of the social issue Democratic migrants held the liberal ground as compared with natives. On the other two groups of issues, differences were much less pronounced, the percentage point distances between migrants and natives being 10 or less on seven of the nine economic and military/defense items. On only one issue in these two categories—spending cuts to balance the budget—did the distance between the two groups approach 20 percent (47 percent of the migrants and 66 percent of the natives approving). Again, the migrants held the liberal ground, although more marginally so than on the social issues.

Black Democrats, while generally liberal on most issues, were notably the most conservative (even more so than the native white group) on several prominent social issues—marijuana, homosexual behavior, environmental protection, prayer in the public schools, and abortion. Differences between migrant blacks and native blacks were very small, exceeding 10 percentage points on only one issue (increasing taxes).

In summary, in-migrants represented a reenforcing conservative influence for the Republicans and a destabilizing liberal influence for the Democrats. Democratic in-migrants, together with native blacks, helped to move that party into the national Democratic mainstream and away from the traditional politics of the region as represented by native white Democrats.[13]

Table 9.3
Issue Positions of Party Delegates (in percent favorable)*

Issue	Democrats				Republicans	
	White Migrant	White Native	Black Migrant	Black Native	White Migrant	White Native
Social Issues						
ERA	89	79	96	97	17	14
Marijuana morally wrong	38	58	64	69	87	84
Homosexual behavior morally wrong	40	65	68	77	91	93
Environmental regulation excessive	16	29	35	31	74	74
Prayer, Bible-reading Amendment	21	42	52	60	79	84
Antiabortion Amendment	14	28	44	52	55	58
Affirmative Action	80	64	99	99	14	12
Handgun control	82	60	90	83	28	21
Nuclear power	17	23	15	12	83	83
Reduction in food stamps	32	61	34	36	95	94
Increase taxes for public educ.	85	82	91	90	23	27
Conservative Christian organizations	5	13	20	19	71	79
Economic Issues						
National health insurance	77	63	93	93	8	8
Spending cuts to balance budget	47	66	49	48	92	91
Tax increase to reduce deficit	60	55	49	36	17	16
Public works to reduce unemploy	62	56	82	72	6	6

Table 9.3 (continued)

| | Democrats | | | | Republicans | |
Issue	White Migrant	White Native	Black Migrant	Black Native	White Migrant	White Native
Military/Defense Issues						
Increase military in Middle East	7	11	8	8	48	55
Increase military in Latin America	9	16	10	10	75	79
More arms control negotiation	97	95	96	91	71	74
Nuclear freeze	94	92	95	92	47	46
Increase defense spending	10	19	10	6	91	92

*Responses of "strongly favor" and "favor" (or "strongly agree" and "agree") have been collapsed into a single favorable category; "undecided" responses have been dropped. Thus the table reports the distribution of opinion among those expressing an opinion. For complete wording of each questionnaire item, see Appendix.

PARTY PENETRATION AND ORIENTATION

In-migrants represent minorities in both parties. Therefore, their potential impact on the state parties and their organizations is dependent on the extent they are active in politics and their success in penetrating the party hierarchy.

Party Penetration

Questionnaire items on previous campaign activity and on current participation in party affairs help to assess the extent to which in-migrants have managed to penetrate party organizations (Tables 9.4 and 9.5). Among both Republicans and Democrats, in-migrants reported substantial previous campaign activity in local, state, and national campaigns. In all instances, however, their participation levels were somewhat lower than those for native whites. This is not surprising as many of these migrants may be relatively new to the region. Perhaps more important than previous campaign activity is the extent to which in-migrants succeeded in gaining current party positions. The data reported in Table 9.5 indicate that in-migrants for both parties succeeded in gaining party offices at rates very similar to other party groups.

The ambitions of in-migrants to hold party office also relate to the extent to which these migrants will be able to realize their potential effects on their respective parties (Table 9.6). In this respect it is clear that in-migrants in both parties were no less ambitious than other party activists. Among Democrats both

Table 9.4
Previous Election Campaign Activity: Delegates Reporting Themselves to Be "Very Active" or "Moderately Active" (in percent)

Type of Campaign	Democrats				Republicans	
	White Migrant	White Native	Black Migrant	Black Native	White Migrant	White Native
Local election	71	79	82	83	68	74
State election	64	75	73	72	64	74
National election	56	59	64	60	65	72

Table 9.5
Current Party Penetration of Delegates

Level of Party Penetration	Democrats				Republicans	
	White Migrant	White Native	Black Migrant	Black Native	White Migrant	White Native
Member of local party committee	54	54	62	54	69	68
Local party officer	26	27	17	23	37	39
State party officer	9	11	13	8	8	12
Delegate to nat'l convention	4	4	10	6	6	7

Table 9.6
Party Organizational Ambitions of Delegates: Delegates Indicating Positions They "Would Like to Hold" (in percent)

Position	Democrats				Republicans	
	White Migrant	White Native	Black Migrant	Black Native	White Migrant	White Native
Member of local party committee	24	21	12	20	16	16
Local party officer	26	23	20	26	14	18
State party officer	29	29	20	33	22	25
Delegate to nat'l convention	43	38	39	44	30	37

Table 9.7
Party History (in percent)

	Democrats				Republicans	
	White Migrant	White Native	Black Migrant	Black Native	White Migrant	White Native
Ever Switched Parties?						
Yes	27	13	5	4	24	34
No	73	87	95	96	76	66
Totals	100	100	100	100	100	100
(N=)	(349)	(1616)	(76)	(703)	(615)	(1197)
Reason for Party Switch?						
Better candidates	15	34	*	29	10	11
Right stand on issues	62	37	60	25	79	78
Friends, relatives, or coworkers	7	4	20	*	1	2
Greater opportunities for personal advancement	2	3	*	25	*	1
Superior organization	4	4	*	4	2	2
Other	10	18	20	17	8	7
Totals	100	100	100	100	100	101
(N=)	(93)	(203)	(5)	(24)	(147)	(393)

*Less than 0.5 percent

the migrant group and black natives were (marginally) the most ambitious in their desire to hold various party positions.

Party Orientation

Finally, each state convention delegate responded to a series of questions relating to personal party history and to orientations toward his party's proper role. We might expect that party switchers would be most numerous among Republican natives given the traditional Republican party weakness in the six states of this study. As Republican growth has occurred in recent years, some native whites might be expected to switch their partisan loyalties. Indeed, the data support this expectation (Table 9.7) as about a third (34 percent) of the Republican natives reported a switch in partisan loyalty. Republican in-migrants reported somewhat more constant party histories with a quarter indicating a party switch.

In somewhat similar fashion we might expect the party histories of Democratic native whites and Democratic blacks to be considerably more stable. Indeed they were. Very few blacks and a higher proportion of Democratic native whites (13 percent) reported a change in partisan identification. Among Democrats, the white migrants were most likely to indicate a party switch (27 percent). A possible explanation may lie in the fact that these in-migrants moved into states with dominant Democratic state party systems, party systems where the Republican parties are typically monolithic in conservative ideology.

Both Republican and Democratic switchers gave similar reasons for their switches when asked to select the motivation most responsible for their change in party identification (Table 9.7). Republicans were much more homogeneous; large majorities of the switchers (nearly 80 percent), regardless of migrant or native status, indicated the "right stand on the issues" constituted the reason for their change to Republican partisanship, a further confirmation of ideological concentration among the Republican delegates. For the Democrats, too, the issues response was quite often given, but particularly so by the migrant groups (62 percent for the white migrants). Native white Democratic switchers tended to be split between those who shifted because of issues and those who shifted because of "better candidates." Native black Democrats who switched political parties, however, almost equally divided their reasons among issues, candidates, and "greater opportunities for personal advancement."

The last series of questions investigated here relates to party orientation: the "amateur" or "purist" orientation versus the "professional" or "pragmatic" orientation of the state party delegates.[14] Essentially, those party activists characterized as "amateurs" or "purists" generally prefer issues and ideology to party or to electoral success. In recent years, an increasing consciousness of issues on the part of both the electorate and party activists was observed[15] with the resulting implication of diminished party loyalty and regularity. Those of a "professional" or "pragmatic" orientation, on the other hand, prefer winning elections to ideological purity.

Each delegate was asked to respond to a series of three party regularity issues: 1) the most important factor in selecting candidates for public office; 2) a dichotomous choice between issues and electability; and 3) the desirability of splitting ballots between candidates of the Democratic and Republican parties. In all of these, in-migrants with shorter party histories as opposed to natives might be expected to favor the purist position. This general tendency is borne out by the data (Table 9.8). On all three party regularity items, the migrants were generally less party oriented.

Among Democrats, white migrants were the most likely group to prefer issues to electability (although this orientation was strongly favored by all groups). They were the group most likely to say they would stop working for their political party if the party adopted an issue position they opposed. Moreover, they were the group most likely to endorse splitting ballots between the parties. White native Democrats demonstrated notably higher levels of party regularity, and both groups of black Democrats reported greater loyalty to the party than either white group. Inasmuch as blacks at both the mass and elite levels have almost exclusively identified with the Democratic party as the vehicle for black advancement, their greater appreciation for party loyalty and service should not

Table 9.8

Amateur-Purist Orientation Versus Professional-Pragmatic Orientation of Delegates (in percent)

Party Issue	Democrats				Republicans	
	White Migrant	White Native	Black Migrant	Black Native	White Migrant	White Native
Most important factor in selecting candidates for public office?						
Party loyalty and prior service	9	17	29	24	5	5
Positions on issues and ideology	84	75	60	64	85	86
Chance for electoral victory	5	5	3	5	8	7
No opinion, DK	2	3	8	7	2	2
Totals	100	100	100	100	100	100
(N=)	(339)	(1613)	(72)	(686)	(606)	(1190)
If I disagreed with a major stand of my party which was important to me, I would stop working for the party	26	14	12	5	28	22
It is more important to me that my party make a broad electoral appeal than for my party to take stands on issues that I personally agree with	60	70	71	78	61	62
No opinion, DK	14	16	18	18	11	16
Totals	100	100	101	101	100	100
(N=)	(334)	(1547)	(68)	(651)	(579)	(1116)
Party supporters justified in splitting ballots?						
Yes, national elections only	5	12	8	4	3	2
Yes, state/local elections only	11	8	12	7	28	31
Yes, both types of elections	32	21	19	14	30	24
No, never	43	52	52	64	29	34
No opinion, DK	9	7	8	11	10	9
Totals	100	100	99	100	100	100
(N=)	(339)	(1627)	(73)	(686)	(604)	(1189)

be surprising. White migrants, with their stronger histories of switching parties to find one more congenial on issues, reflected lower levels of abstract support for their political party. These findings should be interpreted cautiously as the issue items posed the purist-pragmatic conflict in abstract and theoretical terms. Actual *behavior* might well be different. Indeed, it may well be that the dichotomy is a spurious one in that delegates may see little conflict between ideology and party, a theme developed in other recent research on state party activists.[16]

Among Republicans, there were fewer differences on matters of party loyalty. About 85 percent of both migrants and natives valued ideological and issue congruence over electability. Migrants were, however, somewhat less supportive of party regularity on the other two party loyalty items.

CONCLUSION

The importance of party activists makes them a worthwhile subject for data gathering, study, and analysis. Their impact is evident in two ways. First, the activists provide the organizational infrastructure of the party; as Frank Sorauf has written,

It goes without saying that people are the parties' chief organization resource. But different people bring different expectations, goals, and skills to the party. To a considerable extent the goals and activities of a party organization reflect the men and women its incentives are able to recruit.[17]

Second, these activists also define the image the party presents to the public in its efforts to mobilize political support. Samuel Eldersveld has well summarized this function by observing that "The party, in one sense, is what it believes— its attitudes and perspectives, at all echelons. And what the party leaders believe may certainly determine in large part the image it communicates to the public, and the success with which it mobilizes public support."[18]

In qualitative terms, the Republican party at the state activist level has been less influenced by in-migrants than the Democratic party. In terms of background characteristics, ideology and issues, and party penetration and orientation, the Republicans showed remarkable homogeneity, considerably more than the Democrats. On the other hand, in quantitative terms, the Republican party in the six states clearly was more penetrated than the Democratic party by in-migrants. Over a third of all the Republican respondents were nonnative to the South. In short, the Republican in-migration effect essentially has been to confirm and to consolidate the existing character of southern Republicans.

The Democrats, on the other hand, appear more affected by in-migrants in qualitative terms. Migrants were generally better educated, less religious (and less likely to have had a born-again experience as well), and significantly more liberal, both in general philosophy and issue concerns. Like Republicans, the

Democratic migrants politically were at least as ambitious (in party position terms) as natives in their party. But, unlike the Republicans where native southerners were most likely to have switched party identification, the Democratic state party natives were considerably less likely to have changed their partisan affiliation. Indeed, the Democratic migrants were more likely as well to have adopted a philosophically "purist" stance when compared with the native group. Thus they may represent a somewhat less reliable group in terms of party regularity. However, these qualitative differences are diminished by a quantitative factor, the smaller number of in-migrants represented among the Democratic delegates surveyed (about 13 percent of the total number of Democrats, both blacks and whites).

Many of these characteristics associated with migrants to the South are not necessarily unique to the region; other research has indicated that youth, higher levels of education, and more liberal attitudes (at least for the Democrats) characterized in-migrants generally among state party elites.[19]

Finally, it would appear that the impact of population movement varies, not only with the type of political activity measured, but with party as well. For the Republicans, the impact is largely quantitative; for the Democrats, the impact is in large degree qualitative.

NOTES

1. For a summary of these trends in South Carolina, for example, see Laurence W. Moreland, Robert P. Steed, and Tod A. Baker, "Regionalism in South Carolina Politics," in L. F. Carter and D. S. Mann, *Government in the Palmetto State* (Columbia: Bureau of Government Research, University of South Carolina, 1983), 5–12.

2. A large literature addresses the changes that have taken place in the southern political system over the past three and a half decades. See the citations in n. 8 of chap. 1 of this volume.

3. The 1980 percentage of persons not resident in the state five years earlier is as follows for each of the states in this study: Arkansas, 13.0 percent; Louisiana, 9.5 percent; Mississippi, 9.9 percent; North Carolina, 10.6 percent; South Carolina, 12.4 percent; and Texas, 13.6 percent. Calculated from Bureau of the Census, Department of Commerce, *1980 Census of Population: General Social and Economic Characteristics* (Table 61, vols. 5, 20, 26, 35, 42, and 45).

4. Raymond Wolfinger and Robert B. Arseneau, "Partisan Change in the South, 1952–1976," in *Political Parties: Development and Decay*, ed. Louis Maisel and Joseph Cooper (Beverly Hills: Sage Publications, 1978), 179–210.

5. See, for example, Eui-Hang Shin, "Effects of Migration on the Education Levels of the Black Resident Population at the Origin and Destination, 1955–1960 and 1965–1970," *Demography* 15 (February 1978): 41–56; William R. Schriver, "The Industrialization of the Southeast since 1950: Some Causes of Manufacturing Relocation, with Speculation about Its Effects," *American Journal of Economics and Sociology* 30 (January 1971): 47–69; L. H. Long, "How the Racial Composition of Cities Changes," *Land Economics* 60 (1975): 258–267; and Jeanne C. Bigger and Francis C. Biasiolli, "Met-

ropolitan Deconcentration: Subareal In-Migration and Central City to Ring Mobility Patterns among Southern SMSAs," *Demography* 15 (November 1978): 589–603.

6. See, for example, Philip E. Converse, "On the Possibility of Major Political Realignment in the South," in Angus Campbell et al., *Elections and the Political Order* (New York: John Wiley and Sons, 1966), chap. 12; John C. Topping, Jr., John R. Lazarek, and William H. Linder, *Southern Republicanism and the New South* (Cambridge, Mass.: 1966, n.p.); William Lyons and Robert F. Durant, "Assessing the Impact of Immigration on a State Political System," *Social Science Quarterly* 61 (December 1980): 473–484; Bruce A. Campbell, "Patterns of Change in the Partisan Loyalties of Native Southerners: 1952–1972," *Journal of Politics* 39 (August 1977): 730–761; and Susan Welch and Buster Brown, "Correlates of Southern Republican Success at the Congressional District Level," *Social Science Quarterly* 59 (March 1979): 732–742.

For a more detailed review of this literature, see Robert P. Steed, Tod A. Baker, and Laurence W. Moreland, "In-Migration and Southern State Party Elites," paper presented at the 1981 annual meeting of the Southern Political Science Association, 5–7 November 1981, Memphis, Tennessee, 1–5.

7. Angus Campbell, Philip E. Converse, Warren E. Miller, and Donald E. Stokes, *The American Voter* (New York: John Wiley and Sons, abridged ed., 1964), 232–233.

8. Samuel C. Patterson, "Characteristics of Party Leaders," *Western Political Quarterly* 16 (June 1963): 332–353.

9. For an earlier effort at large-scale data collection on party activists (delegates to state party conventions in 11 states, three of which were in the South), see the various analyses in Ronald Rapoport, Alan I. Abramowitz, and John McGlennon, eds., *The Life of the Parties: Activists in Presidential Politics* (Lexington, KY: University of Kentucky Press, 1986), especially Laurence W. Moreland, Robert P. Steed, and Tod A. Baker, "Migration and Activist Politics," 126–141.

10. See, for example, Laurence W. Moreland, Robert P. Steed, and Tod A. Baker, eds., *Blacks in Southern Politics* (New York: Praeger, 1987).

11. See, for example, the discussion of "new class Democrats" among Democratic party activists in Connecticut in James M. Carlson and Barbara Burrell, "A New Cleavage in the Democratic Party? A Comparison of Mondale and Hart Supporters at the Connecticut State Democratic Convention," *Polity* 20 (Fall 1987): 101–113.

12. See, for example, Laurence W. Moreland, "Ideological and Issue Orientations among South Carolina Party Activists at the 1984 State Party Conventions" (paper presented at the 1985 annual meeting of the South Carolina Political Science Association, Clinton, South Carolina, 13 April 1985).

13. James L. Sundquist, *Dynamics of the Party System: Alignment and Dealignment of Political Parties in the United States* (Washington, D.C.: Brookings Institution, rev. ed., 1983), 352–375.

14. See, for example, Thomas H. Roback, "Amateurs and Professionals: Delegates to the 1972 Republican National Convention," *Journal of Politics* 37 (1975): 436–467; E. G. DeFelice, "Separating Professionalism from Pragmatism: A Research Note on the Study of Political Parties," *American Journal of Political Science* 25 (1981): 796–807; and R. A. Hitlin and J. S. Jackson III, "On Amateur and Professional Politicians," *Journal of Politics* 39 (1977): 786–793.

15. See, for example, J. S. Jackson III, J. C. Brown, and B. L. Brown, "Recruitment, Representation, and Political Values: The 1976 Democratic National Convention Delegates," *American Politics Quarterly* 6 (1978): 187–212; Jeane Kirkpatrick, *The New*

Presidential Elite (New York: Russell Sage Foundation and Twentieth Century Fund, 1976); Roback, "Amateurs and Professionals"; and James W. Soule and Wilma E. McGrath, "A Comparative Study of Presidential Nomination Conventions: The Democrats of 1968 and 1972," *American Journal of Political Science* 19 (1975): 501–517.

16. See, for example, Alan I. Abramowitz, John McGlennon, and Ronald B. Rapoport, "The Party Isn't Over: Incentives for Activism in the 1980 Presidential Nominating Campaign," *Journal of Politics* 45 (November 1983): 1006–1015; and Walter J. Stone and Alan I. Abramowitz, "Winning May Not Be Everything, But It's More Than We Thought: Presidential Party Activists in 1980," *American Political Science Review* 77 (1983): 945–956.

17. Frank J. Sorauf, *Party Politics in America* (Boston: Little, Brown, 3d ed., 1976), 102.

18. Samuel J. Eldersveld, *Political Parties: A Behavioral Analysis* (Chicago: Rand McNally, 1964), 180–181.

19. See Moreland et al., "Migration and Activist Politics," 126–141.

Part IV
Party Systems in Transition

10

Realignment among Southern Political Party Activists

Charles Prysby

The transformation that has occurred in the South is not a classic critical realignment, marked by a sudden, rapid, fundamental, and durable transformation of partisan loyalties.[1] Instead, it bears more similarity to what Key referred to as a secular realignment.[2] Change has occurred more gradually and far less thoroughly. Moreover, the partisan shifts have involved dealignment as much as realignment.[3] But the cumulative impact of these shifts has produced a southern electorate that is substantially less loyal to the Democratic party and correspondingly more favorable to the Republican party.

Two basic sources of increased Republican support can be identified. First, switches in party identification and/or voting behavior among existing voters have more frequently been from the Democrats to the Republicans, rather than in the opposite direction. Second, Republicans have been able to capture the support of a substantial proportion of new members of the southern electorate, including both those reaching voting age and those moving into the region from outside. This support for the Republican party among additions to the southern electorate is especially significant when contrasted with the preferences of those leaving the electorate.[4]

These two sources not only describe where the increases in Republican votes have come from; they also suggest potential sources for new Republican activists. This chapter is concerned with one of these sources—state convention delegates who have switched party loyalties. Furthermore, switchers in both directions are analyzed; while there may be more movement from the Democratic to the Republican party, there is Republican to Democratic party movement as well. Of course, not all individuals who switch their partisan identification become active in their new party, any more than all individuals who have remained loyal to their party are actively involved. But among the activists, party switchers may be a substantial group.

The basic theoretical question is whether activists who switched their party affiliation at some point in the past should be different from activists who maintained the same party affiliation. To answer this question, one must first consider why individuals, especially those who are likely to be active in political party organizations, would switch their party identification. The basic hypothesis put forth here is that such switching is a result of individuals feeling that they would be ideologically more at home in the other party.[5] These feelings of ideological compatibility could be based on a wide range of issues, or they could be based on a single issue area that is highly salient to the individual. There are, of course, other reasons why individuals may switch their partisan affiliation, including beliefs that one party is superior to the other in managing the economy or handling foreign affairs.[6] However, party activists represent a segment of the electorate that is well above average in political interest, knowledge, and sophistication, so we would expect them to place more weight on issues of public policy as a basis for their partisan identification.

We also may expect activists who switched political parties to be more ideological or purist in their orientation than activists who have not switched parties. The distinction here is between "amateur" or "purist" and "professional" or "pragmatic" styles of participation.[7] This distinction is best conceptualized as a continuum on which "purist" and "pragmatist" are ideal-type end points. Purists are motivated by issues. They place more emphasis on ideological purity than on electoral success when it comes to such matters as candidate selection, perhaps even to the point of preferring an electoral loss over an abandonment of position. While pragmatists have preferences when it comes to issues, they readily compromise on these matters for the good of the party and candidate electability. This purist-pragmatist dimension is an important one in the research on party activists. One of the controversies in the recent literature is whether the parties have become dominated by purists and therefore are not willing to make significant ideological compromises for the sake of electoral success.[8] While this question is difficult to answer in the abstract, there is good reason to believe that switchers are likely to be purists. If they have switched parties for ideological reasons, this suggests that they place considerable emphasis on this factor.

If the above expectations are correct, they indicate that the realignment process in the South has been occurring on two levels: the level of the voter and the level of the party activist. At the level of the voter, the realignment of party loyalties has produced, and perhaps continues to produce, an electorate in which partisanship is more closely tied to issue positions than in the past. At the party activist level, realignment alters the character of the party organizations by bringing in new activists, who are drawn to the party on the basis of ideology and are concerned that the party maintain certain issue positions. The result of this, unless counterbalanced by other changes, would be to keep the two parties ideologically distinct.

STUDYING SOUTHERN PARTY ACTIVISTS

For this analysis, the activists are divided into two basic types: switchers and loyalists. Switchers are those who reported identifying with a different party at some point in the past. Loyalists are those who have maintained the same partisan affiliation throughout their lives. It should be noted that although the loyalists have not switched their partisan attachment, they could have changed their party identification in more subtle ways, such as moving from being a strong partisan to being a weak partisan. The analysis concentrates on analyzing Democratic and Republican loyalists. This is the soundest approach, given our data. If we find that these two groups of switchers differ from each other or from their loyalist counterparts, these differences should be reflective of real differences among activists. In other words, these data should be adequate because our purpose is to determine basic differences among Democratic and Republican switchers and loyalists, rather than to estimate population parameters.

COMPARING SWITCHERS AND LOYALISTS

As expected, Republican activists are much more likely to be switchers than are Democratic activists. Perhaps more surprising is the fact that a significant minority of white Democratic activists are switchers. Table 10.1 presents the relevant data by state. As we can see, the proportion of Republican activists who are switchers ranges from 24 percent in South Carolina to 41 percent in Texas. Among white Democrats, the figures are lower but still substantial, with the proportion of activists who are switchers ranging from a low of 10 percent to a high of 21 percent across the states. Black Democratic activists, on the other hand, are almost entirely loyalists; switchers represent far less than 10 percent of this group in all but two states, and in these two the number of black activists is so small that the percentages cannot be considered reliable.

Table 10.1 presents the data by state in order to show the variation across states; the remainder of the analysis deals with the activist and loyalist groups as a whole, but note will be made of instances where the aggregate patterns do not reflect the within-state patterns. In the analysis that follows, Republican and Democratic switchers are activists who at some point in the past identified with the opposite party, respectively. Loyalists are those who have never switched their party loyalty.

One important fact to realize about the Republican switchers is that most changed their party affiliation before President Jimmy Carter's election in 1976. Democratic activists display a different pattern, however. The relevant data are in Table 10.2, and the comparisons are striking. Almost one-half of the Repub-

Table 10.1
Party Switchers by Race and State (in percent)*

State	Democratic Activists White	Black	Republican Activists
Arkansas	9.6 (292)	10.0 (20)	30.2 (242)
Louisiana	12.0 (234)	2.2 (90)	------
Mississippi	21.2 (241)	4.4 (225)	38.0 (200)
North Carolina	14.7 (648)	3.0 (198)	35.8 (316)
South Carolina	17.4 (299)	6.2 (193)	23.8 (728)
Texas	19.5 (261)	3.8 (53)	41.0 (427)

*N's are in parentheses

Table 10.2
Year of Party Switch for Democratic and Republican Switchers (in percent)

Year	Democratic Switchers	Republican Switchers
Before 1968	23.4	47.0
1968-1975	26.8	22.2
1976-1979	16.7	14.6
1980-1984	33.1	16.2
	100.0	100.0
(N=)	(269)	(549)

lican switchers changed parties before Nixon's election in 1968, whereas only about one-fourth of the Democratic switchers fall into this category. And while only about one-sixth of the Republican switchers changed parties during the 1980s, one-third of the Democratic activists did so. Of course, the fact that Democratic switchers are disproportionately recent converts does not mean that most of the recent converts are Democrats. The total number of Republicans who are recent converts may be larger than the Democratic total because of the total number of Republican switchers. This question cannot be fully answered because these data are inadequate for the task of estimating population totals. Fortunately, the important point for our purpose is that the distribution of Democratic and Republican switchers is different.

The differences displayed in Table 10.2 are understandable if we refer to the basic working hypothesis that switchers moved to their new party in order to achieve greater ideological compatibility. During the 1960s and early 1970s, the movement in the South would have been very heavily from the Democrats to

Table 10.3
Issue Scale Scores by Party and Switcher Status*

Scale	Democrats		Republicans	
	Loyalists	Switchers	Loyalists	Switchers
Social Welfare	2.71	2.85	4.25	4.16
Tax Increase	2.56	2.59	3.81	3.72
Affirmative Action	2.18	2.50	3.93	3.87
Social-Moral	2.39	2.16	3.76	3.79
Environment	2.34	2.31	3.42	3.44
Foreign Affairs	1.92	2.04	3.63	3.59
Liberal-Conservative	3.05	3.33	5.92	5.85

*Entries are mean scores on the scales. A higher score represents a more
conservative position. The first six items are five-point scales. The
final item is a seven-point scale. See the Appendix at the end of this
chapter for details on these items.

the Republicans because of conservative Democratic dissatisfaction with the
liberal direction of the national Democratic party, especially as manifested in
the presidential nomination of Senators Hubert Humphrey and George Mc-
Govern. With Carter as the Democratic nominee in 1976 and 1980, the party
had a less liberal appearance than in the previous elections, although Walter
Mondale's nomination in 1984 might have reversed some of this. Additionally,
by the late 1970s two issues that had been extremely polarizing, Vietnam and
civil rights, were less important. Thus it seems logical that Republican switchers
would be less likely to be post–1975 switchers.

For Democratic switchers, the opposite arguments apply. In the last ten years
the Republican party has moved to the right, a shift marked not only by the
nomination and election of Ronald Reagan but also by the rise of numerous
"new right" organizations and individuals. This latter phenomenon has been
particularly important within southern Republican parties, as we have seen the
growing prominence of individuals such as Senator Jesse Helms. This rightward
shift on the part of the Republican party, coupled with the above shifts in the
Democrats, means that moderate Republicans should have been more likely to
switch to the Democratic party in the 1980s than in earlier periods.

The hypothesis that switchers changed parties because of ideological considerations is supported by the data in Table 10.3. Mean scores for Democratic and
Republican loyalists and switchers are presented for six issue areas. For five of
these areas (social welfare, tax increases, social-moral, environmental, and foreign affairs), an index was formed from two or more specific items. Details on
these indices are in the appendix. Only one usable civil rights item, a question
about affirmative action, was available, so this single item is used to measure

Table 10.4
Orientation Toward Party by Party and Switcher Status (in percent)

Party Orientation	Democrats		Republicans	
	Loyalists	Switchers	Loyalists	Switchers
Highly Purist	10.6	27.1	21.3	27.0
Somewhat Purist	13.2	16.6	13.0	14.0
Somewhat Pragmatic	54.6	48.1	54.7	48.8
Highly Pragmatic	21.6	8.3	10.9	10.2
	100.0	100.0	100.0	100.0
(N=)	(2155)	(314)	(1135)	(529)

this issue area. In addition to these six measures of issue orientations, mean scores for respondent self-placements on a seven-point liberal-conservative scale are presented. For all seven measures, a similar pattern exists. Democratic switchers and loyalists are very similar, as are Republican switchers and loyalists, and both Democratic groups are far more liberal than both Republican groups. An inspection of the patterns within each state yields the same results in all but one case, adding to the confirmation of the basic hypothesis. The exception exists among Mississippi Democrats, where the loyalists are considerably more liberal than the switchers, but even here the switchers are still ideologically closer to the loyalists than they are to the Republican groups.

There is an alternative interpretation for the above results. Since we do not have data for these individuals before they switched parties, we cannot prove that the ideological positions preceded the change in partisan affiliation. It is possible that the individuals switched parties for other reasons, and then acquired issue orientations that would make them compatible with their new party. While we cannot disprove this empirically, it seems doubtful that this would be the dominant direction of causality, although some of this might occur.

In addition to examining the issue orientations and ideological placement of switchers and loyalists, the emphasis that they place on issue positions also is analyzed. In particular, we are interested in determining whether switchers are more purist in their orientations, as we hypothesized earlier. In order to measure the purist/pragmatist dimension of party orientation, an index was formed from two items (see the appendix for details), and respondents were placed into four categories, from highly purist to highly pragmatic. Table 10.4 presents data on party orientations, and the result is a partial confirmation of our expectations. Among Democrats, it clearly is the case that the switchers are more likely than the loyalists to hold purist views. Among Republicans, the difference between loyalists and switchers is small, but what difference does exist is consistent with our expectations. Actually, the Republican switchers are about as purist in orientation as the Democratic switchers; the difference is that the Republican loy-

Table 10.5
Perceptions of Candidates and Parties by Party and Switcher Status*

Ideological Placement of:	Democrats		Republicans	
	Loyalists	Switchers	Loyalists	Switchers
Reagan	6.23	6.24	5.97	5.96
Hart	3.18	3.01	1.74	1.64
Mondale	2.69	2.64	1.36	1.34
Jackson	1.98	1.85	1.28	1.23
National Dem. Party	3.02	2.91	1.55	1.50
State Dem. Party	3.76	3.97	2.31	2.19
National Rep. Party	5.95	5.65	5.57	5.59
State Rep. Party	6.18	6.07	5.90	5.86

*Entries are mean scores for respondent placements of the candidates and parties on a seven-point liberal-conservative scale. A higher score indicates a more conservative placement.

alists are significantly more purist than the Democratic loyalists. Again, examining the patterns within each state yields the same pattern in almost every case. The only deviation is among South Carolina Republicans, where the switchers are slightly less purist than the loyalists.

The analysis to this point has shown that switchers are highly similar to their loyalist counterparts in issue positions and are more purist in orientation than loyalists, although only slightly more so for Republicans. All this is consistent with our original expectations. A third element needs to be introduced into the analysis, however. We need to look at how switchers perceive the parties. If switchers have changed parties to achieve ideological compatibility, then this movement depends not only on how the switchers define themselves but also on how they perceive the two parties.

The perceptions activists hold of the parties are examined by using a set of items that asked delegates to place candidates and parties on the seven-point liberal-conservative scale. Since the delegates also placed themselves on the scale, we can analyze both their perceptions of the parties and their ideological distance from each party. Placements of four candidates, Reagan plus the top three Democratic presidential contenders, were used. Also, placements of both national and state parties were obtained, on the grounds that southern party activists might distinguish between national and state parties.[9] The relevant data are in Table 10.5.

Two patterns are clear in Table 10.5. First, within each party the switchers are very similar to the loyalists in their placements of the parties and candidates. Second, Democrats and Republicans do not see things the same way. This is especially true when it comes to the Democratic candidates and parties. Repub-

Table 10.6
Ideological Difference Scores by Party and Switcher Status*

| Ideological | Democrats | | Republicans | |
Difference with:	Loyalists	Switchers	Loyalists	Switchers
National Dem. Party	-.01	.38	4.39	4.36
State Dem. Party	-.75	-.70	3.64	3.66
National Rep. Party	-2.93	-2.37	.38	.28
State Rep. Party	-3.17	-2.79	.06	.02

*Entries are mean difference scores which are computed by taking the dif-
ference between the respondent's placement of the party on the seven-point
liberal-conservative scale and the respondent's own placement on that scale.
A positive score indicates that the respondent considers himself more conservative; a negative score indicates the opposite.

licans place them far to the left, whereas Democrats frequently have more moderate perceptions. Differences in the perceptions of Republican candidates and
parties are much smaller, by contrast. This reinforces the belief that Republican
switchers are motivated by ideological considerations. Not only are Republican
switchers quite conservative on average; they also tend to see the Democrats as
far to the left. This suggests that the ideological distance is enormous.

A measure of the ideological distance that activists perceive between themselves and the respective political parties can be obtained by combining self-
placements on the liberal-conservative scale with placements of the parties. By
taking the difference between where an activist places himself on the scale and
where he places a given party, we obtain a simple numerical score, which can
be anywhere from +6.0 to -6.0, where a score of zero indicates no difference
and a positive score indicates the respondent is more conservative. These ideological distance scores were calculated for the national and state Democratic
and Republican parties. The mean scores for switchers and loyalists are presented
in Table 10.6. Only the four items dealing with the political parties are used
because we are primarily interested in more general perceptions that transcend
particular candidates.

The patterns in Table 10.6 are as expected. Democratic loyalists and switchers
are, on average, ideologically close to the national and the state Democratic
parties. Interestingly, they see themselves as closer to the national party than to
their state party. The ideological distances between Democratic activists and the
Republican parties are substantial, as we would predict. The Republican patterns
are quite comparable. There is one important difference, however. Republican
activists perceive an even greater distance between themselves and the opposite
party than was the case for Democrats. These overall patterns are repeated within
each state as well. Thus Republican and Democratic switchers clearly are ide-

Table 10.7
Ideological Placement by Year of Switch for Democratic and Republican Switchers*

Year of Switch	Democratic Switchers	Republican Switchers
Before 1968	2.65 (60)**	5.90 (241)
1968-1975	3.07 (70)	5.78 (116)
1976-1979	3.42 (45)	5.85 (75)
1980-1984	3.78 (88)	5.70 (83)

*Entries are mean scores on the seven-point liberal-conservative scale. For example, the 60 Democratic switchers who changed parties before 1968 have a mean scale score of 2.65. A higher score indicates a more conservative position.

**N's are in parentheses

ologically at home in their new parties when it comes to their own view of the situation. A close inspection of the data suggests that Republican switchers are even more displeased with the ideological character of the national rather than the state Democratic party. Democratic switchers, however, display more dissatisfaction with the state Republican party than with the national Republicans.

Previously we noted differences between Democratic and Republican switchers in the year when the switch occurred. If we look at the ideological self-placement of switchers broken down by period of switch, an interesting pattern emerges (see Table 10.7). While Republican switchers display a similar level of conservatism regardless of when they changed parties, Democratic switchers differ greatly. The recent switchers are considerably less liberal than the earlier switchers. During the 1980s, a significant number of individuals with fairly moderate positions, at least as measured by their ideological categorization, left the Republican party and became Democratic activists. Very little of this occurred in earlier periods; switchers then tended to be more liberal.

While recent Democratic switchers are more moderate in ideological orientation, they are not more pragmatic when it comes to party orientation. In fact, the opposite is the case, as we can see from the data in Table 10.8. More recent Democratic switchers are somewhat more purist. The same pattern is evident among the Republicans. Two explanations for this relationship can be suggested. First, individuals may tend to display a more purist orientation right after switching parties, then become more pragmatic as time passes. Second, those who changed parties in the 1980s may be especially concerned about issues. If the second explanation is correct, and if this pattern continues, the result will be an overall increase in purists within both parties.

Table 10.8

Party Orientation by Year of Switch for Democratic and Republican Switchers*

Year of Switch	Democratic Switchers		Republican Switchers	
Before 1968	2.53	(55)	2.50	(226)
1968–1975	2.55	(64)	2.50	(103)
1976–1979	2.26	(38)	2.36	(72)
1980–1984	2.15	(84)	2.30	(82)

*Entries are mean scores on a four-point party orientation scale. N's are in parentheses. For example, the 55 Democratic switchers who changed parties before 1968 have a mean scale score of 2.53. A higher score indicates a more pragmatic party orientation. See the Appendix at the end of this chapter for details on this item.

DEMOGRAPHIC AND SOCIAL CHARACTERISTICS

Additional insight into the implications of partisan switching for the party organizations may be derived from an analysis of the demographic and social characteristics of loyalists and switchers. As we would expect, Democratic loyalists are more likely than Democratic switchers to be native southerners, but the opposite is true for Republicans, as shown in Table 10.9. This follows logically from the disproportionate number of Republican migrants from outside the region, especially those of higher socioeconomic status, who are more likely to become actively involved in party organizations. It also is no surprise to learn that almost 90 percent of the Democratic switchers are white. The data on age are surprising, however. Democratic loyalists and switchers are very similar to each other and considerably younger than the Republican activists. And among Republican activists, the switchers tend to be older than the loyalists. This does fit with our earlier finding that most Republican switchers had changed parties before the 1976 election. Apparently, southern Republican parties were able to actively involve an older group of switchers, who tend to change parties in the 1960s or early 1970s, but they have been relatively unsuccessful in recruiting younger activists. Whatever success Republican candidates may have had in winning the support of younger voters, the Democratic party organizations seem to be the clear winners when it comes to capturing younger activists.

On the whole, differences in socioeconomic status among loyalists and switchers of both parties are not very great. Given the types of people who become active in party organizations, it is not surprising that party activists are not sharply divided along SES lines. The one interesting point is that Democratic switchers stand out as being higher in educational attainment than the other groups. Further inspection of the data indicates that many of these are younger individuals who switched parties more recently, which fits with earlier findings.

With respect to religious characteristics, not only are Republican activists

Table 10.9
Social Characteristics by Party and Switcher Status (in percent)

	Democrats		Republicans	
	Loyalists	Switchers	Loyalists	Switchers
Demographic Characteristics				
Region: native southerners	90.5	75.4	69.5	81.9
Age: under 40	41.2	42.7	33.1	21.6
Race: white	67.3	87.9	98.4	94.7
Socio-Economic Characteristics				
Education: college graduate	56.8	70.6	57.6	55.5
Income: over $35,000	43.1	50.3	55.3	59.8
Religious Characteristics				
Affiliation: Protestant	84.2	82.6	91.4	88.9
Church Attendance: attend every week	40.8	36.6	48.7	50.2
Fundamentalism: "born again"	37.3	32.2	43.6	40.4

more likely to be Protestants, as we certainly would expect, but they are significantly more likely to be more religious. Religious tendencies are measured by two variables: frequency of church attendance and whether the respondent described himself as "born again." Of course, fundamentalism would be somewhat higher among Republican activists simply because they are more likely to be Protestants, but even if we consider only Protestant activists, Republicans are more likely to express a fundamental orientation. While the Democratic and Republican activists differ from each other, within each partisan camp the differences between loyalists and switchers are minimal. It is not true, as might have been hypothesized, that Republican switchers are disproportionately fundamentalists, at least not as compared to Republican activists.

CONCLUSION

The above findings have two important implications for the party organizations. First, the addition of partisan switchers to the Democratic and Republican organizations has served to maintain the ideological distance between the parties.

Activists who are switchers are not positioned between the two parties. They are ideologically quite at home, both objectively and subjectively, in their new party. The same is true for their basic social characteristics, such as socioeconomic status or religious tendencies. Moreover, they are at least as purist, if not more so, than the loyalists within the party. This suggests that the switchers help to maintain existing party differences, not weaken them.

Second, it is clear that activist switchers are found in both parties. While Republican activists are twice as likely to be switchers as are Democratic activists, there is still a considerable number of Democratic switchers. More significantly, a relatively large number of Democratic activists have switched parties during the post–civil rights period of southern politics. This group of activists is somewhat more purist, less liberal, younger, and better educated than other Democratic activists. Like other switchers, these recent Democratic activist switchers appear to have changed parties to achieve greater ideological compatibility. At the level of the party organization, there has been a true realignment, with movement in both directions.

APPENDIX

Much of the analysis in this chapter relies on indices formed by combining individual items into summary measures of attitudes or orientations, and these indices are described below. For each index, the intercorrelations among the index components were ascertained, and the indices were constructed only from items that were sufficiently interrelated to suggest that an underlying dimension was present.

1. *Party Orientation.* This index is a measure of the respondent's orientation along a pragmatist/purist dimension. The index was formed by combining two items: one asked respondents whether they would work for the candidate of their party if they disagreed with the candidate on issues, and the other asked whether candidates should be selected on the basis of issue positions or on the basis of electability or commitment to the party. Respondents were categorized as: Highly purist, somewhat purist, somewhat pragmatic, and highly pragmatic.

2. *Social Welfare.* This index measures the respondent's orientation on social welfare issues. It is formed by taking the mean score on three items, each measured on a 5–point scale (strongly agree to strongly disagree): (a) whether there should be reductions in the number of people receiving food stamps; (b) whether there should be public works programs to reduce unemployment: and (c) whether there should be national health insurance. The index runs from 1.0 to 5.0, with a low score indicating a more liberal orientation.

3. *Tax Increase.* This index measures the respondent's support for tax increases. It is formed by taking the mean score on two items, each measured on a 5–point scale (strongly agree to strongly disagree): (a) whether an across-the-board tax increase was needed to reduce the deficit; and (b) whether a broadly based tax with the revenues earmarked for education was desirable. The index runs from 1.0 to 5.0, with a low score indicating support for increased taxes.

4. *Social-Moral.* This index measures the respondent's orientation on social and moral issues. It is formed by taking the mean score on three items, each measured on a 5–point scale (strongly agree to strongly disagree): (a) whether the ERA is desirable; (b) whether school prayer should be permitted; and (c) whether legalized abortion should be permitted. The index runs from 1.0 to 5.0, with a low score indicating a more liberal position.

5. *Environment.* This index measures the respondent's orientation on environmental issues. It is formed by taking the mean score on three items, each measured on a 5–point scale (strongly agree to strongly disagree): (a) whether governmental regulations on business to protect the environment were excessive; (b) whether government action to increase energy sources was needed even if it decreased protection of the environment; and (c) whether there should be a more rapid development of nuclear power. The index runs from 1.0 to 5.0, with a low score indicating a more liberal position.

6. *Foreign Affairs.* This index measures the respondent's orientation on foreign and defense matters. It is formed by taking the mean score on three items, each measured on a 5–point scale (strongly agree to strongly disagree): (1) whether defense spending should be increased; (2) whether U.S. military presence in Latin America should be increased; and (3) whether there should be a nuclear freeze. the index runs from 1.0 to 5.0, with a low score indicating a more liberal position.

NOTES

1. For a discussion of realignment see James L. Sundquist, *Dynamics of the Party System: Alignment and Realignment of Political Parties in the United States,* revised edition (Washington, D.C.: Brookings Institution, 1983).

2. V. O. Key, Jr., "Secular Realignment and the Party System," *Journal of Politics* 21 (1959): 198–210.

3. Paul Allen Beck, "Partisan Dealignment in the Postwar South," *American Political Science Review* 71 (1977): 477–496.

4. Beck, "Partisan Dealignment;" Bruce A. Campbell, "Patterns of Change in the Partisan Loyalties of Native Southerners, 1952–1972" *Journal of Politics* 39 (1977): 730–761.

5. Mary Grisez Kweit, "Ideological Congruence of Party Switchers and Nonswitchers: The Case of Party Activists," *American Journal of Political Science* 30 (1986): 184–196; Charles D. Hadley and Susan E. Howell, "The Southern Split Ticket Voter, 1952–1976: Republican Conversion or Democratic Decline?" in Robert P. Steed, Laurence W. Moreland, and Tod A. Baker, eds., *Party Politics in the South* (New York: Praeger, 1980).

6. Morris P. Fiorina, *Retrospective Voting in American National Elections* (New Haven, Conn.: Yale University Press, 1981).

7. James Q. Wilson, *The Amateur Democrat* (Chicago: University of Chicago Press, 1962); Aaron Wildavsky, "The Goldwater Phenomenon: Purists, Politicians, and the Two-Party System," *Review of Politics* 17 (1965): 386–413; Thomas H. Roback, "Amateurs and Professionals: Delegates to the 1972 Republican National Convention," *Journal of Politics* 37 (1975): 436–438; John W. Soule and James W. Clark, "Amateurs and Professionals: A Study of Delegates to the 1968 Democratic National Convention," *American Political Science Review* 64 (1970): 888–898.

8. Jeane Kirkpatrick, *The New Presidential Elite: Men and Women in National Politics* (New York: Russell Sage Foundation, 1976); Walter J. Stone and Alan I. Abramowitz,

"Winning May Not Be Everything, But It's More than We Thought: Presidential Party Activists in 1980," *American Political Science Review* 77 (1983): 945–956; Alan I. Abramowitz and Walter J. Stone, *Nomination Politics* (New York: Praeger, 1984); Ronald B. Rapoport, Alan I. Abramowitz, and John McGlennon, eds., *The Life of the Parties* (Lexington, Ky.: University Press of Kentucky, 1986).

9. Charles D. Hadley, "Dual Partisan Identification in the South," *Journal of Politics* 47 (1985): 254–268.

11

A 1988 Postscript: Continuing Coalitional Diversity

Robert P. Steed and John McGlennon

The previous chapters in this volume examined a variety of factors related to the evolution of contemporary party coalitions and party patterns in the South in some detail. This chapter offers a brief update of these earlier materials, based as they are on surveys of the 1984 state conventions in six states, by analyzing data from surveys of state convention delegates in 1988 in two southern states, South Carolina and Virginia.[1]

Since the 1988 presidential election was the first election in two decades with no incumbent president seeking re-election, spirited competition marked the nomination races in both parties and eventually the general election itself. This election, in turn, provides a good opportunity to explore the intraparty dynamics that surround the nomination contests and the southern Republican and Democratic party coalitions at the end of the 1980s. Variables such as race, gender, residence, in-migration, religion, and party switching were identified as critical elements in understanding and southern politics in earlier discussions in this book. They remain so in 1988.

DEMOCRATIC PARTY DYNAMICS

The 1988 presidential election once again highlighted the central problem facing the post–World War II Democratic party in the South: the difficulty in nominating a presidential candidate capable of uniting and mobilizing the highly diverse coalition—described in previous chapters—in the general election. The national Democratic ticket has fared poorly in the region in recent presidential elections, and the 1988 contest did nothing to change the pattern. While Michael Dukakis was partially successful in solidifying the national Democratic coalition (improving in numerous ways over the showing made by Walter Mondale in

1984), he had almost no success in moving the South back to the Democratic column. In fact, as with the Mondale-Ferraro ticket in 1984, support for the Dukakis-Bentsen ticket was lower in the South than in any other region.[2]

The problem has centered on finding a candidate (or producing a ticket) sufficiently liberal to attract Democrats outside the South and black Democrats in the South, yet sufficiently moderate to conservative to attract white voters in the South. The picture is further complicated within the South by the ideological divisions among white Democrats.[3] With the narrow exception of Jimmy Carter in 1976, the national Democratic party generally has not been successful in walking this tightrope to the satisfaction of southern voters.

1988 was supposed to be different, mainly because the combination of southern presidential primaries on Super Tuesday was expected to increase the likelihood that a more centrist candidate ultimately would receive the Democratic party's nomination.[4] For the Democrats, however, Super Tuesday's results were far from conclusive because three candidates divided the states and delegates. Albert Gore, a native son who had counted heavily on a strong southern showing to boost him into national contention, carried five states. Another native son, Jesse Jackson, combined overwhelming black support with a scattering of white votes to carry five states. Dukakis did better than expected and finished first in Texas and Florida; these two large southern states combined with his victories on the same day in Massachusetts, Maryland, and Rhode Island produced five Super Tuesday wins for him.

The coalitional problems facing the Democratic party in the region were highlighted by the nature of the support given these three candidates. Jesse Jackson was clearly the choice of southern blacks receiving, by various exit poll estimates, between 91 percent and 96 percent of this group's votes. His appeal to Hispanics and especially to whites was much lower (with estimates ranging from 21 percent to 37 percent among Hispanics and from 7 percent to 10 percent among whites). Gore was the leader among whites and white Protestants; he showed substantial appeal among those over 50 years of age. Of particular significance, Gore did especially well among weakly identified Democrats (including those who had voted for Reagan in 1984), conservative voters, those who were concerned with national defense issues, and those who wanted a southern candidate. Dukakis's appeal, in contrast, was to white liberals and Hispanics. As heir apparent to the Democratic liberal wing, he was the top choice of those who voted for Mondale in 1984.[5]

The divisions among the party-in-the-electorate evident for the Democrats in the Super Tuesday voting go far toward clarifying the recent woes of the Democratic party in South. They suggest the possibility of similar divisions among activists in 1988 in the organization of the Democratic party in the region. There is evidence—much of it presented in the previous discussions in this volume— that southern Democratic party activists display the same type of diversity that continues to plague that party in its effort to develop broadly attractive tickets.[6] We, therefore, should expect to find cleavages among the 1988 state convention delegates that generally parallel the electoral cleavages evident in the Super Tuesday voting. The South Carolina and Virginia state convention delegate surveys provide the opportunity to pursue this point. For this analysis, the Democratic delegates are divided by candidate preference. For South Carolina, supporters of Jesse Jackson account for 58 percent of the respondents (n = 363), Albert Gore's supporters account for 22 percent (n = 135), and Michael Dukakis's supporters account for 15 percent (n = 91). In Virginia, the Jackson contingent constituted 28 percent of the convention delegate respondents (n = 192), the Dukakis supporters 33 percent (n = 228), and the Gore delegates 20 percent (n = 135).[7]

A background profile of the delegates participating in these conventions indicates that, while these three groups of delegates were virtually undifferentiated with regard to certain demographic characteristics such as age, they stood in sharp contrast on a number of the others. In both states the Jackson delegates differed most clearly from the other delegates with respect to their race. In South Carolina, over three-fourths of them were black compared to less than 10 percent of those for both Gore and Dukakis. In Virginia two-thirds of the Jackson delegates were black as compared to less than 5 percent of those for either Dukakis or Gore.

Although the contrasts are not nearly as sharp, Jackson's supporters also differed from those of Gore and Dukakis in terms of gender (more likely to be female) and income (considerably less affluent than Gore or, especially, Dukakis delegates). In South Carolina, the Jackson delegates also tended to be longtime residents of the South, a trait they generally shared with Gore activists but not with Dukakis delegates. Similarly, they generally differed with regard to type of residence (less likely to be urban or suburban residents and more likely to be from rural areas or small towns) and education (roughly as well educated as the Gore supporters and less well educated than the Dukakis supporters). In Virginia, the survey did not include items on childhood state or type of residence. However, the Jackson supporters were characterized by a high proportion of Protestants, especially those with a born-again experience. They tended to be middle class or above, but they did not, as a group, enjoy the same levels of socioeconomic status as the Gore and, especially, the Dukakis delegates.

The Gore delegates, at least in South Carolina, were largely native white southerners divided roughly equally between men and women and urban/suburban and rural/small town residents. In both states examined, they were predominantly Protestant, male, and, among white activists, somewhat less well educated than the Dukakis delegates. They also were more likely to have had a born-again religious experience than the Dukakis delegates (but less likely than those for Jackson).

Delegates who supported Dukakis at the South Carolina state convention also were largely white. They consistently stood apart from the Gore and Jackson delegates—less southern in background, more likely to be from urban and suburban areas, better educated, and more affluent. Although a majority of the

Table 11.1

Political Ideologies of Democratic State Convention Delegates in South Carolina and Virginia by Candidate Preference (in percent)

Political Philosophy	South Carolina Delegates			Virginia Delegates		
	Dukakis	Gore	Jackson	Dukakis	Gore	Jackson
Extremely liberal	4	6	13	6	0	18
Liberal	39	14	47	43	20	41
Slighty liberal	34	30	15	21	20	18
Middle-of-the-road	14	17	14	18	31	18
Slightly conservative	6	17	6	8	17	3
Conservative	3	15	4	5	11	2
Extremely conservative	0	2	1	0	0	1
	100	101	100	101	99	100

Source: 1988 South Carolina and Virginia Delegate Surveys.

Dukakis delegates were Protestant, they indicated lower levels of protestantism than either the Gore or Jackson delegates. Thus while a clear racial dividing line existed between the Jackson delegates and those for Gore and Dukakis, there also were some interesting points of division among the white delegates by candidate preference. While the case is somewhat stronger in South Carolina than in Virginia, in very general terms these data suggest that the Dukakis activists tended more to represent "New South" white Democratic activists—urban, affluent, well-educated professionals, often nonsouthern in background, less Protestant and less religiously fundamentalist—while the Gore activists, in contrast, tended more to represent "Old South" white Democrats—less urban/suburban, somewhat less well educated, somewhat less affluent, more in line with the southern religious subculture.

The differences among these three groups of delegates extended beyond their socioeconomic and demographic backgrounds to their self-professed political ideologies and their positions on a series of specific issues. (See Tables 11.1 and 11.2.) While all these delegates tended to be moderate to liberal on this seven-point self-placement scale, the Jackson delegates clearly were the most liberal of the three groups, followed in order by the delegates for Dukakis and Gore. In South Carolina, nearly two-thirds (60 percent) of the Jackson delegates identified themselves as "extremely liberal" or "liberal" on the scale in contrast with 4 percent of the Dukakis delegates and only 20 percent of the Gore delegates. Indeed, about a third (34 percent) of the Gore supporters described themselves in conservative terms in contrast to only about ten percent of the Jackson and Dukakis delegates. The Virginia pattern was similar; 59 percent of the Jackson delegates placed themselves in the two most liberal categories while 49 percent of the Dukakis activists and 20 percent of the Gore activists did so.

These data on ideological self-placement generally were consistent with the re-

Table 11.2

Issue Positions of Democratic Delegates in South Carolina and Virginia by Candidate Preference (percent liberal)

Issue	South Carolina Delegates			Virginia Delegates		
	Dukakis	Gore	Jackson	Dukakis	Gore	Jackson
Social Issues						
Equal Rights Amendment	83	71	94	*	*	*
Affirmative Action Programs	61	43	96	71	61	96
Handgun Control Legislation	83	66	83	*	*	*
School Prayer Amendment	67	35	29	67	54	40
Environmental Protection	97	96	91	*	*	*
Use of Marijuana Immoral	54	31	25	46	34	32
Decriminalize Marijuana	36	22	33	*	*	*
Antiabortion Amendment	76	61	44	82	70	62
Too Much Sexual Freedom	42	24	23	38	24	32
Moral Relativism	43	34	46	52	31	46
Strengthen Family Ties	16	6	7	17	10	16
Biblical View	67	35	17	65	42	31
Pollution Regulation	*	*	*	95	85	93
Defense/Foreign Policy Issues						
Defense Spending**	82	62	85	76	63	75
U.S. Military in Mid. East	72	63	60	*	*	*
U.S. Military in Lat. Am.	75	55	60	*	*	*
INF Treaty	85	70	54	*	*	*
Strategic Defense Initiative	59	42	44	77	61	71
Aid to the Contras	*	*	*	80	63	74
Economic Issues						
Tax Increase to Cut Bud. Def.	45	45	37	*	*	*
Nat. Health Insurance	70	50	84	*	*	*
Spending Cuts to Balance Bud.	26	23	28	*	*	*
Public Works Program	49	40	62	*	*	*
Balanced Budget Amendment	*	*	*	48	41	31
Farmers Aid	*	*	*	55	58	78
Increased Tariffs	*	*	*	49	62	65

*Item not included in survey for this state

**South Carolina question related to increasing defense spending; Virginia question related to maintaining current level of defense spending

Source: 1988 South Carolina and Virginia Delegate Surveys.

spective positions for each of the three groups on a series of specific issues. For example, in both states, the Gore delegates clearly exhibited the most conservative positions on the listed issues. In South Carolina, on half of the 21 issues listed, Gore supporters had the lowest percentage with liberal responses. They never were the group with the largest proportion of liberal responses on any issue. In sharp contrast, the Dukakis delegates took the most liberal position on 12 of the 21 issues, and they never held the lowest level of liberal responses on any issue. The Jackson delegates displayed a mixed pattern. On some issues, especially those in the economic category, they held the most liberal views of the three groups. On other issues, particularly those dealing with moral and religious questions, they held the most conservative views of the three groups. This broad pattern was repeated among Virginia delegates. Of the fifteen issues listed, the Dukakis delegates took the most liberal position on twelve while Gore supporters took the most

liberal position on none. Conversely, the Gore activists were the most conservative on eight of the issues, and the Jackson delegates were the most conservative on
five (again, primarily the moral and religious items).

One irony of these data, especially for South Carolina Democrats, was that
the mostly black Jackson supporters and the mostly white (and "Old South")
Gore supporters were closer in their positions on a number of these issues—
abortion, view of the Bible, and marijuana use, for example—than were either
the Gore and Dukakis delegates or the Jackson and Dukakis delegates. On other
issues such as handgun control, increased defense spending, and affirmative
action, the Jackson and Dukakis supporters were closest in their positions.
Clearly, when these Democratic state convention delegates were divided by
candidate preference, they constitute three distinct ideological/issue groupings
which crosscut racial backgrounds in a variety of ways. This suggests the Super
Tuesday electoral divisions in the South were also present among state level
Democratic activists. It underscores the obvious difficulty for the Democrats in
selecting a candidate capable of holding together a highly diverse coalition. It
also suggests that even without the Super Tuesday primaries that resulted in the
nomination muddle, the selection of an acceptable Democratic candidate would
have been neither easy nor guaranteed.

A final point of comparison among these state delegates concerns their levels
of party commitment. As with their ideological and issue positions, a strong
divisive potential exists for these three groups of delegates if they differed sharply
in their party orientations.

The main evidence on this point is their key motivation for political involvement. In South Carolina, Dukakis delegates were more likely than the other two
groups (and especially the Gore delegates) to give "candidate support" as the
main reason for becoming active in 1988. Party support, although the second
most frequently mentioned motivation, was the main reason for involvement for
only about one-fourth of this group. (See Table 11.3) It was the reverse for the
Gore delegates. Party support ranks first (mentioned by 41 percent) followed by
candidate support (mentioned by 27 percent). For Jackson delegates, party support and candidate support were equally important as the main reason for political
involvement (37 percent each).

In Virginia, the pattern was quite different. While there were variations among
the three groups of delegates, they were not in the same configuration as those
found in South Carolina. For the Gore delegates, party support (50 percent) was
by far the most important motivation (as in South Carolina), but it also was the
motivation most frequently mentioned by the Dukakis supporters as most important (36 percent). Candidate support remained important for the Dukakis
delegates (31 percent), but it was not ranked above party support. The Jackson
supporters in Virginia also differed from their South Carolina colleagues by
ranking specific issues (37 percent) as their most important motivation, followed
by candidate support (32 percent) and, distantly, party support (23 percent). In
this instance, then, there was evidence not only of candidate-based intraparty

Table 11.3
Democratic Delegates' Motivations for Political Activity in South Carolina and Virginia by Candidate Preference (in percent)

Reason for Pol. Involvement	Dukakis Delegates	Gore Delegates	Jackson Delegates
SOUTH CAROLINA			
To support party	27	41	37
To help political career	2	5	4
To enjoy campaign excitement	2	1	1
To meet people	0	2	0
To support particular candidate	43	27	37
To work for issues	17	14	14
To enjoy delegate visibility	0	0	0
To fulfill civic duty	8	9	7
To make business contacts	0	2	0
	99	101	100
VIRGINIA			
To support party	36	50	23
To represent a group	11	18	9
To support particular candidate	31	13	32
To work for specific issues	23	19	37
	101	100	101

Source: 1988 South Carolina and Virginia Delegate Surveys.

divisions but also of differing motivations among the Dukakis and Jackson supporters in the two states analyzed here.

Beyond the data in Table 11.3, the evidence of delegates' orientations toward the party is fragmentary, mainly because the Virginia survey did not pursue this point very fully with additional questions. The South Carolina data is, however, at least suggestive that the variations in the activists' motivations extended as well to other perspectives on the party. For example, the Dukakis delegates were somewhat more likely than the Gore or Jackson delegates to feel that the most important factor in candidate selection should be the person's issue stands and ideological positions rather than party loyalty and service (85 percent for Dukakis to 79 percent to 70 percent for Gore and Jackson respectively). Similarly, while majorities of all three groups said that it is more important for the party to make a broad electoral appeal than to take personally agreeable issue positions, fewer of the Dukakis delegates voiced this view. Conversely, while one-fourth of the Dukakis delegates said that they would stop working for the party if it took disagreeable issue stands, slightly smaller percentages of the Gore (17 percent) and Jackson delegates (13 percent) indicated that they would take such a step.

One final observation is in order. When we look at the South Carolina data on splitting ballots and the 1984 presidential vote, we see further evidence of group differences that are broadly consistent with the previous patterns. The Dukakis and the Gore activists were considerably more supportive of splitting ballots than were the Jackson activists. While over half (52 percent) of the Jackson activists opposed this practice, fewer than 40 percent of the other two groups did so. This, perhaps, is a reflection of recent black loyalty to the Democratic party and, in the case of the Gore delegates, recent southern white disaffection with the national Democratic party and its presidential tickets. The position of the Dukakis activists on ticket splitting, together with their greater candidate support than party loyalty, reflects their weaker ties to the southern Democratic party and their higher mobility. The Gore delegates, on the other hand, were inclined to support the principle of ticket splitting. Forty-five percent indicated it was permissible to split the ballot in national elections or in all elections in contrast to the Dukakis (35 percent) and Jackson delegates (only 17 percent). Not only were the Gore delegates more favorable toward ticket splitting, they were more apt to engage in such behavior. In 1984, for example, only 71 percent of the Gore activists voted for the Democratic presidential ticket, and fully one-fifth voted for Ronald Reagan, a point consistent with their issue and ideological positions. Not surprisingly, the Jackson and the Dukakis delegates were much more comfortable with the Mondale/Ferraro ticket and voted accordingly (85 percent support by Dukakis delegates and 98 percent support by Jackson delegates who voted in 1984).

REPUBLICAN PARTY DYNAMICS

For the first time since 1980, the Republican party joined the Democratic party in nominating its presidential ticket through a series of spirited contests prior to the national convention. Although the Republican party generally has enjoyed a greater degree of unity than the Democratic party in recent years, as indicated in earlier chapters,[8] it is not totally without some internal divisions of its own. For example, Baker's analysis of the impact of the religious right on the southern party system documents cleavages within the Republican party on moral issues.[9] This point was confirmed in research on party and political action committee donors conducted by John Green and James Guth.[10] Within this context, the candidacy of Pat Robertson was particularly important in highlighting these divisions.

The Robertson campaign was a classic example of the candidate with an intense but limited appeal. In a number of states he succeeded in organizing his supporters and mobilizing them in an effort to take over party caucuses and/or local party organizations. For example, in Washington he won in the party caucuses. He swept some of the early caucuses in Virginia, and he successfully placed key supporters in a number of county or state party posts in South Carolina and Louisiana.[11] In many respects, the Robertson candidacy bore a marked similarity to those of other recent presidential aspirants. Barry Goldwater in 1964, George McGovern in 1972, and Jesse Jackson in 1984 and (to a lesser extent in 1988) profited from their abilities to mobilize well-organized movements behind their candidacies. The supporters of these candidates fared remarkably well in caucus states and usually won a much smaller level of support in primaries, as was the pattern for Robertson in 1988. They also tended to be people with less attachment to the political party in which they were participating, with more ideological commitment in their issue positions, and with less experience in partisan politics.

Thus we would anticipate Robertson supporters to differ significantly from other Republican delegates in background, political philosophy, issue positions, and strength of party attachment. Party effectiveness might be hampered by sharp differences between the two Republican groups, or enhanced if party leaders see the new activists as welcome and compatible additions.

The Republican state conventions in Virginia and South Carolina were held after George Bush had essentially captured the party's nomination. Anticipating another attempt at the Republican nomination in 1992 or 1996, however, Robertson encouraged his supporters to follow through on their new party involvement. As a result, Robertson backers comprised the second largest block at GOP conventions. Among those declaring a candidate preference, the Bush and Robertson supporters combine to account for 79 percent of the Virginia delegates (n = 199 for Bush and n = 184 for Robertson) and 76 percent of the South Carolina delegates (n = 266 for Bush and n = 197 for Robertson).

Although the Bush and Robertson backers were very similar racially in that over 90 percent of each group were white, they consistently differed with regard to most other background characteristics. Robertson delegates tended to be younger and slightly less well educated than the Bush delegates. Women were better represented among Robertson's forces, dividing nearly equally by gender while the Bush forces had a three-fifths male majority. Their income levels, too, were significantly different. In Virginia, the percentage of Bush delegates earning over $50,000 per year was twice that of similarly affluent Robertson delegates (60 percent to 30 percent respectively). In South Carolina, over half of the Bush supporters reported an annual income of $45,000 or higher in contrast to just under a third of the Robertson supporters.

By far, the greatest distinctions were in terms of religion. Though both groups were predominantly Protestant, the Robertson delegates were much more likely than the Bush delegates to associate themselves with evangelism. For example, in Virginia 97 percent of the Robertson activists called themselves "Born-again Christians" as compared to only 33 percent of the Bush activists. In South Carolina the comparable figures are 76 percent for the Robertson supporters, 27 percent for the Bush supporters. Similarly sharp differences were evident when the delegates were compared on other indicators of fundamentalism and/or evangelicalism.

Turning from background characteristics to ideological and issue positions, Bush and Robertson backers were again differentiated in a number of ways. While the vast majority of all Republican delegates considered themselves conservative, the Robertson delegates in both states were stronger conservatives than the Bush delegates. (See Table 11.4.) In both states, over half the Robertson supporters were extremely conservative on the seven point scale in contrast to

Table 11.4

Political Ideologies of Republican State Convention Delegates in South Carolina and Virginia by Candidate Preference (in percent)

	South Carolina Delegates		Virginia Delegates	
	Bush	Robertson	Bush	Robertson
Political Philosophy				
Extremely liberal	0	0	0	0
Liberal	0	0	0	0
Slighty liberal	0	0	1	0
Middle-of-the-road	3	0	3	0
Slightly conservative	9	2	20	0
Conservative	69	47	63	47
Extremely conservative	19	51	13	52
	100	100	100	99

Source: 1988 South Carolina and Virginia Delegate Surveys.

less than twenty percent of the Bush supporters. Moreover, in contrast to the Bush activists, hardly any of the Robertson delegates even indicated moderate conservatism.

The ideological conservatism of the Robertson delegates was not quite as uniform as the preceding paragraph might suggest. In South Carolina, for example, barely over half of the Robertson activists took the conservative position on U.S. military involvement in the Middle East and the INF Treaty, and fewer than 10 percent expressed conservative views on governmental efforts to protect the environment. (See Table 11.5.) Similarly, in Virginia the Robertson backers did not evince high levels of conservatism on pollution regulation, aid to farmers, and increased tariffs. However, on most of the issues included in Table 11.5, the Robertson delegates were not only conservative, they were consistently more conservative than the Bush delegates. On 19 of the 21 issues in the South Carolina survey and on 11 of the 15 issues in the Virginia survey, the Robertson delegates were the more conservative of the two groups, sometimes considerably so. On some of the issues—mainly in the areas of defense/foreign policy and economics—the Robertson/Bush differences were quite small. The intraparty variations clearly were most evident on the moral questions and social issues. These issues also could provide the basis for some obvious disputes between Bush and Robertson supporters.

Abortion and school prayer issues stand out as particularly important for the Robertson delegates. They also held highly unified views on the Bible, sexual freedom, and the importance of strengthening traditional family ties. Especially in South Carolina, these issues plus the morality of marijuana use and moral relativism formed the basis of Robertson supporters' unity. In some instances, the aggregate differences between the Bush and the Robertson delegates were remarkable. For example, in South Carolina differences between the Robertson

Table 11.5

Issue Positions of Republican Delegates in South Carolina and Virginia by Candidate Preference (percent conservative)

Issue	South Carolina Delegates		Virginia Delegates	
	Bush	Robertson	Bush	Robertson
Social Issues				
Equal Rights Amendment	71	84	*	*
Affirmative Action Programs	76	66	64	53
Handgun Control Legislation	53	56	*	*
School Prayer Amendment	75	96	69	97
Environmental Protection	13	9	*	*
Use of Marijuana Immoral	78	90	41	71
Decriminalize Marijuana	83	94	*	*
Antiabortion Amendment	43	94	43	98
Too Much Sexual Freedom	88	99	41	90
Moral Relativism	79	95	29	86
Strengthen Family Ties	97	99	65	92
Biblical View	68	99	26	93
Pollution Regulation	*	*	24	26
Defense/Foreign Policy Issues				
Defense Spending**	86	88	86	90
U.S. Military in Mid. East	46	56	*	*
U.S. Military in Lat. Am.	75	78	*	*
INF Treaty	11	57	*	*
Strategic Defense Initiative	92	94	90	90
Aid to the Contras	*	*	88	96
Economic Issues				
Tax Increase to Cut Bud. Def.	64	83	*	*
Nat. Health Insurance	64	72	*	*
Spending Cuts to Balance Bud.	78	83	*	*
Public Works Program	75	76	*	*
Balanced Budget Amendment	*	*	87	93
Farmers Aid	*	*	57	36
Increased Tariffs	*	*	60	41

*Item not included in survey for this state

**South Carolina question related to increasing defense spending;
Virginia question related to maintaining current level of defense spending

Source: 1988 South Carolina and Virginia Delegate Surveys.

and Bush delegates exceeded 50 percentage points on an antiabortion amendment. Similarly large differences existed in Virginia on an antiabortion amendment and on the delegate's views of the Bible. A number of other moral and social issues produced almost as much sharp division between the Robertson/Bush groups.

Somewhat surprisingly, in Virginia at least, the Robertson delegates took a decidedly more liberal stance than the Bush delegates on some of the economic issues considered. They were much more favorably disposed on the issue of increased tariffs and considerably more favorable toward increasing aid to farmers than were the Bush delegates.

It appears, then, that Robertson supporters were most clearly identified as staunch conservatives, ideologically at home in the GOP, on precisely the kinds of social issues over which the Republican party has no consensus. Bush delegates reflected the economic conservatism of the party and were opposed to restriction on abortions. They also were less enthusiastic about promoting prayer in public schools, and though they generally took a conservative stance, were much less united in their belief in the literal interpretation of the Bible and in their concern with sexual freedom. In short, while there was considerable common ground for these activists within the Republican party, there also was a series of issues with the potential for disruption.

Robertson supporters, too, held distinct party orientations, as expected. Given the nature of the Robertson candidacy, his backers were much more likely than those of Bush to be only recently involved in partisan politics. When asked how long they had been active in party politics in the state, three-fourths of the Robertson delegates in both states answered less than five years. In contrast, a majority of Bush delegates had been involved at least five years. The Virginia survey further revealed that the Robertson delegates, although similar to the Bush delegates in the strength of their party attachment, were significantly less likely than the Bush delegates to express a willingness to work "for the party year after year, win or lose, whether or not you like the candidates or issues." Indeed, more than 60 percent of the Robertson supporters would work for the party only when there was a particularly worthwhile candidate or issue.[12]

Robertson supporters held similar views on a slightly different question administered in South Carolina. A majority (51 percent) indicated that issue consistency was the most important factor in selecting a candidate, a position taken by only 15 percent of the Bush delegates. On the other hand, almost three-fourths of the Bush delegates considered electability to be the most important factor in candidate selection in direct contrast to only 25 percent of the Robertson supporters. Along the same lines, the South Carolina survey found helping the party to be the most important motivation for political involvement for 46 percent of the Bush delegates (ranking first on the list of motivations) in contrast to only eight percent of the Robertson delegates. For the Robertson delegates, working for specific issues constituted the most important motivation for political activity (mentioned by 49 percent) followed by supporting a particular candidate (mentioned by 38 percent). These motivations were considered most important by only about one-fifth of the Bush delegates.

The picture that emerges from these data is one of party activists with distinct levels of party commitment, patterns of party involvement, and views of their roles within the party.

CONCLUSION

As the southern party system has changed in the post–World War II period, Democratic strength in the region has steadily declined. Voting patterns and data on party identification both point to the growth of Republican party support, especially among the region's dominant conservative white middle class.[13] The

Democratic party and its regional leaders tried, with some success, to offset this erosion of party support by appealing to a highly diverse coalition. As James L. Sundquist has noted, "Given the continued presence of a traditional Democratic vote, the most successful Democratic candidates have been those who have retarded rather than stimulated the realignment process—in other words, the moderate centrists who are skilled in the political straddle, moving just far enough to the center to attract strong black and liberal support but not so far as to drive a large bloc of moderate-conservative Democrats into Republican ranks."[14] While this strategy was moderately successful for the Democrats in state and local elections, it has not worked at the presidential level. The national Democratic coalition consistently pushed its presidential ticket more toward the liberal end of the scale than has been acceptable to the fairly large contingent of conservative southern white Democrats.

The Super Tuesday primaries failed to produce a clear cut Democratic front-runner of centrist persuasion for a number of reasons. The primaries were not limited to the South, moderate voters failed to unify in support of Gore, Jackson appealed strongly to black voters, some of whom might have supported a moderate rather than Dukakis, and Dukakis, although not running well in the South, successfully targeted two key states in the region to gain enough votes to enhance his image as a national candidate.[15] But the Super Tuesday exit polls, analysis by Harold W. Stanley and Charles D. Hadley of a series of Super Tuesday surveys,[16] and the South Carolina and Virginia state convention delegate data examined in this chapter also suggest an additional reason, namely the southern Democratic coalition is now sufficiently diverse to make agreement on a moderate candidate reasonably difficult.

Even in a Deep South state such as South Carolina, the moderate/conservative white activists who once controlled the party are no longer in a dominant position. They are, however, still a significant force within the state Democratic party. More liberal white activists, while not dominant either, are also a presence of significance.[17] Black Democratic activists (and voters) constitute a third Democratic party segment that is closer to the traditional white activists in some instances and closer to the more liberal white activists in other instances. Their intraparty activists, especially in the presidential nomination process, are also understandably influenced by the presence of attractive black candidates (e.g., Jesse Jackson). All three segments bring into the party somewhat different sets of experiences, political philosophy and issue positions, and party orientations. In short, the problems faced by the national Democratic party in finding a presidential candidate deemed suitable by a heterogeneous constituency are also faced by its regional party, and, perhaps to a lesser degree, by its various state parties in the South.

The Democratic party is not alone in its struggle to unite a diverse and changing coalition. Although it has not commonly received the same amount of attention, the southern Republican party also faces a special version of this same struggle. The examination of Bush and Robertson delegates to the 1988 state conventions in South Carolina and Virginia provides an impression of a party confronting the challenge of incorporating a significant new group of activists. In this context, the party faces a large delegation of younger, much more religiously involved partisans of somewhat more modest means, a delegation lacking a pattern of experience in party politics. The Robertson activists professed a conservatism that seems in some ways more extreme and more intense than that of the experienced party members, especially on questions of moral policy.

At the same time, these self-professed conservative ideologues were less committed to the Republican principles of economic conservatism (limited government involvement and limited government expenditure) than were their counterparts who supported George Bush. Issues such as abortion and school prayer motivated their involvement in party politics.

George Bush apparently found a way of accommodating this new force. The Robertson supporters appear to have accepted him pragmatically as the party nominee. Since his nomination and election, Bush has taken a position supportive of the antiabortion movement, bringing a substantial reward to the Robertson supporters for their continued involvement in his campaign after the national convention. But the broader question facing the Republican party is how to maintain a broader coalition by integrating social conservatives who may not be highly committed to economic conservatism with economic conservatives who may not be highly supportive of social conservatism. This is clearly a type of internal cleavage with high potential for intensification and disruption.

While our focus in this chapter was on party activists in two states and, within that context, the 1988 presidential nominating contests, the implications of these data go well beyond these immediate concerns. The future directions of both the Democratic and Republican parties and their prospects in the region clearly lie in the way these coalitional questions—and others raised elsewhere in this volume—are resolved (if they are resolved). This, in turn, undoubtedly will affect the future direction and strength of the national parties and help shape the national party system, as well.

NOTES

1. A preliminary note regarding the data used in this chapter is in order. The 1988 state convention surveys that this chapter utilizes are not completely comparable. The key difference lies in the relationship of the conventions to the party's presidential nominating process. In South Carolina, the Democratic party convention was an integral part of the caucus-convention process for selecting the Democratic delegation to the national convention. The Republican party convention in South Carolina and the Democratic party convention in Virginia followed presidential primaries and were, therefore, essentially ratification conventions for the national convention delegations. Even the Virginia Republican convention met after the Super Tuesday advisory primary to ratify the selection of national convention delegates chosen earlier at the congressional district level. In all conventions, a variety of other state party business also was on the agenda. The second difference in these data is rooted in slight variations in the questionnaire design. The South Carolina and Virginia studies overlap in important ways, but they are not identical.

While this limits some of the analysis, it is not a major detriment to the discussion that follows.

The South Carolina conventions were surveyed in April 1988 as an extension of the 1984 Comparative State Party Activist Survey. Questionnaires were administered to all delegates attending the two state party conventions. The number of usable questionnaires returned was quite high (1,325) with correspondingly high response rates (an average of approximately 60 percent). The delegates were nearly evenly divided between the two parties—680 Democrats and 645 Republicans. A similar approach was used at the Virginia conventions held later in the summer. At the Republican convention, the return rate was 49 percent (n = 534), while that for the Democratic convention was 62 percent (n = 684).

2. For data and discussion of the 1988 election, see Gerald M. Pomper, "The Presidential Election," in Gerald M. Pomper et al. (eds.), *The Election of 1988: Reports and Interpretations* (Chatham, N.J.: Chatham House, 1989), chap. 5; for more detailed discussion of the 1988 election in the South, see Laurence W. Moreland, Robert P. Steed, and Tod A. Baker (eds.), *The 1988 Presidential Election in the South* (New York: Praeger, 1989).

3. In addition to the materials presented in the present volume, the heterogeneity of the Democratic party in the South and the related problems of coalitional unity is addressed in Earl Black and Merle Black, *Politics and Society in the South* (Cambridge, Mass.: Harvard University Press, 1987), chap. 11; Harold W. Stanley, "Southern Partisan Changes: Dealignment, Realignment or Both?" *Journal of Politics* 50 (February 1988); 64–88; David M. Brodsky, "Partisan Change: An Overview of a Continuing Debate," in Robert H. Swansbrough and David M. Brodsky (eds.), *The South's New Politics* (Columbia: University of South Carolina Press, 1988), chap. 2; and Alexander P. Lamis, *The Two-Party South* (New York: Oxford University Press, 1984), 229–231.

4. There is some debate over the goals of those who designed Super Tuesday. Indeed, it is likely that a variety of goals played at least some part. However, the most extensive analyses point to the centrality of nominating a candidate attractive to southern voters. For an extended discussion of the background of Super Tuesday, see Charles D. Hadley and Harold W. Stanley, "Super Tuesday 1988: Regional Results, National Implications," *Publius* 19 (Summer 1989), forthcoming; and Harold W. Stanley and Charles D. Hadley, "The Southern Presidential Primary: Regional Intentions with National Implications," *Publius* 17 (Summer 1987): 83–100. Also see David S. Castle, "A Southern Regional Presidential Primary in 1988: Will It Work as Planned?" *Election Politics* (Summer 1987); 6–10; and Charles S. Bullock, III, "Super Tuesday," in Moreland, Steed, and Baker, *The 1988 Presidential Election in the South*.

5. Summarized from Bullock, "Super Tuesday."

6. For example, see the discussion in Chapter 6 in this volume. These issue patterns are broadly confirmed by research on local party officials in Florida and South Carolina. See, for example, Lewis Bowman, William E. Hulbary, and Anne E. Kelley, "Party Sorting at the Grass Roots: Stable Partisans and Party Changers among Florida's Precinct Officials," in Robert P. Steed, Laurence W. Moreland, and Tod A. Baker (eds.), *The Disappearing South: Studies in Regional Change and Continuity* (Tuscaloosa: University of Alabama Press, 1989), chap. 4; and Laurence W. Moreland, Robert P. Steed, and Tod A. Baker, "Ideology, Issues, and Realignment among Southern Party Activists," in Swansbrough and Brodsky (eds.), *The South's New Politics*, chap. 18.

7. The remaining delegates have been excluded from the analysis inasmuch as they

were scattered widely among the other candidates for the nomination or indicated no preference.

8. See, for example, the discussions by Moreland, chap. 6, and Steed, chap. 3.

9. Baker, chap. 7 in the current volume.

10. John C. Green and James L. Guth, "The Transformation of Southern Political Elites: Regionalism among Party and PAC Contributors," in Steed, Moreland, and Baker (eds.), *The Disappearing South?*, chap. 3. See also their "The Christian Right in the Republican Party: The Case of Pat Robertson's Supporters," *Journal of Politics* 50 (February 1988); 150–165.

11. See, for example, Charles D. Hadley, "Louisiana," in Moreland, Steed, and Baker (eds.), *The 1988 Presidential Election in the South*, chap. 6; Laurence W. Moreland, Robert P. Steed, and Tod A. Baker, "South Carolina," in Moreland, Steed, and Baker (eds.), *The 1988 Presidential Election in the South*, chap. 8; and Larry Sabato, "Virginia," in Moreland, Steed, and Baker (eds.), *The 1988 Presidential Election in the South*, chap. 14.

12. For elaboration, see John McGlennon, "Religious Activists in the Republican Party: Robertson and Bush Supporters in Virginia" (paper presented at the 1989 annual meeting of the Midwest Political Science Association, Chicago, Illinois, April, 1989).

13. Black and Black, *Politics and Society in the South*, chaps. 11–14. Also see Stanley, "Southern Partisan Changes."

14. James L. Sundquist, *Dynamics of the Party System*, rev. ed. (Washington, D.C.: Brookings Institute, 1983), 374. For elaboration of a similar argument, see Black and Black, *Politics and Society in the South*, chap. 14, esp. 315.

15. For an elaboration of this material, see Harold W. Stanley and Charles D. Hadley, "Super Tuesday Surveys: Insights and Hindsights" (paper presented at the 1989 annual meeting of the Midwest Political Science Association, Chicago, Illinois, April 1989).

16. Stanley and Hadley, "Super Tuesday Surveys," 12–13.

17. Research on the 1980 and the 1984 state convention delegates in a number of southern states has confirmed this increased presence of white liberals within the Democratic party organization. See, for example, this volume, chap. 3; and Tod A. Baker, Robert P. Steed, and Laurence W. Moreland, "Dancing Out of Step: Deviant Delegates at the 1984 State Party Conventions" (paper presented at the 1989 annual meeting of the Western Political Science Association, Salt Lake City, Utah, March 29–April 2, 1989).

Conclusion: Southern Party Coalitions

Lewis Bowman

The national political party reforms and southern economic and cultural changes have put the southern party system under great stress. Indeed the major political party coalitions in the region seem to have been transformed significantly since 1948. The outcome of these changes helps us understand the evolution of the southern traditional one-party system into the current variety of party system configurations. These systems range from one and one-half party systems in some southern areas to competitive two-party systems in other southern areas.[1] These changes also help us understand the role that the transformation of the southern party system from 1948 to 1988 has played in the results of recent presidential elections in the region and in the nation.

Utilizing data derived mainly from a survey of the delegates to the 1984 state conventions in six southern states, but augmented as well by surveys of delegates in two states in 1988, the authors have examined the southern party activist coalitions. They have described who the delegates were, and have examined how national political party reforms and economic and cultural changes appear to have impacted the selection of delegates, their views, and their party loyalties.

BACKGROUND

One has to look earlier than 1948 to observe the panorama of change that produced the forces pushing toward a transformation of the southern party system. Examples of earlier manifestations of pressures toward party coalitional change abound. The dropping of the two-thirds rule at the party convention in 1936 began the weakening of the political veto the South had used to maintain its substantial leverage in the Democratic party. Also massive economic and cultural changes resulting from the burgeoning population migrations of the World War

I, the Great Depression, the World War II, and the post–World War II eras already were impacting upon the major party coalitions before 1948. As Alexander Heard[2] pointed out, the germ of Republicanism was never completely dormant among conservative white southern voters in a number of areas of the South; it was awaiting the forces of change that would enable it to become a viable part of the southern party system.

These changes evolved much more rapidly after events at the 1948 presidential nominating convention. For the first time the Democratic party's coalition, in which southern whites were such a major component, threatened white southerners directly on the issue most dear to them—the race issue. "Their" Democratic party dared to place a civil rights plank in the 1948 platform. The "world of southern presidential politics" was turned on its head.[3] Since the moment southern whites have not been a "solid" component of the traditional New Deal Democratic party coalition. From 1948 southern whites formed a steadily increasingly available source for Republican party efforts, or for third party efforts.[4]

After signing the Civil Rights Act of 1964, President Johnson told an aide, "I think we just delivered the South to the Republican Party for a long time."[5] He was correct. Even in Lyndon Johnson's sweeping Democratic electoral victory in 1964 white southerners shifted toward Barry Goldwater in response to his attack on Johnson's support of civil rights legislation and Goldwater carried four Southern states. As Bernard Cosman reported:

The salience of race for the mass public of the Deep South was made abundantly clear by the election returns. Race was a force strong enough to override whatever misgivings many white Deep South voters may have had about Senator Goldwater's economic views.[6]

In recent years revisionists have pointed out that many observers of political activism in the 1960s were so dazzled by the admittedly spectacular efforts of the liberal activists that they failed to give due credit to the concommitant development of the activism of the "new conservatism" in both the Republican party and George Wallace's American Independent Party. This conservative movement was evolving as counterpoint to the liberal activities, and as an inevitable split in the American political ethos of the time; much of this ensued in reaction to the multitude of particularly critical and polarizing political and cultural events of 1948, 1954, 1964, 1965, 1968, 1972, and 1974.[7]

Since the 1960s white southerners have constituted the solid portion of the Republican presidential party coalition in the South.[8] This addition of Southern whites (in disproportionately male numbers) seems to have become the major core of southern Republicanism. The bloc of "sure" southern electoral votes that this phenomenon produced has assured Republican preeminence in southern presidential politics.[9] In view of these party coalitional changes the presidential election results of 1988 were no surprise; the Republican, President Bush, won the South easily, taking approximately 67 president of the white southern vote and 70 percent of the white male southern vote.[10]

THE EVOLVING SOUTHERN PARTY COALITIONS:
A SUMMARY

These evolving transformations of the Democratic party and the Republican party are based on significant changes in each party's coalition. By the 1984 state party conventions the components of the transforming southern major party coalitions were clearly visible, and this was reinforced by the 1988 state party conventions delegate data.

In comparison to the Republican party delegates, the Democrats were more heterogenous as a group. During a generation of party organizational change, fueled mainly by Democratic intraparty struggles, the Democrats introduced substantially more women and blacks into party activism as state party delegates.[11]

Among the Democratic convention delegates, women were more likely to be black, younger, native-born southerners, in families making less income, and better educated than Republican women delegates. They were also more involved in political activities and were more ambitious than the Republican women delegates. Women delegates in both parties tended to be more liberal than the men, but overall the Republican delegates were conservative regardless of gender. Among the Democratic delegates, however, the women were substantially more liberal than the men.

The young (18–34) Republican delegates reported much more party office-holding than the Democrats. They also reported greater political activity levels during the last eight years in state and national campaigns, although not in local campaigns. Whether these variations represented greater opportunity in the minority party structure, or whether they reflected a disparate political zeal, is unclear. If the latter, then the Republicans gradually have acquired an important component in their new coalition.

The young Democratic delegates reported being much more liberal on issues than older Democratic delegates. This differentiation was not the case among the Republican delegates. Age was also strongly related to reported activity in religious groups. Young Democratic delegates were less likely than older Democrats to be active in religious groups; just the opposite was the case for the Republican delegates. This places younger Republican delegates closer to traditional southern values than either their older Republican colleagues or any of the Democratic age groups, and it particularly differentiates them from the young Democratic group that scored lower on this activity than any other age grouping in either of the two party coalitions.

Blacks constituted an important component in the southern Democratic party organizational coalition; however, they were not significant among the Republican coalition. The blacks and whites among the Democratic delegates were quite similar except for their practice of religion, in which the blacks were more likely to attend church regularly and to accept a literal interpretation of the scriptures.

Contrary to some expectations, in 1984 the Jackson supporters among the black Democratic delegates differed little from the white Democratic delegates on liberal and conservative measures. However, in comparison to the white Democratic delegates, the black Democratic delegates reported stronger support for their party; this was the case both in terms of the role they saw for the Democratic party and their personal identification with the Democratic party. Among the 1988 delegates, however, the Dukakis delegates rather than the Jackson delegates were the most liberal group of Democratic delegates.[12] The Jackson delegates' economic liberalism, accompanied by social conservatism on religion-related issues, accounts for this differentiation. In turn, this ideological inconsistency among the Jackson delegates was related to their lessened party commitment.

Civil rights activists constitute another important element in the party coalition changes in the South. Almost one-fifth of the party state convention delegates in the six states reported involvement at some time with civil rights organizations. Almost a third of the Democratic delegates reported involvement with these organizations, but only three percent of the Republicans reported any involvement with civil rights organizations. The civil rights activists were much more likely to be liberal than the non–civil rights activists; these delegates bring an unusual attachment to liberalism to their party organizational work in both parties. This is particularly important in the Democratic party because 70 percent of the civil rights activists reported being liberal whereas only 35 percent of the non–civil rights activists did so. Also, this civil rights activist component of the Democratic party organization was particularly active in support of Jesse Jackson in 1984. Among the civil rights activists 44 percent supported Jackson compared to only 8 percent of the non–civil rights activists. Surprisingly, the civil rights activists were no more likely to be organizational amateurs than were the non–civil rights activists in the party organization.

The two parties attracted in-migrants differentially. Overall the Republicans attracted a greater proportion of the in-migrants who had become party state convention delegates. However, the Democrats disproportionately accumulated in-migrant delegates who were young and who had urban or professional backgrounds; the Republicans drew on older, more traditional in-migrants. Hence the Democrats' in-migrants tended to reinforce the liberalism of the Democratic party coalition while the Republican in-migrants reinforced that party's conservatism. However, because the Republicans attracted more in-migrants overall, the in-migrants augmented the Republicans' efforts to penetrate southern politics. The Democrats' in-migrants produced more qualitative change in their party coalition and served as another factor increasing the party's heterogeneity.

Urbanization appears to be a major factor in the breaking of the grip of traditionalism on the Democratic delegates. However, in 1984 this change was occurring in only one of the two major party organizations. The Democratic delegates from urban areas were different from the rural Democratic delegates in terms of membership in activist, often more liberal-oriented groups (such as civil rights, labor, women's, and environmental groups), as well as in terms of many nonfundamentalist stands about religious practices. This clearly was not the case for the Republican delegates.

The Democrats were substantially more heterogeneous than the Republican state convention delegates in ideological beliefs about political conservatism-liberalism, in views about social and political issues, and in religious practice. By all measures, the Republican delegates were heavily conservative socially and politically. The Democrats were more diverse ideologically, although they tended to be much more liberal overall in comparison to the Republicans. The most striking aspect of this was that the delegates in each party thought the parties were becoming more differentiated and competitive ideologically. This perception probably has been a factor in the party switching or party sorting that has been taking place among southern party activists. The push towards ideological congruence with one's party organization certainly fits the delegates' attitudes and perceptions.

The religious right, in particular, seems to have played a major role in the breakup of the Democratic party's one-party system in the South. It is likely to continue to push the parties toward ideological clarification and polarization. Persons of that orientation among the Democratic party delegates articulated little attachment to the national Democratic party. The blacks among the Democratic delegates tended to be oriented toward the views of the religious right also, but the factor was not sufficient to override the black delegates' view that the Democratic party was more conducive to their policy concerns. However, the continuing attraction of these social conservatism issues to black delegates is demonstrated in the 1988 surveys among Virginia and South Carolina black delegates. This raises questions about the long-term impact of social conservatism on the Democratic party coalition.

IMPLICATIONS

What implications do these findings have for the party organizations and party coalitions in the South? And, what are the implications for possible restructuring of southern and national politics?[13]

For Party Coalitions

The Republican party activists' coalition has incorporated delegates who disproportionately embody traditional conservative southern political and cultural values and who are disproportionately in-migrants. Hence the Republican coalition has been formed by Republicans of long standing who essentially have been carried over from an earlier era, in combination with two newer cohorts—those Democrats who are abandoning the Democratic party because it is increasingly perceived as less interested in defending the traditional values of the region, and those Republicans moving into the state who continue their loyalty to the Republican party.

The Democratic contemporary party activists' coalition has been formed disproportionately from liberal white males, women, blacks, and civil rights activists. This gives the Democratic coalition a more heterogeneous character socially and ideologically than the Republican. Also even though the Democrats have drawn fewer in-migrants than the Republicans, the Democrats have been more affected by their in-migrants because these tend to be better educated, to be less religious, to have more professional women, and to be significantly more liberal, more politically ambitious, and of greater ideological purity than the native portion of the Democratic coalition. On the contrary, the Republican in-migrants have confirmed and reinforced the existing political and social character of southern values, and probably have made the Republicans more homogeneous. Delegates to national conventions have been increasingly polarized ideologically in the 1970s and into the 1980s.[14] Our data do not enable us to look at this over time on a southwide basis, but the 1988 delegate data reported from Virginia and South Carolina do not argue against the suspicion that this is what has been happening at the state convention level in the South as well.

For Realignment[15]

The processes of conversion, mobilization, and demographic change were present in varying degrees in the restructuring and formation of the delegations to the party conventions in the six southern states in 1984. Hence all three of the general processes of realignment seemed to be at work among the volatile southern party coalitions.[16]

The amount of conversion present among the party activists may seem surprising; however, it is certainly in line with findings from other studies.[17] Even though the Democratic party suffered a net loss, conversion among the party delegates cut both ways in 1984, rather than merely reducing the majority party's advantage in the spectacular fashion that is often visualized as a part of critical realignments. This is significant because it shows that polarization around issues is occurring in both directions, bringing the party elites into greater congruency with the southern electorates and with the national parties' electorates and elites. Over the long haul this is clearly one of the processes through which secular realignment is taking place.

Present also in 1986 was mobilization, a realignment process helping to transform the southern party coalitions. This was especially the case among blacks and women who were attracted to the Democratic coalition in larger numbers. Similarly housewives and retirees were being brought into the Republican coalition.

Several demographic changes have provided a third realignment process for the reshuffling of the two major parties' activists in the South. In-migration, generational change, changing patterns of religiosity, and changing patterns in the economic workforce are reflected in the shifts taking place in the transformation of the party coalitions.

Taken together, and applied throughout the South to fit the variation in pressures for change *or* status quo for party elites, these three processes of realignment fit Thomas Jahnige's conceptual framework for the forces causing realignment.[18] Broad and deep demographic changes have been sweeping the South for years. No region of the United States has experienced more uneven economic development; national and regional policy and social efforts often have viewed large portions of the South to be "developing areas." As a result a situation has arisen in which economic growth *or* decline at various times have impacted upon economic and ethnic groupings very differentially. The resulting southern sectional changes in the composition of the ethnic and class populations have produced great social and cultural stress for various ethnic and economic groupings in the South.[19]

The tradition of Democratic party dominance, reinforced by the powerful myths of Southern political history, delayed the final alienation with the "old politics" and the restructuring of new party elites. However, these 1984 findings in the Comparative State Party Activist Study (CSPAS), and the additional data from two states in 1988, illustrate that the frustration and incongruence of these patterns have been giving way, and that considerable transformation of the party elites have been occurring. As these southern party coalitions solidify they are likely to continue, and even increase, their emphases on the major political and cultural symbols of the region. Eventually the ideological and representational congruence this is developing among the party elites will promote the interests of economic and social groups in each of the major coalitions and, at that point, a "new politics" will be in place.[20] The southern party coalitions in the new politics era will be increasingly congruent with those in national politics because the blocs forming the two major southern party coalitions are increasingly representative of those forming the national major party coalitions.

NOTES

1. This is a party system in which the issues are fought out, in the main, in the majority party, while the second party serves as a moon reflecting the light of the sun of the majority party. This metaphor seems particularly appropriate for the evolutionary stage of several party systems in the South as the Republican party struggles to become sufficiently heterogeneous to serve as a majority party. This is an application of the configuration of political parties explicated by Samuel Lubell in his *Future of American Politics* (New York: Doubleday and Co., 1956, 2d ed., rev.), chaps. 10 and 11. (This book remains amazingly contemporary, speaking directly and prophetically to the current problems of the national and southern Democratic party, and to the problems of the current party system.)

2. See Alexander Heard, *A Two-Party South?* (Chapel Hill: University of North Carolina Press, 1952).

3. For a vivid description of the forces and personalities involved in this and earlier

southern bolts from the national Democratic party see: V. O. Key, Jr., *Southern Politics* (New York: Alfred A. Knopf, 1949), chap. 15.

4. As Crotty details in his "Introduction" to this volume, the changes wrought in the South in a generation were spectacular. One assumes these were likely to be accompanied by profound changes in party politics, particularly in the area of party coalition changes.

5. Cited in Joseph A. Califano, Jr., "Tough Talk for Democrats," *New York Times Magazine* (January 8, 1989): 28.

6. Bernard Cosman, *Five States for Goldwater* (Tuscaloosa: University of Alabama Press, 1966), 120. (He also noted that outside the Deep South nationalization of southern politics begun by the forces of urbanization, migration, and related phenomena of the Eisenhower era were continuing apace. See 121ff.)

7. For an interesting discussion of this point of view see: Robert Reinhold, "The Past Examined," *New York Times* (January 8, 1989, sect. 4A): 16–18.

8. Of course this did not occur as an instantaneous realignment of the moment; it has been occurring over time through various processes; and it still is in process. See discussions in: Martin P. Wattenberg and Arthur H. Miller, "Decay in Regional Party Coalitions: 1952–1980," in Seymour Martin Lipset, ed., *Party Coalitions in the 1980s* (San Francisco: Institute for Contemporary Studies, 1981, 341–370); and Harold W. Stanley, "Southern Partisan Changes: Dealignment, Realignment, or Both?" *Journal of Politics* 50 (February); esp. 84–6.

9. Earl Black and Merle Black, *Politics and Society in the South* (Cambridge: Harvard University Press, 1987), chaps. 11 and 12.

10. E. J. Dionne, Jr., "Solid South Again, But Republican," *New York Times* (Sunday, November 13, 1988): 17.

11. This was happening at other levels in the organization too. For a discussion of this at the county precinct committee persons level in one southern state see: Lewis Bowman, William E. Hulbary, and Anne E. Kelley, "Party Sorting at the Grassroots: Stable Partisans and Party Changers among Florida's Precinct Officials," in Robert F. Steed, et al. eds., *The Disappearing South? Studies in Regional Change and Continuity* (Tuscaloosa: University of Alabama Press, forthcoming, 1989), chap. 4.

12. Among the Jackson delegates two-thirds of those in Virginia were black, as were three-fourths of those in South Carolina. (See Steed and McGlennon in this volume.)

13. Of course, one must be careful in drawing answers to these questions from a survey of a set of delegates at one point in time. As Miller and Jennings have warned: "A single convention, and its participants, captures only part of the action and a portion of the actors in what is in reality a much larger array of interconnected scenes in the ongoing drama of . . . politics."

14. For information about the national delegates over time see Warren E. Miller and M. Kent Jennings, *Parties in Transition: A Longitudinal Study of Party Elites and Party Supporters* (New York: Russell Sage Foundation, 1986), 252: passim.

15. The discussion here is about "realignment" with little consideration of "dealignment" because the data are about party activists—state party convention delegates—that are partisan by definition. Of course differentiations between the two concepts are helpful for evaluations of what is taking place in the system. See the general discussion of this conceptual problem, and data supporting the occurrence of both simultaneously among southern electorate, in Harold W. Stanley, "Southern Partisan Changes: Dealignment, Realignment, or Both?" *Journal of Politics* 50 (February 1988): 64–88.

16. For a good summary of these processes of realignment, and for extensive references to works utilizing various of the processes as explanations of realignment, see: David M. Brodsky, "Partisan Change: An Overview of a Continuing Debate," in Robert H. Swansbrough and David M. Brodsky, eds., *The South's New Politics: Realignment and Dealignment* (Columbia: University of South Carolina Press, 1988), 13ff.

17. See: Alan I. Abramowitz, "Party Leadership, Realignment, and the Nationalization of Southern Politics" (Paper delivered at the 1981 annual meeting of the Southern Political Science Association, November 5–7); Bowman, Hulbary, and Kelley, "Party Sorting at the Grassroots."

18. Thomas Jahnige, "Critical Elections and Social Change," *Polity* 3 (Summer 1971); 465–500.

19. It is often overlooked that just as significant changes can occur in political, social, and economic institutions in "bad" times, so can significant changes occur in "good" times. Murray Havens did a fascinating study of the political havoc that can result from the cultural stress and confrontation produced through the interplay of this set of variables: migration to urbanizing areas, increases in technical education, substantial increases in income, and difficulties of being accepted in the recognized cultural, social, economic, and political institutions of the society. In this study he found "good times," usually upwardly mobile success, to be a root cause of the rapid spread of the political radical right. See his "The Radical Right in the Southwest: Community Response to Shifting Socio-Economic Patterns" (Paper presented at the 1964 annual meeting of the American Political Science Association, Chicago, September).

20. This has already been having wider impact on the outcomes of southern electoral politics than is often appreciated. Even though their gains sometimes are interpreted as not impressive, the Republicans have made significant headway in elections at all levels in the South. The southern Republicans started almost from ground zero and, thereby, have not achieved majorities at legislative levels, but when compared regionally their gains have been significant. See Charles S. Bullock III, "Regional Realignment from an Officeholding Perspective," *Journal of Politics* 50 (August 1988): 553–576.

Appendix
1984 State Convention Delegate Survey

1. Are you a regular delegate or an alternate delegate to this
   convention?

	Percent	Frequency
Regular delegate	89	4410
Alternate delegate	11	540

2. How many years have you lived in this state?

	Percent	Frequency
Five years or less	6	302
6-10 years	8	376
11-15 years	7	360
16-20 years	6	330
Over 20 years	73	3672

3. How many years have you been active in party politics in this state?

	Percent	Frequency
Five years or less	32	1593
6-10 years	21	1043
11-15 years	13	634
16-20 years	12	600
Over 20 years	23	1170

4. How would you describe the area where you now live?

	Percent	Frequency
Urban	28	1395
Suburban	23	1151
Rural small town	32	1580
Rural	17	819

5. What county is that in? [data not reported here]

6. Please indicate which, if any, of the following positions you now
   hold, have held in the past, or would like to hold in the future.

	Percent	Frequency
Now member of local party committee	59	2937
Past member of local party committee	24	1168
Would like to be member of local party committee	18	897
Now local party officer	30	1493
Past local party officer	15	742
Would like to be local party officer	21	1029
Now state party officer	10	509
Past state party officer	7	333
Would like to be state party officer	28	1344
Now delegate to national convention	5	252
Past delegate to national convention	5	246
Would like to be delegate to national convention	38	1843
Now hold elected public office	8	375
Past elected public office	5	252
Would like to hold elected public office	24	1180
Now hold appointed public office	7	349
Past appointed public office	5	261
Would like to hold appointed public office	23	1112

7. During the past 8 years, have you been a delegate to a previous state
   party convention (number attended)?

	Percent	Frequency
One	20	999
Two or more	32	1562
No previous conventions	48	2383

8. During the past 8 years, how actively have you worked in each of the
   following types of campaigns?

	Percent	Frequency
Local election campaigns		
very actively	58	2751
moderately actively	19	911
somewhat actively	14	653
not at all actively	9	455
State election campaigns		
very actively	48	2183
moderately actively	25	1133
somewhat actively	15	704
not at all actively	12	543
National election campaigns		
very actively	40	1746
moderately actively	24	1055
somewhat actively	20	888
not at all actively	16	709

9a. Is there any particular issue which caused you to become involved in
    this year's election campaign?

	Percent	Frequency
Yes	53	2507
No	47	2212

9b. What issue was that?

	Percent	Frequency
Economic issues	17	428
Social welfare/public services issues	8	193
Energy and natural resources issues	2	48
Morality and conduct issues	11	276
Race relations issues	2	43
National defense issues	2	52
General governmental/political issues	47	1177
Foreign policy issues	4	108
State and local issues	3	65
Miscellaneous	4	105

10. How did you vote in the 1980 presidential election?

	Percent	Frequency
Jimmy Carter	52	2586
Ronald Reagan	43	2103
John Anderson	3	127
Other	1	31
Did not vote	2	103

11. During the past 8 years, which of the following activities, if any, have you performed for your party? (Check as many as apply.)

	Percent	Frequency
Getting out the vote	81	4014
Communicating with the public	63	3086
Representing a particular group	29	1409
Recruiting candidates	28	1368
Building party organization	52	2551

12. If you checked one or more of the activities listed in Question 11 above, which ONE of the checked activities do you consider the MOST important? (Check only one.)

	Percent	Frequency
Getting out the vote	58	2630
Communicating with the public	21	950
Representing a particular group	3	117
Recruiting candidates	4	188
Building party organization	14	610

13. What method do you prefer for the selection of your state's delegates to your party's national nominating convention?

	Percent	Frequency
Caucus-convention system	45	2162
Primary election system	43	2027
Other	3	155
No preference	9	425

14. How would you describe your own party affiliation in STATE politics?

	Percent	Frequency
Strong Democrat	49	2419
Democrat, but not too strong	7	341
Independent, closer to Democrats	4	188
Completely independent	1	44
Independent, closer to Republicans	3	143
Republican, but not too strong	4	190
Strong Republican	32	1594

15. How would you describe your own party affiliation in NATIONAL
    politics?

	Percent	Frequency
Strong Democrat	45	2203
Democrat, but not too strong	9	464
Independent, closer to Democrats	4	222
Completely independent	2	75
Independent, closer to Republicans	3	128
Republican, but not too strong	2	112
Strong Republican	35	1712

16a. Have you ever switched parties (that is, from Democratic to
     Republican, or from Republican to Democratic)?

	Percent	Frequency
No	80	3925
Yes	20	969

16b. In what year did you switch? (Asked of those who answered "yes" to
     Question 16a above)

	Percent	Frequency
Before 1970	49	406
1970-1974	11	92
1975-1978	16	136
1979-1983	21	177
1984	3	26

16c. Which ONE of the following was MOST important in your decision to
     switch? (Asked of those who answered "yes" to Question 16a above)

	Percent	Frequency
The party to which I switched had better, more appealing candidates	17	164
The party to which I switched was much more likely to take the right stand on issues	64	603
I switched because friends, relatives, or fellow workers persuaded me to do so	3	26
The party to which I switched offered greater opportunities for personal advancement	3	24
The party to which I switched is more active and has a superior organization	3	28
Other	10	94

17. Which ONE of the following statements more clearly expresses your
    opinion? (Check only one.)

	Percent	Frequency
If I disagreed with a major stand of my party which was important to me, I would stop working for the party	17	799
It is more important to me that my party make a broad electoral appeal than for my party to take stands on issues that I personally agree with	67	3079
Can't decide, no opinion	16	715

18. Look at the reasons listed below for becoming involved in politics this year. Please indicate how important each of them was for you.

	Percent	Frequency
To support my party		
very important	77	3660
somewhat important	19	881
not important	4	200
To help my political career		
very important	14	567
somewhat important	20	817
not important	66	2723
To enjoy the excitement of the campaign		
very important	24	1007
somewhat important	43	1821
not important	33	1425
To meet other people with similar interests		
very important	37	1593
somewhat important	46	1996
not important	17	726
To support a particular candidate I believe in		
very important	82	3748
somewhat important	14	651
not important	4	165
To work for issues		
very important	78	3471
somewhat important	19	818
not important	3	142
To enjoy the visibility of being a delegate		
very important	14	597
somewhat important	25	1040
not important	61	2555
To fulfill my civic responsibilities		
very important	60	2682
somewhat important	31	1391
not important	10	437
To make business or professional contacts		
very important	10	399
somewhat important	22	926
not important	68	2815

19. Which ONE of the following is the MOST important to you for becoming involved in politics this year? (Check only one.)

	Percent	Frequency
To support my party	39	1948
To help my political career	3	130
To enjoy the excitement of the campaign	2	76
To meet other people with similar interests	1	68
To support a particular candidate I believe in	22	1073
To work for issues	22	1096
To enjoy the visibility of being a delegate	*	18
To fulfill my civic responsibilities	9	425
To make business or professional contacts	2	119

20. How would you describe your own political philosophy?

	Percent	Frequency
Extremely liberal	7	311
Liberal	22	1034
Slightly liberal	12	552
Middle-of-the-road	13	596
Slightly conservative	11	534
Conservative	29	1386
Extremely conservative	7	359

21. You may have been active in some of the following groups. If so,
    check those groups to which you belong. (Check as many as apply.)

	Percent	Frequency
Labor unions	12	552
Business organizations	35	1702
Religious-related groups	44	2146
Civil rights groups	19	936
Teachers or school administrators groups	22	1058
Conservation or ecology groups	13	615
Anti-abortion groups	7	342
Farm or agricultural groups	11	536
Women's rights groups	16	785
Public interest groups	35	1728

22. Please indicate your position on each of the following issues.

	Percent	Frequency
Equal Rights Amendment to the Constitution		
strongly favor	35	1691
favor	18	882
undecided	8	366
oppose	19	895
strongly oppose	20	982
Constitutional amendment to prohibit abortions except when the mother's life is endangered		
strongly favor	24	1143
favor	14	648
undecided	12	558
oppose	21	1025
strongly oppose	29	1411
Continued increase in defense spending even if it requires cutting domestic programs		
strongly favor	18	848
favor	22	1070
undecided	11	501
oppose	24	1164
strongly oppose	25	1192
Government sponsored national health insurance program		
strongly favor	17	822
favor	21	1016
undecided	18	854
oppose	19	907
strongly oppose	25	1184
More rapid development of nuclear power		
strongly favor	12	545
favor	23	1103
undecided	21	966
oppose	24	1125
strongly oppose	21	980

Across-the-board cuts in spending to
balance the federal budget

strongly favor	29	1386
favor	34	1611
undecided	14	651
oppose	17	815
strongly oppose	6	309

Affirmative action programs to
increase minority representation
in jobs and higher education

strongly favor	23	1072
favor	23	1101
undecided	14	642
oppose	25	1181
strongly oppose	16	768

Increasing America's military
presence in the Middle East

strongly favor	4	189
favor	14	687
undecided	25	1186
oppose	37	1750
strongly oppose	19	912

Increasing America's military
presence in Latin America

strongly favor	9	438
favor	21	1011
undecided	20	924
oppose	29	1362
strongly oppose	21	982

More intensive negotiation with
the Soviet Union on arms control

strongly favor	35	1661
favor	44	2088
undecided	9	420
oppose	8	392
strongly oppose	4	204

A nuclear freeze agreed to by the
U.S. and the Soviet Union

strongly favor	35	1675
favor	32	1516
undecided	10	483
oppose	12	561
strongly oppose	11	506

An across-the-board tax increase
to reduce the federal budget deficit

strongly favor	7	348
favor	22	1045
undecided	18	842
oppose	30	1417
strongly oppose	23	1085

Stricter legislation to control handguns

strongly favor	22	1027
favor	24	1129
undecided	11	512
oppose	22	1046
strongly oppose	22	1028

Governmental action to increase energy
sources even though it might decrease
protection for the environment

strongly favor	5	255
favor	20	954
undecided	22	1056
oppose	37	1736
strongly oppose	15	702

A public works program to reduce
unemployment even if it means an
increase in inflation

strongly favor	9	419
favor	21	1001
undecided	19	897
oppose	31	1472
strongly oppose	20	964

23. How would you rate the political philosophy of each of the following
    on a 7-point scale ranging from very liberal to very conservative?

	Percent	Frequency
Ronald Reagan		
very liberal	2	81
liberal	1	50
slightly liberal	1	36
middle-of-the-road	4	167
slightly conservative	6	263
conservative	46	2114
very conservative	40	1840
Gary Hart		
very liberal	24	1072
liberal	33	1457
slightly liberal	20	900
middle-of-the-road	14	634
slightly conservative	6	254
conservative	3	119
very conservative	1	27
Walter Mondale		
very liberal	37	1659
liberal	34	1527
slightly liberal	15	680
middle-of-the-road	10	428
slightly conservative	2	111
conservative	1	62
very conservative	*	24
Jesse Jackson		
very liberal	59	2605
liberal	27	1181
slightly liberal	8	336
middle-of-the-road	4	197
slightly conservative	1	46
conservative	1	36
very conservative	1	30
John Glenn		
very liberal	4	183
liberal	13	545
slightly liberal	20	855
middle-of-the-road	32	1390
slightly conservative	17	752
conservative	11	488
very conservative	3	114
The average American voter		
very liberal	1	50
liberal	3	148
slightly liberal	14	608
middle-of-the-road	42	1906
slightly conservative	32	1445
conservative	7	317
very conservative	*	22

```
The average voter in this state
     very liberal                         1              56
     liberal                              4             191
     slightly liberal                    11             481
     middle-of-the-road                  19             845
     slightly conservative               38            1722
     conservative                        24            1091
     very conservative                    2              99

The national Democratic party
     very liberal                        27            1234
     liberal                             31            1401
     slightly liberal                    25            1122
     middle-of-the-road                  10             474
     slightly conservative                4             185
     conservative                         2              80
     very conservative                    *              23

The Democratic party in this state
     very liberal                        14             611
     liberal                             24            1063
     slightly liberal                    24            1054
     middle-of-the-road                  18             825
     slightly conservative               14             610
     conservative                         5             243
     very conservative                    1              59

The national Republican party
     very liberal                         1              68
     liberal                              1              67
     slightly liberal                     1              65
     middle-of-the-road                   5             227
     slightly conservative               18             794
     conservative                        50            2239
     very conservative                   23            1024

The Republican party in this state
     very liberal                         2              75
     liberal                              1              62
     slightly liberal                     1              52
     middle-of-the-road                   4             157
     slightly conservative               10             433
     conservative                        44            1971
     very conservative                   39            1741
```

24. Who is NOW your first choice for your party's presidential nomination?

	Percent	Frequency
Ronald Reagan	41	1886
Gary Hart	14	629
Walter Mondale	32	1483
Jesse Jackson	11	507
John Glenn	*	24
Ernest Hollings	*	9
Reuben Askew	0	0
Other	2	96

25. Who WAS your first choice for your party's presidential nomination as of January 1984?

	Percent	Frequency
Ronald Reagan	41	1893
Gary Hart	12	541
Walter Mondale	25	1141
Jesse Jackson	11	514
John Glenn	5	254
Ernest Hollings	2	97
Reuben Askew	*	6
Other	3	155

26. How good a chance do you think each of the following candidates would have of winning the November election if nominated by his party?

	Percent	Frequency
Ronald Reagan		
definitely would win	39	1768
probably would win	32	1444
might win	22	1006
probably would lose	4	192
definitely would lose	4	174
Gary Hart		
definitely would win	3	126
probably would win	10	448
might win	36	1580
probably would lose	34	1465
definitely would lose	17	734
Walter Mondale		
definitely would win	11	491
probably would win	15	703
might win	31	1411
probably would lose	27	1215
definitely would lose	17	763
Jesse Jackson		
definitely would win	2	78
probably would win	3	119
might win	6	274
probably would lose	24	1032
definitely would lose	66	2872
John Glenn		
definitely would win	1	38
probably would win	2	106
might win	15	631
probably would lose	31	1337
definitely would lose	50	2141

27. At present, how important a role DOES your STATE party organization play in each of the following areas?

	Percent	Frequency
Providing campaign assistance to candidates		
very important	44	1998
somewhat important	35	1589
not important	10	470
not sure	12	540
Taking positions on issues to influence elected officials		
very important	33	1491
somewhat important	42	1858
not important	16	700
not sure	10	433
Providing services and information to elected officials and local party organizations between campaigns		
very important	43	1917
somewhat important	37	1661
not important	10	467
not sure	10	435
Recruiting candidates		
very important	38	1662
somewhat important	35	1544
not important	15	678
not sure	12	527

Informing the electorate about party goals
and positions

very important	44	1998
somewhat important	33	1490
not important	14	624
not sure	8	377

28. Of the following roles for your state party organization, which ONE
    of the following do you consider the MOST important? (Check only
    one.)

	Percent	Frequency
Providing campaign assistance to candidates	29	1362
Taking positions on issues to influence elected officials	18	854
Providing services and information to elected officials and local party organizations between campaigns	21	962
Recruiting candidates	7	319
Informing electorate about party goals and positions	25	1136

29. With regard to the party activities listed in Question 28 above, in
    your opinion has your party's organization in this state generally
    IMPROVED or DETERIORATED in the last few years?

	Percent	Frequency
Improved	66	2969
Deteriorated	14	633
No change	20	926

30. Was there ever a time when you thought that your party supporters
    would have been justified in splitting their ballots between
    Democratic and Republican candidates? (Check only one.)

	Percent	Frequency
Yes, in national elections only	6	308
Yes, in state/local elections only	17	798
Yes, in both national and state/local elections	23	1071
No	45	2132
Not sure	9	409

31. Which ONE of the following statements MOST closely expresses your own
    opinion? (Check only one.)

	Percent	Frequency
The most important factor in selecting candidates for public office is their party loyalty and prior service to the party	13	608
The most important factor in selecting candidates for public office is their positions on issues and ideology	78	3660
The most important factor in selecting candidates for public office is their chance for electoral victory	6	280
Not sure; no opinion	3	155

32. Please indicate whether you agree or disagree with each of the
    following statements.

	Percent	Frequency
The use of marijuana is morally wrong		
strongly agree	40	1911
agree	22	1061
undecided	10	462
disagree	19	888
strongly disagree	9	434
Governmental regulation of business to protect the environment is excessive		
strongly agree	13	603
agree	27	1262
undecided	12	569
disagree	33	1536
strongly disagree	14	669
Homosexual behavior is morally wrong		
strongly agree	48	2246
agree	21	970
undecided	10	493
disagree	13	609
strongly disagree	8	391
A constitutional amendment to permit prayers and Bible-reading in the public schools		
strongly agree	34	1577
agree	21	982
undecided	8	375
disagree	17	816
strongly disagree	20	964
A broad-based tax to increase funding for public education		
strongly agree	23	1053
agree	30	1407
undecided	14	671
disagree	20	941
strongly disagree	13	587
Steps should be taken to reduce the number of people getting food stamps		
strongly agree	28	1307
agree	31	1444
undecided	15	694
disagree	17	816
strongly disagree	9	435

33. What is your attitude toward conservative Christian organizations such as Moral Majority and Christian Voice?

	Percent	Frequency
Member	4	198
Sympathizer	26	1214
Opponent	48	2228
Am not familiar with these organizations; no opinion	21	963

34. How politically active were your parents when you were growing up?

	Percent	Frequency
Both parents active	23	1117
Father active, Mother inactive	17	825
Mother active, Father inactive	5	237
Neither parent active	49	2336
Not sure	6	265

35. How would you describe your parents' party affiliation or party identification (ID) at the time when you were growing up?

	Percent	Frequency
Father's state party ID		
strong Democrat	38	1641
Democrat, but not too strong	19	829
independent, closer to Democrats	7	313
completely independent	4	172
independent, closer to Republicans	6	269
Republican, but not too strong	7	291
strong Republican	11	469
not sure	9	383
Father's national party ID		
strong Democrat	31	1167
Democrat, but not too strong	19	717
independent, closer to Democrats	7	262
completely independent	4	156
independent, closer to Republicans	8	291
Republican, but not too strong	8	302
strong Republican	14	540
not sure	8	287
Mother's state party ID		
strong Democrat	32	1308
Democrat, but not too strong	22	876
independent, closer to Democrats	8	324
completely independent	5	193
independent, closer to Republicans	6	227
Republican, but not too strong	8	323
strong Republican	10	385
not sure	10	389
Mother's national party ID		
strong Democrat	28	1019
Democrat, but not too strong	21	756
independent, closer to Democrats	8	282
completely independent	5	186
independent, closer to Republicans	7	260
Republican, but not too strong	9	331
strong Republican	12	443
not sure	9	331

36. In what state did you spend most of your childhood? [Data reported by South and non-South]

	Percent	Frequency
South	74	3752
Non-South	26	1288

37. What is your age?

	Percent	Frequency
Under 35 years old	22	1114
35-54 years old	45	2257
Over 54 years old	33	1669

38. What is your sex?

	Percent	Frequency
Female	48	2315
Male	52	2514

39. What is your race?

	Percent	Frequency
White	81	3889
Black	17	826
Hispanic	1	64
Asian-American	*	9
American Indian	1	29

40. How much formal schooling have you completed?

	Percent	Frequency
None	*	4
Grade school only	1	31
Some high school	2	88
Graduated from high school	10	464
Vocational or trade school	4	181
Some college	26	1262
Graduated from college	21	1027
Post-college work	36	1748

41. What is your current occupation? (If retired, check pre-retirement occupation.)

	Percent	Frequency
Professional	38	1790
Business/managerial	23	1067
Clerical/sales	8	395
Skilled/semi-skilled/service worker	6	281
Public official	7	322
Housewife	9	417
Student	3	122
Unemployed	1	58
Other	6	277

42. What would you estimate your family's income to be this year before taxes?

	Percent	Frequency
0 to $14,999	10	480
$15,000 to 24,999	19	885
$25,000 to 34,999	22	998
$35,000 to 44,999	18	855
$45,000 to 59,999	15	682
$60,000 or more	16	736

43. What is your religious preference?

	Percent	Frequency
Reform Era Protestant	22	1015
Pietistic	56	2521
Neo-Fundamentalist	4	186
Non-traditional Christian	2	93
Roman Catholic	10	443
Jewish	1	40
Eastern Orthodox	*	4
Other	5	227

44. How often would you say you go to church or synagogue?

	Percent	Frequency
Every week	44	2092
Almost every week	20	972
Once or twice a month	12	565
A few times a year	18	887
Never	6	289

45. Some people have had deep religious experiences commonly described as being "born again"; other religious people have not had such experiences. Have you had an experience of this sort?

	Percent	Frequency
Yes	39	1842
No	53	2487
Don't know	8	354

46. Of the following statements about the Bible, which ONE is CLOSEST to your own view? (Check only one.)

	Percent	Frequency
The Bible is God's word and all it says is true	43	2019
The Bible was written by men inspired by God but it contains some human errors	46	2204
The Bible is a good book because it was written by wise men, but God had nothing to do with it	5	233
The Bible was written by men who lived so long ago that it is worth very little today	1	40
Other, don't know	5	241

Note: Percentages reported are based on the number of valid responses for each question or item. Totals may not add to 100 because of rounding.

Selected Bibliography

Abramowitz, Alan I., John McGlennon, and Ronald Rapoport. "The Party Isn't Over: Incentives for Activism in the 1980 Presidential Nominating Campaign." *Journal of Politics* 45 (1983): 1006–1015.

———. "Presidential Activists and the Nationalization of Party Politics in Virginia." In *Contemporary Southern Political Attitudes and Behavior*, edited by Laurence W. Moreland, Tod A. Baker, and Robert P. Steed. New York: Praeger Publishers, 1982.

Abramowitz, Alan I., and Walter J. Stone. *Nomination Politics: Party Activists and Presidential Choice*. New York: Praeger Publishers, 1984.

Althoff, Phillip, and Samuel C. Patterson. "Political Activism in a Rural County." *Midwest Journal of Political Science* 10 (1966): 39–51.

Baker, Tod A., and Robert P. Steed. "Southern Political Elites and Social Change: An Explanatory Study." In *Politics '74: Trends in Southern Politics*, edited by Tinsley E. Yarbough. Greenville, N.C.: East Carolina University Press, 1974.

Baker, Tod A., Robert P. Steed, and Laurence W. Moreland. "Fundamentalist Beliefs and Southern Distinctiveness: A Study of the Political Attitudes of State Party Activists." In *Religion and Politics in the South: Mass and Elite Perspectives*, edited by Tod A. Baker, Robert P. Steed, and Laurence W. Moreland. New York: Praeger Publishers, 1983.

———, editors. *Religion and Politics in the South*. New York: Praeger Publishers, 1983.

———. "Southern Distinctiveness and the Emergence of Party Competition: The Case of a Deep South State." In *Contemporary Southern Political Attitudes and Behavior*, edited by Laurence W. Moreland, Tod A. Baker, and Robert P. Steed. New York: Praeger Publishers, 1982.

Bartley, Numan V. "The South and Sectionalism in American Politics." *Journal of Politics* 38 (1976): 239–257.

———. *The Rise of Massive Resistance: Race and Politics in the South in the 1950s*. Baton Rouge: Louisiana State University Press, 1969.

————, and Hugh D. Graham. *Southern Politics and the Second Reconstruction*. Baltimore: Johns Hopkins University Press, 1975.

Bass, Jack, and Walter DeVries. *The Transformation of Southern Politics: Social Change and Political Consequence since 1945*. New York: Basic Books, 1976.

Bass, Jack, and Thomas E. Terrill, editors. *The American South Comes of Age*. New York: Alfred A. Knopf, 1986.

Beck, Paul Allen. "Partisan Dealignment in the Postwar South." *American Political Science Review* 71 (1977): 477–496.

————, and Paul Lopatto. "The End of Southern Distinctiveness." In *Contemporary Southern Political Attitudes and Behavior*, edited by Laurence W. Moreland, Tod A. Baker, and Robert P. Steed. New York: Praeger Publishers, 1982.

Bensel, Richard Franklin. *Sectionalism and American Political Development, 1880–1980*. Madison: University of Wisconsin Press, 1984.

Black, Earl. *Southern Governors and Civil Rights*. Cambridge, Mass.: Harvard University Press, 1976.

————. "The Militant Segregationist Vote in the Post Brown South: A Comparative Analysis." *Social Science Quarterly* 54 (173): 66–84.

————, and Merle Black. *Politics and Society in the South*. Cambridge, Mass: Harvard University Press, 1987.

Boles, Janet. *The Politics of the Equal Rights Amendment*. New York: Longman, 1979.

Bone, Hugh A. *Party Committees and National Politics*. Seattle: University of Washington Press, 1958.

Botsch, Robert. *We Shall Not Overcome: Populism and Southern Blue-Collar Workers*. Chapel Hill: University of North Carolina Press, 1980.

Bowman, Lewis, and G. R. Boynton. "Activities and Role Definitions of Grassroots Party Officials." *Journal of Politics* 28 (1966): 121–143.

————. "Recruitment Patterns among Local Party Officials." *American Political Science Review* 60 (1966): 667–676.

Bowman, Lewis, Dennis S. Ippolito, and William S. Donaldson. "Incentives for Maintenance of Grassroots Political Activism." *Midwest Journal of Political Science* 13 (1969): 126–139.

Bromley, David G., and Anson D. Shupe, editors. *New Christian Politics*. Macon, Georgia: Mercer University Press, 1984.

Brudney, Jeffrey L., and Gary W. Copeland. "Evangelicals as a Political Force: Reagan and the 1980 Religious Vote." *Social Science Quarterly* 65 (1984): 1072–1079.

Buell, Emmett, and Lee Sigelman. "An Army That Meets Every Sunday: Popular Support for the Moral Majority in 1980." *Social Science Quarterly* 66 (1985): 426–434.

Campbell, Angus, Philip E. Converse, Warren E. Miller, and Donald E. Stokes. *White Attitudes toward Black People*. Ann Arbor: University of Michigan Institute for Social Research, 1971.

————. *The American Voter*. New York: John Wiley and Sons, 1960.

Campbell, Bruce A. "Change in the Southern Electorate." *American Journal of Political Science* 21 (1977): 37–64.

————. "Patterns of Change in the Partisan Loyalties of Native Southerners, 1952–1972." *Journal of Politics* 39 (1977): 730–761.

Carmines, Edward G., and Harold W. Stanley. "Ideological Realignment in the Contemporary South: Where Have All the Conservatives Gone?" In *The Disappearing South? Studies in Regional Change and Continuity*, edited by Robert P. Steed,

Laurence W. Moreland, and Tod A. Baker. Tuscaloosa: University of Alabama Press, 1989.

Carmines, Edward G., and James A. Stimson. "On the Structure and Sequence of Issue Evolution." *American Political Science Review* 80 (1986): 901–920.

———. "Racial Issues and the Structure of Mass Belief Systems." *Journal of Politics* 44 (1982): 2–20.

———. "Issue Evolution, Population Replacement, and Normal Partisan Change." *American Political Science Review* 75 (1981): 107–118.

Carter, Hodding. *Southern Legacy*. Baton Rouge: Louisiana State University Press, 1950.

Cash, Wilbur J. *The Mind of the South*. New York: Alfred A. Knopf, 1941.

Cassel, Carol A. "Change in Electoral Participation in the South." *Journal of Politics* 41 (1979): 907–917.

Ceasar, James W. *Reforming the Reforms: A Critical Analysis of the Presidential Selection Process*. Cambridge, Mass.: Ballinger, 1982.

Clotfelter, C. T. "Urban School Desegregation and Declines in White Enrollment: A Reexamination." *Journal of Urban Economics* 6 (1979): 352–370.

Converse, Philip E. "On the Possibility of Major Political Realignment in the South." In *Elections and the Political Order*, Angus Campbell, Philip E. Converse, Warren E. Miller, and Donald E. Stokes. New York: John Wiley and Sons, 1966.

Conway, Margaret, and Frank B. Feigert. "Motivation and Task Performance among Party Precinct Workers." *Western Political Quarterly* 27 (1974): 693–709.

———. "Motivation, Incentive Systems, and Political Party Organization." *American Political Science Review* 62 (1968): 1169–1183.

Cook, Samuel D. "Political Movements and Organizations." *Journal of Politics* 26 (1964): 130–153.

Cosman, Bernard. *Five States for Goldwater*. University, Ala.: University of Alabama Press, 1966.

Cotter, Cornelius P., James L. Gibson, John F. Bibby, and Robert J. Huckshorn. *Party Organizations in American Politics*. New York: Praeger Publishers, 1984.

Crotty, William, editor. *Political Parties in Local Areas*. Knoxville: University of Tennessee Press, 1986.

———. *Party Reform*. New York: Longman, 1983.

———. *Decision for the Democrats*. Baltimore: Johns Hopkins University Press, 1978.

———, and John S. Jackson III. *Presidential Primaries and Nominations*. Washington: Congressional Quarterly Press, 1985.

Darcy, R., Susan Welch, and Janet Clark. *Women, Elections, and Representation*. New York: Longman, 1987.

DeJong, Gordon F., and Thomas R. Ford. "Religious Fundamentalism and Denominational Preference in the Southern Appalachian Region." *Journal for the Scientific Study of Religion* 5 (1965): 24–43.

Eldersveld, Samuel J. *Political Parties in American Society*. New York: Basic Books, 1982.

———. *Political Parties: A Behavioral Analysis*. Chicago: Rand McNally, 1964.

Elifson, Kirk W., and C. Kirk Hadaway. "Prayer in Public Schools: When Church and State Collide." *Public Opinion Quarterly* 49 (1985): 317–329.

England, Robert E. "The Gospel and Racial Equality." *Fundamentalist Journal* (1986): 10.

England, Robert E., Ed Dobson, and Ed Hinson, editors. *The Fundamentalist Phenomenon*. Garden City: Doubleday, 1981.

England, Robert E., and Kenneth J. Meier. "From Desegregation to Integration: Second-Generation Discrimination as an Institutional Impediment." *American Politics Quarterly* 13 (1985): 227–247.

Fichter, Joseph H., and George Maddox. "Religion in the South, Old and New." In *The South in Continuity and Change*, edited by John C. McKinney and Edgar T. Thompson. Durham: Duke University Press, 1965.

Flinn, Thomas A., and Frederick M. Wirt. "Local Party Leaders: Groups of Like-Minded Men." *Midwest Journal of Political Science* 9 (1965): 77–98.

Fowlkes, Diane L., Jerry Perkins, and Sue Tolleson Rinehart. "Women in Southern Party Politics: Roles, Activities, and Futures." In *Party Politics in the South*, edited by Robert P. Steed, Laurence W. Moreland, and Tod A. Baker. New York: Praeger Publishers, 1980.

Franklin, John Hope. *The Militant South: 1800–1861*. Cambridge, Mass.: Belknap, 1956.

Gastil, Raymond D. *Cultural Regions of the United States*. Seattle: University of Washington Press, 1976.

Gibson, James L., Cornelius P. Cotter, John F. Bibby, and Robert J. Huckshorn. "Assessing Party Organizational Strength." *American Journal of Political Science* 27 (1983): 193–222.

Glazer, Amihai, and Marc Robbins. "Voters and Roll Call Voting: The Effect on Congressional Elections." *Political Behavior* 5 (1983): 377–389.

Glenn, Norval D. "Class and Party Support in the United States: Recent and Emerging Trends." *Public Opinion Quarterly* 37 (1973): 1–20.

—— and J. L. Simmons. "Are Regional Cultural Differences Disappearing?" *Public Opinion Quarterly* 31 (1967): 172–180.

Grantham, Dewey W. *The Democratic South*. New York: Norton, 1963.

Green, John C., and James L. Guth. "The Christian Right in the Republican Party: The Case of Pat Robertson's Supporters." *Journal of Politics* 50 (1988): 150–165.

Hadley, Charles D. "The Continuing Transformation of Southern Politics." In *Political Ideas and Institutions*, edited by Edward V. Heck and Alan T. Leonhard. Dubuque, Iowa: Kendall/Hunt, 1983.

——. "The Impact of the Louisiana Open Electronics System Reform." *State Government* 58 (1986): 153–154.

——. "Dual Partisan Identification in the South." *Journal of Politics* 47 (1985): 254–268.

——. "The Nationalization of American Politics: Congress, the Supreme Court, and the National Political Parties." *The Journal of Social and Political Studies* 4 (1979): 359–380.

——, and Susan E. Howell. "The Southern Split Ticket Voter, 1952–1976: Republican Conversion or Democratic Decline?" In *Party Politics in the South*, edited by Robert P. Steed, Laurence W. Moreland, and Tod A. Baker. New York: Praeger Publications, 1980.

Hanks, Lawrence J. *The Struggle for Black Empowerment in Three Georgia Counties*. Knoxville: University of Tennessee Press, 1987.

Havard, William C., editor. *The Changing Politics of the South*. Baton Rouge: Louisiana State University Press, 1972.

Hawkey, Earl W. "Southern Conservatism 1956–1976." In *Contemporary Southern*

Political Attitudes and Behavior, edited by Laurence W. Moreland, Tod A. Baker, and Robert P. Steed. New York: Praeger Publishers, 1982.

Heberle, Rudolf. "Regionalism: Some Critical Observations." *Social Forces* 21 (1943): 280–286.

Hero, Alfred O., Jr. *The Southerner and World Affairs*. Baton Rouge: Louisiana State University Press, 1965.

Hertzler, J. O. "Some Notes on the Social Psychology of Regionalism." *Social Forces* 18 (1940): 331–337.

Hill, Samuel S., Jr., editor. *Religion in the Southern States: A Historical Study*. Macon, Ga.: Mercer University Press, 1983.

———. *Southern Churches in Crisis*. New York: Holt, Rinehart and Winston, 1967.

Huckshorn, Robert J. "The Role Orientations of the State Party Chairmen." In *The Party Symbol*, edited by William J. Crotty. San Francisco: Freeman, 1980.

———. *Party Leadership in the States*. Amherst: University of Massachusetts Press, 1976.

Ippolito, Dennis S. "Political Perspectives of Suburban Party Leaders." *Social Science Quarterly* 49 (1969): 800–815.

———, and Lewis Bowman. "Goals and Activities of Party Officials in a Suburban Community." *Western Political Quarterly* 22 (1969): 572–580.

Jewell, Malcolm E., and David M. Olson. *American State Political Parties and Elections*. Homewood, Ill.: Dorsey, 1978.

Johnson, Stephen D., and Joseph B. Tamney. "Support for the Moral Majority: A Test of a Model." *Journal for the Scientific Study of Religion* 23 (1984): 183–196.

———. "The Christian Right and the 1980 Presidential Election." *Journal for the Scientific Study of Religion* 21 (1982): 123–131.

Johnston, W. Lee. "The New Right in North Carolina: From a Minority Faction in the State's Democratic Party to the Dominant Faction in the State's Republican Party." *Journal of the North Carolina Political Science Association* 3 (1983): 9–23.

Key, V. O., Jr. *Southern Politics in State and Nation*. New York: Alfred A. Knopf, 1949.

Killian, Lewis. *White Southerners*. New York: Random House, 1970.

Kirby, Jack Temple. *Media Made Dixie: The South in the American Imagination*. Baton Rouge: Louisiana State University Press, 1978.

Kirkpatrick, Jeane J. *Dismantling the Parties: Reflections on Party Reform and Party Decomposition*. Washington, D.C.: American Enterprise Institute, 1978.

———. *The New Presidential Elite: Men and Women in National Politics*. New York: Russell Sage Foundation and Twentieth Century Fund, 1976.

———. *Political Women*. New York: Basic Books, 1974.

Kolbe, Richard L. *American Political Parties: An Uncertain Future*. New York: Harper and Row, 1985.

Kousser, J. Morgan. *The Shaping of Southern Politics: Suffrage Restriction and the Establishment of the One-Party South, 1880–1910*. New Haven: Yale University Press, 1974.

Ladd, Everett Carll, Jr., and Charles D. Hadley. *Transformation of the American Party System: Political Coalitions from the New Deal to the 1970s*, 2d ed. New York: W. W. Norton, 1978.

Lamis, Alexander P. *The Two-Party South*. New York: Oxford University Press, 1984.

Lea, James F. *Contemporary Southern Politics*. Baton Rouge: Louisiana State University Press, 1988.

LeBlanc, Hugh L. *American Political Parties*. New York: St. Martin's Press, 1982.

Leiserson, Avery, editor. *The American South in the 1960's*. New York: Praeger Publishers, 1964.

Liebman, Robert C., and Robert Wuthnow, editors. *The New Christian Right*. Hawthorne, New York: Aldine, 1983.

Lienesch, Michael. "Right-Wing Religion: Christian Conservatism as a Political Movement." *Political Science Quarterly* 97 (1982): 403–425.

Lipset, Seymour Martin. "Beyond 1984: The Anomalies of American Politics." *PS* 19 (1986): 222–236.

McKern, Sharon. *Redneck Mothers, Good Ol' Girls, and Other Southern Belles: A Celebration of the Women of Dixie*. New York: Viking, 1979.

McKinney, John C., and Linda B. Bourque. "The Changing South: National Incorporation of a Region." *American Sociological Review* 36 (1971): 399–412.

———, and Edgar T. Thompson, editors. *The South in Continuity and Change*. Durham: Duke University Press, 1965.

Marshall, Thomas R. *Presidential Nominations in a Reform Age*. New York: Praeger Publishers, 1981.

Marvick, Dwaine. "Party Organizational Personnel and Electoral Democracy in Los Angeles, 1963–1972." In *The Party Symbol*, edited by William J. Crotty. San Francisco: W. H. Freeman, 1980.

———. "Political Linkage Functions of Rival Party Activists in the United States: Los Angeles, 1969–1974." In *Political Parties and Linkage*, edited by Kay Lawson. New Haven: Yale University Press, 1980.

Matthews, Donald R., and James W. Prothro. *Negroes and the New Southern Politics*. New York: Harcourt, Brace and World, 1966.

———. "Stateways v. Folkways: Critical Factors in Southern Reactions to *Brown* v. *Board of Education*." In *Essays on the American Constitution*, edited by Gottfried Dietze. Englewood Cliffs: Prentice-Hall, 1964.

Mezey, Michael L. "The Minds of the South." In *Religion and Politics in the South*, edited by Tod A. Baker, Robert P. Steed, and Laurence W. Moreland. New York: Praeger Publishers, 1983.

Miller, Arthur H., and Martin Wattenberg. "Politics from the Pulpit: Religiosity and the 1980 Elections." *Public Opinion Quarterly* 48 (1984): 301–317.

Miller, Warren E., and M. Kent Jennings. *Parties in Transition: A Longitudinal Study of Party Elites and Party Supporters*. New York: Russell Sage Foundations, 1986.

Moreland, Laurence W., Tod A. Baker, and Robert P. Steed, editors. *Contemporary Southern Political Attitudes and Behavior*. New York: Praeger Publishers, 1982.

Moreland, Laurence W., Robert P. Steed, and Tod A. Baker, editors. *The 1988 Presidential Election in the South*. New York: Praeger Publishers, 1989.

———, editors. *Blacks in Southern Politics*. New York: Praeger Publishers, 1987.

———. "Migration and Activist Politics." In *The Life of the Parties: Activists in Presidential Politics*, edited by Ronald B. Rapoport, Alan I. Abramowitz, and John McGlennon. Lexington, Ky.: University Press of Kentucky, 1986.

Morland, J. Kenneth, editor. *The Not So Solid South: Anthropological Studies in a Regional Subculture*. Athens: University of Georgia Press, 1971.

Morris, Willie, editor. *The South Today: 100 Years after Appomattox*. New York: Harper and Row, 1965.

Murray, Albert. *South to a Very Old Place*. New York: McGraw-Hill, 1971.

Myrdal, Gunnar. *An American Dilemma*. New York: Harper and Brothers, 1944.

Newby, I. A. *The South: A History*. New York: Holt, Rinehart, and Winston, 1978.

O'Brien, Michael. *The Idea of the American South, 1920–1941*. Baltimore: Johns Hopkins Press, 1979.

Patel, Kent, Denny Pilant, and Gary Rose. "Born-Again Christians in the Bible Belt." *American Politics Quarterly* 10 (1982): 255–271.

Patterson, Samuel C. "Characteristics of Party Leaders." *Western Political Quarterly* 16 (1963): 332–352.

Perkins, Jerry. "Ideology in the South: Meaning and Bases in Masses and Elites." In *Contemporary Southern Political Attitudes and Behavior*, edited by Laurence W. Moreland, Tod A. Baker, and Robert P. Steed. New York: Praeger Publishers, 1982.

———, Donald Fairchild, and Murray Havens. "The Effects of Evangelism on Southern Black and White Political Attitudes and Voting Behavior." In *Religion and Politics in the South*, edited by Tod A. Baker, Robert P. Steed, and Laurence W. Moreland. New York: Praeger Publishers, 1983.

Petrocik, John R. "Realignment: New Party Coalitions and the Nationalization of the South." *Journal of Politics* 49 (1987): 347–375.

———. *Party Coalitions: Realignments and the Decline of the New Deal Party System*. Chicago: University of Chicago Press, 1981.

Phillips, Ulrich B. "The Central Theme of Southern History." *American Historical Review* 34 (1928): 30–43.

Polsby, Nelson W. *Consequences of Party Reform*. Oxford: Oxford University Press, 1983.

Pomper, Gerald. "From Confusion to Clarity: Issues and American Voters, 1956–1968." *American Political Science Review* 66 (1972): 415–428.

Potter, David. *The South and the Concurrent Majority*. Baton Rouge: Louisiana State University Press, 1972.

———. *The South and the Sectional Conflict*. Baton Rouge: Louisiana State University Press, 1968.

Price, David E. *Bringing Back the Parties*. Washington, D.C.: Congressional Quarterly, 1984.

Ranney, Austin. *Curing the Mischiefs of Faction*. Berkeley: University of California Press, 1975.

Rapoport, Ronald B., Alan I. Abramowitz, and John McGlennon, editors. *The Life of the Parties: Activists in Presidential Politics*. Lexington, Ky.: University Press of Kentucky, 1986.

Reed, John Shelton. *Southerners: The Social Psychology of Sectionalism*. Chapel Hill: University of North Carolina Press, 1983.

———. "For Dixieland: The Sectionalism of *I'll Take My Stand*." In *A Band of Prophets: The Vanderbilt Agrarians after Fifty Years*, edited by Walter Sullivan and William C. Havard. Baton Rouge: Louisiana State University Press, 1982.

———. *One South: An Ethnic Approach to Regional Culture*. Baton Rouge: Louisiana State University Press, 1982.

————. *The Enduring South: Subcultural Persistence in Mass Society*. Lexington, Mass.: Lexington Books, 1971.

————, and Daniel Singal, editors. *Regionalism and the South: Selected Papers of Rupert Vance*. Chapel Hill: University of North Carolina Press, 1982.

Reichley, James A. "The Rise of the National Parties." In *New Directions in American Politics*, edited by John E. Chubb and Paul E. Petersen. Washington, D.C.: Brookings Institution, 1985.

Riemer, Svend. "Theoretical Aspects of Regionalism." *Social Forces* 21 (1943): 275–280.

Roback, Thomas H. "Motivation for Activism among Republican National Convention Delegates: Continuity and Change, 1972–1976." *Journal of Politics* 42 (1980): 181–201.

Roland, Charles P. *The Improbable Era: The South since World War II*. Lexington, Ky.: University Press of Kentucky, 1975.

Rubin, Louis D., Jr., editor. *The American South: Portrait of a Culture*. Baton Rouge: Louisiana State University Press, 1980.

Sabato, Larry J. *The Party's Just Begun: Shaping Political Parties for America's Future*. Glenview, Ill.: Scott, Foresman, 1988.

Salisbury, W. Seward. "Religiosity, Regional Sub-Culture, and Social Behavior." *Journal for the Scientific Study of Religion* 2 (1962): 94–101.

Scott, Anne Firor. *The Southern Lady from Pedestal to Politics: 1830–1930*. Chicago: University of Chicago Press, 1970.

Seagull, Louis M. *Southern Republicanism*. Cambridge, Mass.: Schenkman, 1975.

Sellers, Charles G., Jr., editor. *The Southerner as American*. New York: E. P. Dutton, 1966.

Sharkansky, Ira. *Regionalism in American Politics*. Indianapolis: Bobbs-Merrill, 1970.

Shortridge, James R. "A New Regionalization of American Religion." *Journal for the Scientific Study of Religion* 13 (1977): 143–153.

Sindler, Allan P., editor. *Change in the Contemporary South*. Durham: Duke University Press, 1963.

Smidt, Corwin. "Born Again Politics: The Political Behavior of Evangelical Christians in the South and Non-South." In *Religion and Politics in the South*, edited by Tod A. Baker, Robert P. Steed, and Laurence W. Moreland. New York: Praeger, 1983.

Sorauf, Frank J. *Money in American Elections*. Glenview, Ill.: Scott, Foresman and Company, 1988.

Soule, James W., and Wilma E. McGrath. "A Comparative Study of Nominating Conventions: The Democrats of 1968 and 1972." *American Journal of Political Science* 19 (1975): 501–517.

Soule, James W., and James W. Clarke. "Issue Conflict and Consensus: A Comparative Study of Democratic and Republican Delegates to the 1968 National Conventions." *Journal of Politics* 33 (1971): 72–91.

Stanley, Harold W. "Southern Partisan Changes: Dealignment, Realignment, or Both?" *Journal of Politics* 50 (1988): 64–88.

————. *Voter Mobilization and the Politics of Race: The South and Universal Suffrage, 1952–1984*. New York: Praeger, 1987.

————. "The 1984 Presidential Election in the South: Race and Realignment." In *The 1984 Presidential Election in the South: Patterns of Southern Party Politics*, edited by Robert P. Steed, Laurence W. Moreland, and Tod A. Baker. New York: Praeger, 1986.

Stedman, Murray S., Jr. *Religion and Politics in America.* New York: Harcourt, Brace and World, 1964.

Robert P. Steed, Laurence W. Moreland, and Tod A. Baker. "Politics and Race in the South." *Blacks in Southern Politics,* edited by Laurence W. Moreland, Robert P. Steed, and Tod A. Baker. New York: Praeger Publishers, 1987.

————. *The 1984 Presidential Election in the South.* New York: Praeger, 1986.

————. "Religion and Party Activists: Fundamentalism and Politics in Regional Perspective." In *Religion and Politics in the South: Mass and Elite Perspectives,* edited by Tod A. Baker, Robert P. Steed, and Laurence W. Moreland. New York: Praeger Publishers, 1983.

————. *Party Politics in the South.* New York: Praeger Publishers, 1980.

Stone, Walter J. and Alan I. Abramowitz. "Winning May Not Be Everything, But It's More than We Thought: Presidential Party Activists in 1980." *American Political Science Review* 77 (1983): 945–956.

Strong, Donald S. *Issue Voting and Party Realignment.* University, Ala.: University of Alabama Press, 1977.

————. "Further Reflections on Southern Politics." *Journal of Politics* 33 (1971): 239–256.

————. *Urban Republicanism in the South.* University, Ala.: University of Alabama Bureau of Public Administration, 1960.

Sundquist, James L. *Dynamics of the Party System: Alignment and Realignment of Political Parties in the United States.* Revised edition. Washington, D.C.: Brookings Institution, 1983.

Swansbrough, Robert H., and David M. Brodsky, editors. *The South's New Politics: Realignment and Dealignment.* Columbia: University of South Carolina Press, 1988.

Tindall, George Brown. *The Disruption of the Solid South.* Athens: University of Georgia Press, 1972.

————. *The Ethnic Southerners.* Baton Rouge: Louisiana State University Press, 1977.

Trilling, Richard J. *Party Image and Electoral Behavior.* New York: Wiley, 1976.

Twelve Southerners. *I'll Take My Stand: The South and the Agrarian Tradition.* New York: Harper Torchbooks, 1962.

Walton, Hanes, Jr. *Invisible Politics: Black Political Behavior.* Albany: State University of New York Press, 1985.

Wattenberg, Martin P. *The Decline of American Political Parties: 1952–1984.* Cambridge, Mass.: Harvard University Press, 1986.

Watters, Pat, and Reese Cleghorn. *Climbing Jacob's Ladder, The Arrival of Negroes in Southern Politics,* New York: Harcourt, Brace, and World, 1967.

Wiggins, Charles W., and William L. Turk. "State Party Chairmen: A Profile." *Western Political Quarterly* 23 (1970): 321–332.

Woodward, C. Vann. *The Burden of Southern History.* New York: Vintage Books, 1960.

Wright, Gavin. *Old South, New South.* New York: Basic Books, 1986.

Zelinsky, Wilbur. *The Cultural Geography of the United States.* Englewood Cliffs: Prentice-Hall, 1973.

Index

ABOUT THE EDITORS AND CONTRIBUTORS

TOD A. BAKER is professor of political science at The Citadel.

CHARLES D. HADLEY is professor of political science at the University of New Orleans.

ROBERT P. STEED is professor of political science at The Citadel.

LAURENCE W. MORELAND is professor of political science at The Citadel.

WILLIAM CROTTY is professor of political science at Northwestern University.

HAROLD W. STANLEY is associate professor of political science at the University of Rochester.

ROBERT DARCY is professor of political science and statistics at Oklahoma State University.

JANET M. CLARK is professor of political science at the University of Wyoming.

STEPHEN D. SHAFFER is associate professor of political science at Mississippi State University.

CHARLES PRYSBY is associate professor of political science at the University of North Carolina at Greensboro.

JOHN McGLENNON is associate professor of political science at The College of William and Mary.

LEWIS BOWMAN is professor of political science at the University of South Florida.